MACROMEDIA® DREAMWEAVER® 4

Creating Web Pages

AGAINST THE CLOCK
PERFORMANCE SUPPORT & TRAINING SYSTEMS

Prentice
Hall

Upper Saddle River, NJ 07458

Library of Congress Cataloging-in-Publication Data

Macromedia Dreamweaver 4: Creating Web Pages/Against The Clock.
     p.cm. -- (Against the Clock series) Includes Index
ISBN 0-13-094191-3
1.Dreamweaver (Computer File). 2. Web Sites--Authoring Programs.
3. Web Publishing. I. Against The Clock (Firm) II. Series.
TK.5105.8885.D74M33 2002
005.7'2 — dc21

2001021678

Editor-in-Chief: Stephen Helba
Director of Production and Manufacturing: Bruce Johnson
Executive Editor: Elizabeth Sugg
Managing Editor-Editorial: Judy Casillo
Editorial Assistant: Anita Rhodes
Managing Editor-Production: Mary Carnis
Production Editor: Denise Brown
Composition: Against the Clock, Inc.
Design Director: Cheryl Asherman
Senior Design Coordinator: Miguel Ortiz
Cover Design: LaFortezza Design Group, Inc.
Icon Design: James Braun
Prepress: Photoengraving, Inc.
Printer/Binder: Press of Ohio

The fonts utilized in this training course are the property of Against The Clock, Inc., and are supplied to the legitimate buyers of the Against The Clock training materials solely for use with the exercises and projects provided in the body of the materials. They may not be used for any other purpose, and under no circumstances may they be transferred to another individual, nor copied or distributed by any means whatsoever.

A portion of the images supplied in this book are Copyright © PhotoDisc, Inc., 201 Fourth Ave., Seattle, WA 98121. These images are the sole property of PhotoDisc and are used by Against The Clock with the permission of the owners. They may not be distributed, copied, transferred, or reproduced by any means whatsoever, other than for the completion of the exercises and projects contained in this Against The Clock training material.

Against The Clock and the Against The Clock logo are trademarks of Against The Clock, Inc., registered in the United States and elsewhere. References to and instructional materials provided for any particular application program, operating system, hardware platform, or other commercially available product or products do not represent an endorsement of such product or products by Against The Clock, Inc. or Prentice Hall, Inc.

Photoshop, Acrobat, Adobe Type Manager, Illustrator, InDesign, PageMaker, Premiere, and PostScript are trademarks of Adobe Systems Incorporated. Macintosh is a trademark of Apple Computer, Inc. Macromedia Flash, Generator, FreeHand, Dreamweaver, FireWorks and Director are registered trademarks of Macromedia, Inc. CorelDRAW! and Painter are trademarks of Corel Corporation. FrontPage, Publisher, PowerPoint, Word, Excel, Office, Microsoft, MS-DOS, Windows, and Windows NT are either registered trademarks or trademarks of Microsoft Corporation. QuarkXPress is a registered trademark of Quark, Inc. TrapWise and PressWise are registered trademarks of ScenicSoft.

Other products and company names mentioned herein may be the trademarks of their respective owners.

Prentice Hall International (UK) Limited, London
Prentice Hall of Australia Pty. Limited, Sydney
Prentice Hall Canada Inc., Toronto
Prentice Hall Hispanoamericana, S.A., Mexico
Prentice Hall of India Private Limited, New Delhi
Prentice Hall of Japan, Inc., Tokyo
Pearson Education Asia Pte. Ltd., Singapore
Editora Prentice Hall do Brasil, Ltda., Rio de Janeiro

10 9 8 7 6 5 4 3 2

ISBN 0-13-094191-3

Contents

FREE-FORM PROJECT #2

REVIEW #2

PROJECTS:

GLOSSARY

INDEX

Purpose

The Against The Clock series has been developed specifically for those involved in the field of computer arts and now — animation, video and multimedia production. Many of our readers are already involved in the industry in advertising and printing, television production, multimedia and in the world of Web design. Others are just now preparing for a career within these professions.

This series will provide you with the necessary skills to work in these fast-paced, exciting and rapidly expanding fields. While many people feel that they can simply purchase a computer and the appropriate software and begin designing and producing high-quality presentations, the real world of high-quality printed and Web communications requires a far more serious commitment.

The Series

The applications presented in the Against The Clock series stand out as the programs of choice in professional computer arts environments.

We've used a modular design for the Against The Clock series, allowing you to mix and match the drawing, imaging and page-layout applications that exactly suit your specific needs.

Titles available in the Against The Clock series include:

Macintosh: Basic Operations
Windows: Basic Operations
Adobe Illustrator: Introduction and Advanced Digital Illustration
Macromedia FreeHand: Digital Illustration
Adobe InDesign: Introduction and Advanced Electronic Mechanicals
Adobe PageMaker: Introduction and Advanced Electronic Mechanicals
QuarkXPress: Introduction and Advanced Electronic Mechanicals
Microsoft Publisher: Creating Electronic Mechanicals
Microsoft PowerPoint: Presentation Graphics with Impact
Microsoft FrontPage: Designing for the Web
MetaCreations Painter: A Digital Approach to Natural Art Media
Adobe Photoshop: Introduction and Advanced Digital Images
Adobe Premiere: Digital Video Editing
Macromedia Director: Creating Powerful Multimedia
Macromedia Flash: Animating for the Web
Macromedia Dreamweaver: Creating Web Pages
File Preparation: The Responsible Electronic Page
Preflight: An Introduction to File Analysis and Repair
TrapWise and PressWise: Digital Trapping and Imposition

For the Reader

On the CD-ROM, you will find a complete set of Against The Clock (ATC) fonts, as well as a collection of data files used to construct the various exercises and projects.

The ATC fonts are solely for use while you are working with the Against The Clock materials. These fonts will be used throughout both the exercises and projects, and are provided in both Macintosh and Windows formats.

A variety of resource files have been included. These files, necessary to complete both the exercises and projects, are also provided in Macintosh and Windows formats. These files may be found on the CD-ROM within the RF-Dreamweaver folder.

For the Instructor

The Instructor's CD-ROM includes various testing and presentation materials in addition to the files that are supplied with this book.

- **Overhead Presentation Materials** are provided and follow along with the book. These presentations are prepared using Microsoft PowerPoint and are provided in both native PowerPoint format as well as Acrobat Portable Document Format (PDF).

- **Extra Projects** are provided along with the data files required for completion. These projects may be used to extend the training session, or they may be used to test the reader's progress.

- **Test Questions and Answers** are included on the Instructor's CD-ROM. These questions may be modified and/or reorganized.

- **Finished Artwork** for all projects is supplied on the CD-ROM.

Chapter openers provide
the reader with specific objectives.

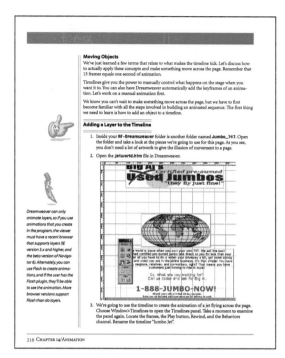

Sidebars and **hands-on
activities** supplement concepts
presented in the material.

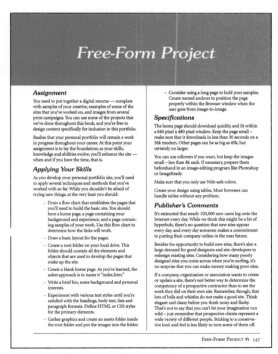

Free-Form projects allow you to use
your imagination and your new skills
to satisfy a client's needs.

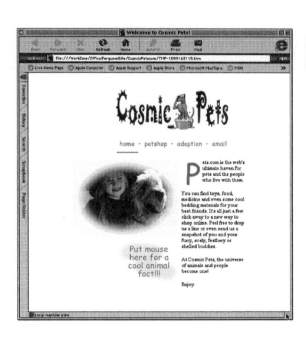

Step-by-step projects result in
finished artwork — with an emphasis
on proper file-construction methods.

In addition to explanatory text and illustrations, Against The Clock books have been constructed with two primary building blocks: exercises and projects. Projects always result in a finished piece of work — digital imagery built from the ground up, utilizing images, vector artwork and type elements from the library supplied on your CD-ROM.

This book, *Macromedia Dreamweaver: Creating Web Pages*, uses step-by-step projects on which you will work during your learning sessions. There are also free-form projects immediately preceding the two reviews. You will find images of the step-by-step projects you will complete displayed on the inside front and back covers of the book. Here's a brief overview of each:

Project A: Cosmic Pets

The Cosmic Pets project is a small but compelling commercial site. A real-world job, the site was designed to be a cost-effective and simple way for a pet adoption service to communicate with their supporters and their pets' potential parents. The site requires the use of a placed logo, and uses tables to facilitate a strong sense of coordination and design. Rollover images are used throughout the site, and provide a touch of humor to this effective Internet presence.

Project B: Tropiflora Order Form

This is another project based on an actual client requirement. Tropiflora is a world leader in the cultivation and sales of tropical plants. This project is based on a re-design of their customer order form. Using text fields, radio buttons, jump menus, pop-up lists and proven design techniques, the order form you'll create is very structured, graphically pleasing and easy for the user to fill out. You'll use forms, objects, layers, tables and a range of Dreamweaver's powerful tools to complete the assignment.

Project C: Diehard Digital

The home page of contributing author Dwayne Ferguson, this project is a perfect example of an entry point into a site-designer's portfolio. Using a variety of advanced features, the project relies on a powerful combination of dark grays and blacks, and provides an example of how controlling the background color of a site — combined with objects of a similar tonal range — can create a sense of mood. You'll use sliced images positioned in a layered document to build the page, and use animated layers to provide a changing tag line that provides some insight and humor into the designer's profile.

Project D: Mr. BlockHead's Challenge

Going where no Web page authoring tool has ever gone before, Dreamweaver provides a set of behaviors and JavaScript tools that are showcased in this fun and free game. Using layers, behaviors, animation, stacking order and a variety of other methods, you'll build a functional puzzle game that includes sounds, interactivity and even a trashcan to dispose of the extra pieces. As is the case in all the projects, you're provided with all the objects you'll need to complete this game.

Acknowledgments

I would like to give special thanks to the writers, illustrators, editors and others who have worked long and hard to complete the Against The Clock series.

Thanks to the dedicated teaching professionals whose comments and expertise contributed to the success of these products, including Michelle Ratliff and Jamey Weare of Santa Fe Community College, David McGill of Azusa Pacific University and Janet O'Neal of Sussex County Community College.

Thanks to Dean Bagley and Michael Barnett for their technical, editorial and production expertise.

A big thanks to Judy Casillo, developmental editor, and Denise Brown, production editor, for their guidance, patience and attention to detail.

— *Ellenn Behoriam, April 2001*

Our History

Against The Clock (ATC) was founded in 1990 as a part of Lanman Systems Group, one of the nation's leading systems integration and training firms. The company specialized in developing custom training materials for such clients as L.L. Bean, *The New England Journal of Medicine*, the Smithsonian, the National Education Association, *Air & Space Magazine*, Publishers Clearing House, the National Wildlife Society, Home Shopping Network, and many others. The integration firm was among the most highly-respected in the graphic arts industry.

To a great degree, the success of Lanman Systems Group can be attributed to the thousands of pages of course materials developed at the company's demanding client sites. Throughout the rapid growth of Lanman Systems Group, founder and general manager Ellenn Behoriam developed the expertise necessary to manage technical experts, content providers, writers, editors, illustrators, designers, layout artists, proofreaders and the rest of the chain of professionals required to develop structured and highly-effective training materials.

Following the sale of the Lanman Companies to World Color, one of the nation's largest commercial printers, Ellenn embarked on a project to develop a new library of hands-on training materials engineered specifically for the professional graphic artist. A large part of this effort is finding and working with talented professional artists, writers and educators from around the country.

The result is the ATC training library.

Gary E. Poyssick

Gary Poyssick, co-owner of Against The Clock, is a well-known and often controversial speaker, writer and industry consultant who has been involved in professional graphics and communications for over 15 years.

A respected author, Poyssick penned the highly popular *Workflow Reengineering* (Adobe Press), *Teams and the Graphic Arts Service Provider* (Prentice Hall), *Creative Techniques: Adobe Illustrator*, and *Creative Techniques: Adobe Photoshop* (Hayden Books).

Dwayne Ferguson

Dwayne Ferguson is the CEO of DIEHARD Studio, which specializes in illustration, 3D animation and writing. Ferguson is the art director of the animated TV series *Mutant League* and the author of the childrens' novel series, *Kid Caramel: Private Investigator*, nominated for the Coretta Scott King award.

Julie Bath

Julie Bath has been an instructor at the Wichita Area Technical College in the Graphic Communications Technology department for four years. Prior to beginning her career in education, Julie spent two years as a graphic artist, animator and editor for a video production company. Julie holds an associates degree in Graphic Communications Technology, a bachelors degree in Fine Arts, and is currently working toward a masters degree in Liberal Studies focusing in e-curriculum and distance learning.

Getting Started

Platform

With only few exceptions — those being books targeting at teaching how specific operating systems function — the entire Against The Clock series is designed to work for both Macintosh and Windows learners. This book will serve you equally well if you're a Macintosh user, or are working with Windows 95, NT, 98, Millennium, or Windows 2000.

We should note, however, that there are a number of differences between how Dreamweaver works on a Macintosh as compared to the same software on a Windows machine. Almost all of these variances are essentially cosmetic; some things look different, while working exactly the same. Many examples come to mind — the Preview in Browser command — arguably the one thing you'll do more than any other — is called Preview/Debug in Browser on the Macintosh. The keyboard equivalent for the command is F12 in Windows; you have to use Option-F12 if you're a Macintosh user. If you ever find yourself working with Dreamweaver on both platforms at the same time, you'll spot dozens of these discrepancies.

Of all the differences, one really stands out — and it's not a difference in wording or descriptions. If you're using Dreamweaver on a Windows platform and you close all the open windows, the program quits. On the Macintosh, you can close all open windows and the application is still active — you can open existing documents and create new ones.

Naming Conventions

In the early days of the PC, the Windows operating system placed several restrictions on what you could call your files. All file names consisted of two parts: a name, which could contain no more than eight alphanumeric characters; and a three character suffix. The suffix defined the nature of the file. Applications generally ended with the .exe (for executable) suffix, while documents used suffixes like .doc (document), .txt (text file), .wav (wave, a sound format), .htm (HTML documents, and the native file format used by Dreamweaver) as well as many others. The Macintosh operating system never imposed this limitation. Nor did it use extensions, or suffixes, to identify files to the operating system.

For at least the past five years, Windows systems no longer restrict you to eight characters for the name; you can use 256 characters. Every application appends a three character suffix to its files. You might not see these extensions, however. By default, the Windows operating system hides extensions for "known" file types. These known file types include just about every file you're going to use in this book.

To configure your system so that file extensions are visible, click the Start button (in the lower-left part of your screen), and select Settings>Folder Options from the pop-up menu. Select the View tab, and uncheck the "Hide file extensions for known file types."

While viewing file extensions isn't required in order to use the book, changing the setting will ensure that what you see on your monitor matches the screen shots and illustrations used in the discussions and exercises. If you're on a Macintosh, we still recommend using the suffixes — it ensures that your host servers will properly recognize the components that make up your site.

Key Commands

There are two keys generally used as *modifier* keys — they do nothing when pressed, unless they are pressed in conjunction with another key. Their purpose is to alter the normal functions of the other key with which they are pressed.

The Command (Macintosh) or Control (Windows) key is generally used when taking control of the computer. When combined with the "S" key, it functions to save your work. When combined with "O," it opens a file; with a "P," it prints the file.

Another special function key is the Option (Macintosh) and Alt (for alternate) (Windows) key. It, too, is a modifier key, and you must hold it down along with whatever other key (or keys) is required for a specific function. The Option and Alt keys are often used in conjunction with other keys to access typographic characters having an ASCII number higher than 128. Under Windows, they are used in conjunction with the numeric keypad.

The Macintosh and Windows access context-sensitive menus in similar but different ways. On the Macintosh, holding down the Control (not the Command) key while clicking the mouse button will bring up context-sensitive menus. Under Windows, this is accomplished by clicking the right mouse button (right-clicking). We generically call accessing the context menu "context-clicking."

The CD-ROM and Initial Setup Considerations

Before you begin using your Against The Clock course book, you must set up your system to have access to the various files and tools to complete your lessons.

Resource Files

This course comes complete with a collection of resource files. These files are an integral part of the learning experience — they're used throughout the book to help you construct increasingly complex elements. Having these building blocks available to you for practice and study sessions will ensure that you will be able to experience the exercises and complete the project assignments smoothly, spending a minimum of time looking for the various required components.

In the Resource Files folders, we've created sets of data. Locate the **RF-Dreamweaver** folder and drag the icon onto your hard disk drive. If you have limited disk space, you may want to copy only the files for one or two lessons at a time.

Creating a Project Folder

Throughout the exercises and projects you'll be required to save your work. Since the CD-ROM is "read-only," you cannot write information to it. Create a "work in progress" folder on your hard disk and use it to store your work. Create the folder at the highest level of your system, where it will always be easy to find. Name this folder "Work in Progress".

System Requirements

On the Macintosh, you will need a Power PC 604 processor or above, running the 8.5 operating system or later; 32MB* of application memory (with Virtual Memory on); 110 MB of available hard-disk space (after install); a monitor with a resolution of at least 800×600 or greater; and a CD-ROM drive. Version 4.0 or later of Netscape Navigator or Microsoft Internet Explorer

On a Windows operating system, you'll need a Pentium II or faster processor; Windows 98/NT 4.0, or Windows 2000† or higher; 32 MB* application memory; 135 MB of available hard-disk space (after installation); a monitor with a resolution of at least 800×600 pixels; and a CD-ROM drive. Version 4.0 or later of Netscape Navigator or Microsoft Internet Explorer.

Prerequisites

This book assumes that you have a basic understanding of how to use your system.

You should know how to use your mouse to point and click, and how to drag items around the screen. You should know how to resize a window, and how to arrange windows on your desktop to maximize your available space. You should know how to access pull-down menus, and how checkboxes and radio buttons work. Lastly, you should know how to create, open, and save files.

If you're familiar with these fundamental skills, then you know all that's necessary to utilize the Against The Clock courseware library.

Notes:

Introduction

In its early days, the Internet was the sole domain of the technically adept. Without plenty of time, and an in-depth knowledge of HTML — the language upon which the Web depends — there was little chance that a non-technical person could successfully develop compelling Web pages.

For the artist or designer working in the world of print media, there were plenty of powerful, relatively easy-to-use page layout programs. Although the first incarnations of these "desktop publishing" applications lacked the horsepower they currently offer, they nonetheless provide a visual environment within which the artist could import and arrange page elements.

Nature, as they say, abhors a vacuum, and the adage certainly holds true for the commercial software marketplace. As the Web rapidly gained in popularity, a number of Web page design packages began to appear. Among the first was Adobe's PageMill. With it, a lay designer could build Web pages using a visual workspace. Much like the company's PageMaker program, or the highly-popular QuarkXPress, the software provided a drag-and-drop interface. Images and text could be imported, positioned and rearranged quite easily.

At the same time, HTML was evolving as well. Spearheaded by the World Wide Web consortium (which you'll read about in the chapter 1, "Dreamweaver and the Web"), the programming language was being enhanced with features such as tables, Cascading Style Sheets and more. Programs like PageMill — and others like Microsoft's FrontPage — offered access to even these more esoteric functions.

The applications, however, were not without their share of problems. First and foremost — particularly in the eyes of the techie crowd — the HTML these programs generated behind the scenes was riddled with errors, was far too verbose and couldn't even be used unless an army of programmers "cleaned up" the code. While this wasn't totally true, the applications certainly didn't produce clean HTML.

Dreamweaver first appeared on the scene about four years ago. The dyed-in-the-wool coders out there turned up their noses on Dreamweaver just as they did on PageMill, FrontPage and other Web layout packages. As the software evolved, even the most devoted HTML programmer had to admit things were getting better.

Today, it's estimated that over 70% of all major sites were built and are being maintained using Dreamweaver. Arguably, there's still a need for someone that understands what's going on under the hood — inside the HTML code that the program generates; but the requirement is far less pressing than ever. Many of the most technically-demanding functions can be applied to your Dreamweaver pages without a single minute being spent tweaking the code. JavaScript behaviors, layer animations, Cascading Style Sheets, rich-media management and much more are all at your fingertips when you're in the Dreamweaver authoring environment.

We've designed this book to provide you with a solid knowledge of this powerful program. As is often the case with evolving technologies, we can't teach you everything there is to know; even long hours of study, experimentation and experience building commercial sites will only build on your knowledge. Learning to use a program like Dreamweaver, in addition to HTML, XML, Cascading Style Sheets, JavaScript, extensions and Active Server pages, is an ongoing process, not an event.

We can assure you, however, that once you've had a chance to study the discussions, work through the exercises, complete the projects and project assignments and absorb what you've learned, you'll be on your way to achieving almost any creative vision you might have. And — most importantly — you'll be able to deliver your compelling content to the millions of potential viewers using the global Internet.

We hope that you enjoy the book — we certainly enjoyed writing it.

1 Dreamweaver and the Web

Chapter Objective:

In chapter 1, we begin our exploration into using Dreamweaver by taking a brief look at the Internet. In chapter 1 you will:

- Learn about the origin of the Internet, and how it developed into the phenomena it is today.

- Learn the definition and use of HTML, the basic language of the Internet.

- Explore the concept of Web servers, and their role in the World Wide Web.

- Learn about ISPs (Internet Service Providers), and how they work with site-developers to make Web sites available to the general public.

- Become comfortable with the concept of a Web browser, which interprets HTML and displays it on your monitor.

- Discuss the importance of proper planning in the development of your own Web sites.

Projects to be Completed:

- Cosmic Pets (A)

- Tropiflora Order Form (B)

- Diehard Digital (C)

- Mr. BlockHead's Challenge (D)

Dreamweaver is published by Macromedia, the preeminent provider of Web development and management tools. Among their portfolio of products are Flash, the most popular vector graphics and animation program; Director, the leading multimedia development application; Fireworks, a bitmap and painting program designed specifically for Web graphics; and a variety of other authoring and site-management components.

Internet services include the World Wide Web (HTTP), a secure version (HTTPS), email (POP, IMAP, SMTP), news (NNTP), file transfer protocol (FTP) and Gopher (an older text-based medium largely displaced by the Web).

Dreamweaver and the Web

In a few short years, Dreamweaver has risen from relative obscurity to become the tool of choice among a majority of leading Web designers, not only in the United States, but around the world. In this book, you're going to learn how the program's many features provide you with the ideal authoring environment for creating and publishing your Web designs and content.

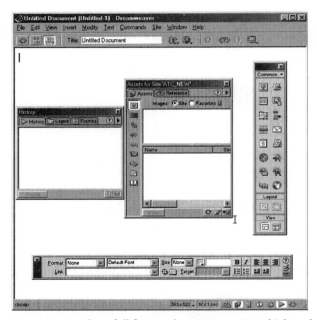

Dreamweaver provides a full-featured environment in which to design and construct individual pages and management tools to maintain your Web sites.

The Internet

Before we begin working with Dreamweaver, let's briefly examine the Web and the ingredients that make it work. It's difficult to believe that the World Wide Web (WWW) is a relatively new technology dating back only to 1990. Commercial use of the Web has been growing in the last five years, so that no matter where you turn these days, you're directed by television, radio and print advertising to one Web site or another. The Web has something to offer everyone — from government agencies providing access to public information, to nonprofit organizations garnering support for their causes, individuals sharing personal information and companies seeking innovative ways to market their products and services.

Components

The World Wide Web (WWW) is one of several services distributed via the Internet, and, aside from email, is the most widely used.

The Internet is the world's largest network of computers communicating through the use of a common, uniform networking protocol called "TCP/IP" (Transmission Control Protocol/Internet Protocol).

A Web site is a collection of interconnected Web pages that are accessed from a personal computer equipped with a connection to the Internet and browser software, which interprets HTML and displays it on the user's monitor. A site can have as few as one page or as many as thousands.

There are an increasing number of alternative connections to the Internet. Among them are special high-speed phone lines "called DSP, for Digital Signal Processing" and cable modems, special devices supplied by a cable supplier that provide fast connections at reasonable rates. These options can offer connection speeds of up to 50 times that of a conventional dial-up modem. Actual results may vary from provider to provider, and from region to region.

The Internet originated in the 1960s as a research project. The U.S. Department of Defense sought to create a cross-connected information network that could span a large geographical area and withstand disruption during a possible nuclear war. The idea behind this was to create a built-in fail-safe mechanism that would reroute data through the network should any part of the network fail. So the Internet was born — initially used only by the military and university scientists.

How does the Internet work? It relies on what's known as "client/server technology." *Clients* are individual computers that issue requests for information and services from other, higher-end computers called "servers." One example of a client is the personal computer that you use to access the Internet.

A *server* is a computer that receives and processes requests by "delivering or serving" files back to the requesting computer. Servers generally have a faster connection to the Internet, greater memory and a faster hard drive than the typical personal computer. Most servers are optimized to process numerous requests from many clients at once.

Hosted Web server space contains a full-time connection to the Internet and is, therefore, available for others to browse anytime, from anywhere else on the Internet.

How can you get on the Internet? You could purchase a direct connection, although the expense generally limits this option to larger office installations or to ISP companies whose business is reselling Internet access through this connection. ISPs enable you to connect to the Internet for a fee. Most ISPs also provide users with one or more email addresses and with server space to host their Web pages. You'll need this sort of server space to make the pages you've created with Dreamweaver available for viewing on the Web. Many ISPs offer some amount of server space free of charge, but if you're creating a complex commercial site, you can count on paying a monthly fee for the service.

To access the Internet, you usually establish an account with an ISP. You'll also need an Internet-ready computer that includes a *modem*, a device that allows you to communicate with other computers via your telephone line or cable connection. This computer also includes a *Web browser*, a software application that allows you to view Web pages, and mail software to exchange email with other users. Most new computers come with a Web browser and email client software already installed.

The Web

In March of 1989, Tim Berners-Lee, working at CERN (The European Organization for Nuclear Research), published a proposal for a global hypertext medium that he called "the World Wide Web." This proposal was presented as a justification to develop a mechanism for CERN to address the problem of information access within the organization through a complex of linked information systems to allow scientists to share research information.

The *World Wide Web*, also known as "the Web," consists of a huge collection of documents stored on computers around the world. These documents, called "Web pages," have been created in accordance with an agreed-upon standard called "HyperText Markup Language" (HTML). HTML defines the way information on a Web page should appear when you access that page with your browser. Web pages can include text, graphics, sound, even video. The ability to include multimedia makes the Web a powerful tool for sharing information.

Every Web page has a unique "address," or location on the Web. The address is called a "Uniform Resource Locator," or "URL." (Http**://** is the protocol designation that precedes the URL.) The following are examples of URLs:

Macromedia's Home Page:	http://www.macromedia.com
The Library of Congress:	http://loc.gov
Prentice Hall:	http://www.prenhall.com
Against The Clock:	http://www.againsttheclock.com

You can access a Web page by typing its URL into your Web browser. Your system then locates the server on which the URL resides and displays the page. Most Web pages are part of a collection of pages called a "Web site." For example, if you visit Macromedia's home page, you'll find links to many different areas, such as company information, products, technical support, employment opportunities and so forth. The combination of these pages comprise the Macromedia Web site.

Multimedia means the use of more than one presentation medium. Multimedia on the Web commonly refers to some combination of text, graphics, sound, animation or video.

Search Engines

Search engines are programs that look for requested topics on Web sites throughout the Internet (or, in some cases, within a Web site). Many popular search engines, each of which has varying levels of functionality, can be accessed on the Internet. Some of the most popular search engines include yahoo.com, excite.com, lycos.com, altavista.com, hotbot.com and nbci.com.

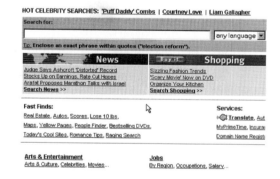

Altavista.com is one of the Web's most popular search engines.

HTML – Speaking Webese

Most Web visitors find the sites they visit by using one or more search engines.

HyperText Markup Language (HTML) is the standard programming language for Web pages. The World Wide Web Consortium (W3C, http://www.w3c.org) is responsible for the definition of HTML standards.

HTML has been specifically designed to easily and accurately transmit information to all Internet users. One of the crippling factors in information-sharing has always been a lack of compatibility. For example, how will pages created on a PC using Microsoft Publisher appear to a person accessing them on a Macintosh with Adobe PageMaker? Will the information display at all? Will the layout and image positioning translate to other users?

While still considered relatively primitive compared to page layout programs designed to create printed material, HTML overcomes many compatibility issues by providing a universal standard for displaying information. This standard works on any platform or software used by either the page designer or the viewer. Web pages coded with HTML will be similar in appearance on any computer that uses a compatible Web browser.

Many traditionalists feel that the only way to build Web pages is by using a simple text editor — plowing through hundreds of lines of arcane code to eventually develop the perfect page, without any extraneous HTML.

Basic Hypertext Programming

The primary characteristic of the World Wide Web is the use of links, formally referred to as "hyperlinks," that allow the Web browser to move through information in a unique, reader-selectable, nonlinear fashion.

A book, for example, is linear. You begin at the first page and read each page in turn. With hypertext, you can select a link to jump to another page and then back again. Or you can branch off in a nearly infinite number of different directions.

"Surfing the Web" refers to the practice of jumping from site to site by clicking on links that attract your attention. New users of the Web often find this an interesting and consuming experience, although it can also become a huge time-waster. More experienced users realize the value of carefully targeted searches that bring you efficiently to the desired information.

Web Hosting Services

Both free and commercial Web hosting are available to you. If you are creating a personal Web site, some of the free options may work for you. Most ISPs provide an optional free site in your access charges. If not, you can find several sites on the Web that will provide you with a site in exchange for displaying their advertisements to you and your site visitors.

If your site is intended to market your business or sell products, a commercial hosting service that will provide a site with your own domain name is probably more appropriate.

Browsers

The key to effective Web design is accessibility. As you'll discover, making certain that your Web pages are accessible, that they display properly in all of the different Web browsers available, can be a task in and of itself. Why? Here's the short list:

- The HTML standard continually evolves to provide Web designers with new and improved capabilities. Older versions of browsers may not recognize the more advanced features.

- Some Web browsers display only text. You must make certain that text-only viewers have access to an appropriate text alternative when viewing your pages. Using HTML attributes to embed such text into your graphic links ensures that this will occur. Since Web sites are now almost entirely graphically-dependent, this need is all but ignored. But that will change as we begin to address the need to provide access to Web sites via hand-held devices.

- The two most popular Web browsers, Internet Explorer and Netscape Navigator, offer features that aren't part of the HTML standard. While these browser-specific tags give you more control over the appearance of your pages, they don't translate well for other browsers. This is why many Web pages claim to be "best viewed" using a specific browser.

The first use of hypertext dates back to 1945, although the Web did not appear until 1990.

In the next chapter, we're going to provide you with a primer on basic HTML, and teach you some of the language's simpler functions. You don't have to know how to code HTML to use Dreamweaver — that's the beauty of using a visual tool for page design.

A good reason to design your sites to alternatively be presented in "text only" is to provide access for people with disabilities. Programs such as Dragon Naturally Speaking and others can read these sites, offering access for those who would normally be restricted from visiting your site and enjoying your content. As of May 2001, all government sites must be compliant with the American's for Disabilities Act (ADA).

So how can you design for the Web and ensure compatibility with your site visitors? First, you should know what browsers your visitors are using. Many hosting services include an activity-monitoring service such as WebTrends. Monitoring the browser usage of visitors to your site will probably reveal that more than 85 to 90% of your visitors are using either Microsoft Internet Explorer (MSIE) 4 (or greater) or Netscape Navigator (NS) 4. The rest are using other browsers, each in numbers so small that it may not justify modifications to your Web pages or alternate Web pages to accommodate them.

Secondly, you can test your pages in multiple browsers to see how they display. Compatibility testing should be a standard part of your design process, at a minimum using MSIE 5 and NS 4. Most designers also make certain that their pages are backward-compatible to some degree with older browsers. In these cases, the goal is to have advanced Web page features degrade gracefully when viewed in an older browser. Of course, you'll need to access older browsers to do this. You'll find older Web browsers at http://tucows.com. For example, search for "Internet Explorer 3."

Lastly, you should also make certain that you have the latest version of both Internet Explorer and Netscape Navigator. You can upgrade these for free at the TuCows archive or at the publishers' own URLs: Internet Explorer (http://www.microsoft.com) and Netscape Navigator (http://www.netscape.com).

With Dreamweaver, you'll be able to design specifically for Internet Explorer or Navigator. However, you should make certain that your pages work for other browsers as well. The new Netscape browser is version 6; version 5 was skipped because the developers abandoned the former proprietary technologies. The new open standard browser layout technology — Gecko — has been designed to be compatible with W3C standards and recommendations. This marks the first significant move to end the "browser wars" and is generally good for both Web developers and users.

Web Design 101

A glance at the shelves of any bookstore should convince you that Web design — the "look and feel" of your Web pages — is an entirely separate discipline. This book isn't meant to guide you through the design of your pages, but you will learn how to make them work. Following a few simple design strategies, however, can make a huge difference in your results.

Planning Your Site

Before you begin creating your pages, you should organize your content. This means working out exactly what you want to say and what you want to include on your pages. Consider your purpose in designing the site. If you want to put up your resume, get your text together before you start your pages. If you're designing a business site, consider what the business is looking to achieve through its Web presence. Do you want to provide product information? Give customers access to technical support information and staff? Allow customers to purchase items from the site?

These are just a few of the areas you should think about before you begin to design your site.

Knowing Your Target Audience

Who is your target audience — the collective group of people whom you expect to visit your site? Do you think they'll fall into a particular age group? Or do they share a profession or some common interest? This is important because if you know who your audience is, you can make some assumptions about their technical capabilities as well as what they're likely to expect from your site.

For example, let's assume that your site is geared toward graphic designers. Because the field of graphic design requires the use of sophisticated technology and greater processing speeds, you can assume that your viewers will probably be using state-of-the-art equipment and connections. This means that they'll be able to handle a site with many complex images. You can probably also safely include a variety of features that require plug-in applications that typical Web viewers might not have. You can do this because you have a good idea of your audience's technical capabilities and expectations. Keeping the site accessible to everyone on the Web by sacrificing images and advanced technologies may not be a priority for you. In fact, one of your strategies to attract viewers might be through the inclusion of sophisticated images and functions.

Creating Storyboards

Once you've outlined your plan and made some determinations about your audience, you can start developing ideas by making sketches of your layout. One effective way to sketch out your layout is by creating storyboards. The term "storyboard" was borrowed from the film industry and is very loosely defined. Storyboards can be as basic as hand-drawn sketches of your page on scrap paper or as elaborate as complex, computerized minipages that show samples of your chosen graphics, fonts and page colors.

Plugins are miniprograms that work inside other, larger programs. Web plugins extend the capabilities of your Web browser. Some common plugins include Shockwave and Flash. For more information on plugins, visit http://www.browserwatch.internet.com/plug-in.html.

Creating storyboards doesn't have to be a formal activity. You may want to make storyboards that are simple sets of notes that outline what you think you might put on each page. Until you gain substantial experience, designing for the Web can be challenging. If you take the time to plan your design in advance, however, you can easily overcome this limitation.

Developing Flowcharts

A *flowchart* is a graphical representation of the navigation, or flow, of a Web site. Flowcharts are great tools for mapping out the page-to-page navigation on your site. To develop a flowchart for your site, answer these questions:

- How many pages will I create? Use an index card to represent each page.
- What is a logical flow of information? Arrange the index cards accordingly.

Use this method to create your flowchart. Be careful, however, not to lock yourself into the flowchart. You may find that you need to add or remove Web pages during the design process, and you should allow yourself the flexibility to do so. The idea behind flowcharting is to organize your ideas and establish the logical flow of information.

If you aren't certain exactly what to include on your site, consider asking the people whom you expect to visit your site. Ask them what kind of information they're interested in: product descriptions, pricing, contact information, financial statements? Another critical task is to visit sites that offer similar content, and examine the way in which their designers approached the project. The idea is to benchmark, not copy; take the time to see what they did well and what you might do better or differently.

Programs like Visio2000 are often used by professional designers to map out initial flowcharts before they begin building their site.

There are many programs available that can dramatically improve the flowcharting process, letting you develop the most complex charts imaginable. Many professional designers use such third-party applications to develop the fundamental structure of their sites. It's a good idea to do so before you even launch Dreamweaver.

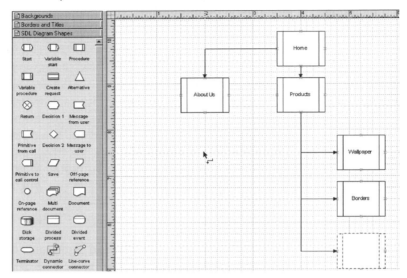

The flowchart, or map of the site, is also something that should be discussed with all parties involved: clients, copywriters, marketing people, even the legal department if necessary. The more time you spend initially designing the map of the site, the less major reconstruction you'll have to do later when you realize something isn't wired correctly.

Create a Storyboard

1. Divide a blank sheet of paper into four even sections by drawing a vertical line in the center of the page. The line should start at the top of the page and run to the bottom.

2. Draw a horizontal line from the left side to the right side of the page. The line should appear in the center of the page.

3. Use this sheet to create a four-page storyboard for a beachfront restaurant that serves seafood. The upper-left quadrant will represent the main page. This page will introduce the restaurant and welcome viewers. The second page will list the services the restaurant offers. The third page will outline the restaurant's wine list. The last page will be a form that allows viewers to make dinner reservations online.

4. The sample storyboard above illustrates just one way you might design the restaurant's Web pages. Be creative. Spend time thinking about the most effective way you can present the information on each page. Here are some ideas:

When laying out your storyboard pages, use a wide, or landscape, orientation, since the browser window, as viewed on the typical monitor, will usually be wider than it is tall. The top of the Web page that is seen without scrolling is the most important area, and should receive careful attention. Often, if a user is not hooked by what is in this first window view, he or she will not bother scrolling to see the rest of the page.

Home Page

- A brief introduction to the restaurant and the Web site.
- An attractive photograph of the interior or exterior of the restaurant or a typical dish served.
- Location, phone number and other information of importance to viewers.

Services

- A list of services (for example, does the restaurant have a catering service? Does it provide takeout service?).
- A description of the services.

Wine

- A list of the most popular wines served.
- Prices of wine by the glass and by the bottle.

Reservations

- A form to gather customer information such as name and phone number.
- Hours of operation.
- Date, time and type of dining in which the customer is interested.

Deciding upon a navigation system is an important factor in determining the usability of your Web site. You should understand that you may not be the best judge of how people will view your site; it's important to solicit input from unbiased individuals outside the Web development group.

Pages should be designed on a 600 × 400 pixel page model so that even a low-resolution display will show the page without the need to scroll. The smallest monitor that a user is likely to be viewing is a 14-inch screen, which translates to 640 pixels × 480 pixels. Staying slightly below that will give them room for the browser's menus and tools.

Determine a Navigation System

1. Tear blank sheets of paper into four equal parts (or, if you have index cards, use four cards). Give each piece of paper or index card a descriptive title. The title should represent the page or area of the Web site being created. For example, you might name the pages: Home, Parties, Banquets, Contacts, Recipes, Meals, Chef's Choice, Birthday Club, Wine List, and Reservations. Include a short description of what will appear on the page.

2. Ask several people to arrange the paper or cards in different categories to determine what they think is the most logical navigation flow for the Web site. They should ask where viewers should start and where will they want to go next.

3. Ask each person how they came up with the categories they chose. Look for patterns to emerge, and use these as the basis of your navigation system.

Building the Web Page

The page colors and fonts that you use on your Web pages are an important consideration because they set the tone for your site. Take the time to visit sites that are similar to the one you envision creating. How did the colors and fonts on those sites make you feel? Did the colors flow together smoothly? Did they blend well? What colors would you change? Why?

As you design your navigational scheme, consider your viewers. Above all, navigation should be clear and easy to follow. Viewers should be able to find what they're looking for, and find it quickly.

The purpose of soliciting opinions is to gain insight into how people will view your site, not to take a vote on the design of the navigation system. Sometimes equally logical categories emerge from this process. In that case, it makes sense to consider cross-linking sections of the site, or listing information under more than a single category.

Make certain that your text is easy to read. Be careful that the size of your text isn't too small and doesn't overuse bold or italic typefaces. Test your color schemes to make certain that the text doesn't fade into the background.

Unless your audience requires it, avoid cluttering your site with unnecessary graphics and animations, since this can increase the time it takes to load your pages (and seriously frustrate your viewers). The best overall designs follow a theme. If you choose to use a theme for your pages, make certain that you stick to it. Select images that flow well with the rest of the design.

Don't re-invent the wheel. Instead of wasting a lot of time experimenting with colors and typefaces, spend that time researching design on the Web. You'll find thousands of sites dedicated to the development of interesting and effective Web design.

Chapter Summary

In chapter 1 you have been introduced to the concept of the Internet and the World Wide Web. You have learned how a standard language, HTML, is used to develop pages that can be stored on a Web server to be sent out, on request, to people using Web browser software. You have learned the importance of planning the development of your Web site, and have seen some approaches for the process.

2 An Introduction to HTML

Chapter Objective:

In chapter 2 we will learn more about HTML, or Hypertext Markup Language — the fundamental building block of the Internet. To begin understanding how to work with HTML, in chapter 2 you will:

- Learn how HTML is interpreted by various browser applications.

- Understand how Dreamweaver actually writes HTML code behind the scenes, while you're building your sites in a graphic environment.

- Experiment with the different page views — Design view, Code view and Code and Design views.

- Learn to change HTML code in order to modify your pages.

- Learn to change pages visually in order to alter HTML code.

- Explore the use of HTML "tags" — special codes that effect a range of page attributes.

- Learn to use the most common HTML tags — and why using Dreamweaver dramatically reduces the need to understand or work directly with HTML codes.

- Explore the built-in reference tools — the highly-popular O'Reilly HTML and CSS reference books.

Projects to be Completed:

- Cosmic Pets (A)

- Tropiflora Order Form (B)

- Diehard Digital (C)

- Mr. BlockHead's Challenge (D)

An Introduction to HTML

Dreamweaver provides a visual method for creating Web pages. You can add copy, drop in images, import external objects (such as Flash movies, QuickTime movies, "real" content and sounds), create backgrounds, and do it all without actually typing in complex and tedious HTML code.

The ability to visualize what the final product will look like is a feature that dates back to the early days of page layout programs. With applications such as QuarkXPress or Adobe PageMaker, you can design printed material using a blank piece of paper, importing and positioning elements as you construct each page. The same holds true with Dreamweaver.

Dreamweaver is known as a "WYSIWYG" (What You See Is What You Get) Web page editor; that is, a program that enables you to design, produce and manage Web pages and Web sites without having to learn and key all of the detailed and exacting code into your design as you work. Yet behind the scenes, Dreamweaver is actually writing the HTML code required to create the page that you're seeing during the construction process.

Web pages are written in a standard, generally agreed-upon language called "HyperText Markup Language" (HTML) based originally on the international Standard Generalized Markup Language (SGML) used for the exchange of electronic documents. The browsers that are used to browse Web pages have been developed, for the most part, with the HTML standards in mind. In this chapter you will learn to recognize the elements of an HTML document and the formats of those elements.

Dreamweaver isn't the first visual Web authoring environment. It is, however, the first Web page editor that writes HTML code that's mostly compliant with established standards. Dreamweaver also allows you to edit the code it produces, and you can even enter HTML codes that Dreamweaver doesn't recognize.

HTML Document Structure

HTML works through the use of special tags that tell a browser how to display text, images and other content. The tags themselves are not displayed in the browser; they are interpreted by the browser to format the text and graphics that are displayed. When you create a Web page, you use HTML tags to define the way in which you want your content to appear. By adhering to the HTML standard, Web authors around the globe create pages that can be displayed in a common browser.

The World Wide Web Consortium (W3C) is the organization responsible for setting HTML standards. W3C is a group of organizations that attempts to iron out variations in Web technologies and ensures that HTML continues to be accessible to all. W3C members include AT&T, CompuServe, Microsoft, and Netscape Communications, among others. You can visit W3C on the Web at http://www.w3c.org.

Tags

The format of HTML tags includes first an opening "less than" symbol (<), followed by an element and possibly one or more attributes and associated values, and closes with the "greater than" symbol (>). Following the word(s) to be formatted, comes a closing element tag, indicated by the "/" symbol, which marks the end of the format application. Some other tags do not have a closing element, and are referred to as "Empty Elements."

Using Dreamweaver to see HTML

1. Launch the Dreamweaver application.

2. In the upper-left corner of the Document window, click the Show Design View icon to make sure that it's selected.

3. Select Modify>Page Properties, and select a sandy-brown color for the background of the page. The number of the color is #996600.

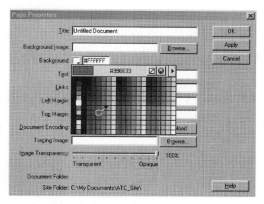

Most Web design applications allow you to select colors by entering their hexadecimal code.

4. Enter the following text (with returns after each line) onto the colored page: "Fishing Tampa Bay," "An Online Resource for Gulf Coast Anglers," "About Us," "Fishing Reports," "Chat Rooms," "Weather and Tides," "Tackle Shop," "Guides".

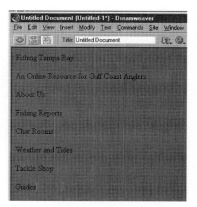

5. The view icons are in the upper-left corner of the Document window. You used one a minute ago to make certain that the window was in Design view. Design view shows the page only the way in which it will most likely appear in a browser window. There are three icons in the row. Click on the center one (Show Code and Design Views). This selection will show you both the HTML code that the program created, as well as the WYSYWYG design.

6. In the bottom (Design view) of the window, double-click the word "Fishing." Look at the top (Code) window. Whatever you select in one window is automatically selected in the other.

We're assuming that you're familiar enough using a computer that you know to press the OK button once you've made selections in a dialog box.

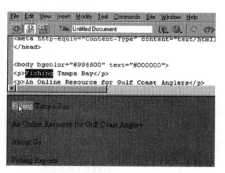

7. Change the copy to read "Sportfishing in Tampa Bay". Notice that the change is simultaneously occurring in the HTML code.

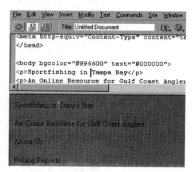

When saving files on a Macintosh, Dreamweaver automatically adds ".html" to the file name, as the extension. On the Windows platform only ".htm" is added.

8. Save the file as "fishing.htm" in your **Work in Progress** folder. Keep it open for the next exercise.

Clearly, being able to format and design your pages visually is a major advantage. You can concentrate on how your pages look, how they work and how effective the content is — all without having to learn how to code directly in HTML. Although it's not impossible, programming is far more tedious than visual page layout and design.

All pages, however, rely on the underlying HTML to function correctly, and there will be times when you'll have to get into the code to fix problems or make adjustments that can't be made visually.

Throughout the following chapters, you'll be studying at the various tags, structures, styles and formatting created by Dreamweaver whenever you design or modify a page.

While it isn't necessary for you to memorize all of the details of HTML tags, it will prove helpful to be familiar with the basics.

Tag Structure

Some tags require that the instructions be enclosed within two similar tags. For example, the title of a document — the name at the top of the browser when the page is loaded — requires that you start with <title> and end with </title>, which is the closing code.

The title is different from the file name. You can choose to display whatever you want to in the browser's Title bar, and use a completely different name for the file itself. For example, you might choose to enter <title>Enjoy backwater fishing in Tampa Bay</title> as the message seen in the browser window whenever the fishing.htm file is loaded.

When we created the document named fishing.htm, Dreamweaver automatically began inserting HTML tags in the document. Let's work with the file to see how tags affect the page view.

Seeing Tags in Action

1. If it's not already open, open the file **fishing.htm**. Click the Show Code and Design Views icon to view both the page and the corresponding HTML.

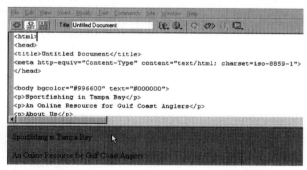

The method in which HTML (or any programming language) is structured is known as the language's "syntax." The syntax is the set of rules that determines the codes, tags, styles and other components that are required for proper interpretation within a browser window.

2. Scroll to the top of the Code window. You can see that the document begins with the <html> tag. This code tells the browser that the document that follows is to be interpreted as HTML.

3. The next code that you see is the <head> code. The head information usually contains the title and the meta information. Meta information is used by search engines to locate and display your pages when certain words are found. A list of appropriate words and phrases would be inserted here. We'll cover this issue in-depth in a later chapter. You can see the closing tag (</head>) at the end of the section.

4. Highlight the title (it currently reads "Untitled Document"). Change it to "Enjoy backwater fishing in Tampa Bay". Click in the Design view, and you'll see the title change at the top of the window. Next to that, in parentheses, you'll see the folder where the file resides, and the name of the file — in this case fishing.htm.

5. Position your cursor inside of the first line of text on the page: the words "Sportfishing in Tampa Bay". If it's not visible on your monitor, activate the Property inspector by selecting Window>Properties, or by pressing Command/Control-F3. Position it near the upper-left corner of the window so that you can see what's happening to the code and the page when you change the settings in the panel.

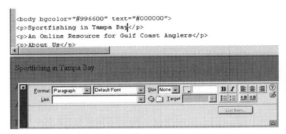

This line of text is currently a regular paragraph, as you can see from the <p> and </p> tags.

6. Use the Format pop-up menu to select Heading 1. This is the first of several heading tags used by HTML to assign special attributes to specific lines of text. Much like writing an outline, HTML lets you create Headings 1, 2, 3, and so on so that you can structure your documents in a logical manner.

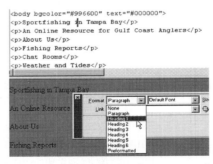

7. Look at the code and the view on the page when you make this change. Notice that the actual HTML code for Heading 1 is <h1> and the closing tag is </h1>.

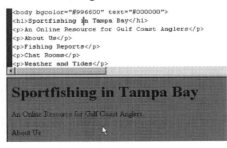

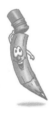

The title of a page is critically important — it's used to bookmark pages, and search engines place more weight on the title then they do on the information stored in the <meta> section.

8. Working in the Code editor, change the <p> in front of "An Online Resource for Gulf Coast Anglers" to an <h2> and the closing code to </h2>. Click the lower-portion of the window and preview the page.

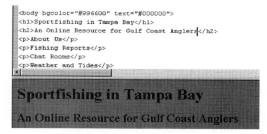

```
<body bgcolor="#996600" text="#000000">
<h1>Sportfishing in Tampa Bay</h1>
<h2>An Online Resource for Gulf Coast Anglers</h2>
<p>About Us</p>
<p>Fishing Reports</p>
<p>Chat Rooms</p>
<p>Weather and Tides</p>
```

Sportfishing in Tampa Bay

An Online Resource for Gulf Coast Anglers

9. Save the file. If you are on a Windows machine, Dreamweaver will quit if you close the file. It works just fine on the Macintosh; the program remains active even if there aren't any open documents.

As you can see, you have the option of entering or changing the HTML code created by Dreamweaver, or you can change an item in the Design view and have Dreamweaver automatically create or update the HTML code.

HTML Tag List

The following pages contain a list of various HTML tags along with a brief explanation of how they are used in Web pages. It's important that you understand in general the basis for the codes generated by Dreamweaver. We will be examining an HTML view of the pages we create, and sometimes making changes directly to this code. The listing here is not intended to be memorized, but you may wish to use it as a reference.

Head Elements

- **<TITLE>…</TITLE>** — These tags enclose the exact words which appear in the Title bar of the browser window, and comprise the title that shows up in the Bookmark (Netscape) or Favorites (MS Internet Explorer) list. It is also an important component for some Internet search engines.

- **<BASE>…</BASE>** — These optional tags enclose the document's URL, which can be helpful in locating linked material if the document is accessed from a local copy.

- **<META>** — This empty tag includes various attributes and provides keyword, description, authorship or automatic redirection to a different Web page; it is an essential part of achieving search engine placement.

- **<SCRIPT>…</SCRIPT>** — These tags enclose embedded VBScript or JavaScript code that is used within the page.

- **<LINK>…</LINK>** — The text enclosed by these tags makes a connection to external, non-embedded resources such as a style sheet or a script.

Body Elements

- **<BODY>…</BODY>** — The <BODY> opening tag has a number of attributes:
  - **<BODY BGCOLOR=?>** — This tag sets the background color for the page.
  - **<BODY TEXT=?>** — This tag sets the text color.
  - **<BODY LINK=?>** — This tag sets the color of hyperlinks in the text.
  - **<BODY VLINK=?>** — This tag sets the color of followed hyperlinks in the text.

Web page markup language standards are constantly evolving due to the frequent release of new versions and formats. Check the W3C.org Web site for the latest official releases. (http://www.w3c.org/).

As specific tags become nonessential in the current HTML specification, they are designated as "deprecated," and in later versions, "obsolete." Almost all attributes that specify the presentation of an HTML document (e.g., colors, alignment, fonts, graphics, and so forth) have been deprecated in favor of style sheets. It is likely that in some future HTML version, these tags and attributes will become obsolete.

- **<BODY ALINK=?>** — This tag sets the color of hyperlinks when clicked.

• **<H1>…</H1>, <H2>…</H2>, <H3>…</H3>, <H4>…</H4>, <H5>…</H5>, and <H6>…</H6>** — These are the format tags for the different available sizes of headings within the Web page. The largest size is H1, and the smallest H6.

• **<P>…</P>** — These paragraph tags wrap the enclosed text according to the current browser window width, and add space above each paragraph.

- **<P ALIGN="?">** — This (alternate) opening paragraph tag includes an attribute which aligns a paragraph to the left, right or center.

• **<PRE>** — This tag creates preformatted text.

• **<I>…</I>** — These tags cause the enclosed text to become italic text.

• **<TT>…</TT>** — These tags create teletype- or typewriter-style text from the enclosed text.

• **<CITE>…</CITE>** — These tags render the enclosed text as a citation, usually in italic styling.

• **<EM>…</EM>** — These tags emphasize the enclosed word(s) (with italic or bold styling). <b> works the same way in most browsers.

• **<STRONG>…</STRONG>** — These tags emphasize enclosed words (also with italic or bold styling). Again, <b> works the same in most browsers.

• **<BLOCKQUOTE>…</BLOCKQUOTE>** — These tags indent enclosed text from both sides.

• **<DL>…</DL>** — These tags create a definition list of enclosed text.

- **<DT>** — This tag precedes each definition term.

- **<DD>** — This tag precedes each definition.

• **<OL>…</OL>** — These tags make the enclosed text a numbered (ordered) list.

• **<UL>…</UL>** — These tags make enclosed text into a bulleted (unordered) list.

• **<LI>…</LI>** — These tags precede each list item, and add a number for items in a numbered or ordered list, or add a bullet for items in a bulleted or unordered list.

• **<DIV ALIGN=?>…</DIV>** — This generic tag is used to format large blocks of HTML and is also used for style sheets.

• **<FONT SIZE=?>…</FONT>** — These tags set the size of font for the enclosed text from 1 to 7, with 1 being large and 7 being small.

• **<FONT COLOR=?>…</FONT>** — These tags set the font color for the enclosed text, using name or hex value.

• **
** — This tag inserts a break in a line of text without generating additional space between paragraphs. Break is an example of an empty element that does not have content and therefore does not use the closing element tag.

• **<HR>** — This empty element tag inserts a horizontal line or rule. Its available attributes (which are enclosed within the tag are:
  - **WIDTH**   in pixels or a percentage of the window width.
  - **HEIGHT**   in pixels.
  - **ALIGN**   left, center or right.
  - **COLOR**   hue.
  - **NOSHADE**   eliminates the default shadow.

Hyperlink Tags

- **<A HREF= "URL">...</A>** — These tags make the enclosed text a hyperlink.
- **<A HREF= "MAILTO:SOMEBODY@THEDOMAIN.COM">...</A>** — These tags create a "mailto" link to send a message to "somebody@thedomain.com".
- **<A NAME= "NAME">...</A>** — These tags create a target location within a document to which another link points and jumps.
- **<A HREF= "#NAME">...</A>** — These tags link enclosed text to that target location from elsewhere in the document.

Picture Tags

- **<IMG SRC="NAME">** — This tag adds an image.
- **<IMG SRC="NAME" ALIGN=?>** — This tag adds an image and aligns it left, right, center, bottom, top or middle. Other alignments include baseline, absolute top, middle and bottom.
- **<IMG SRC="NAME" BORDER=?>** — This tag adds an image and sets the size of a border around the image.

Table Tags

- **<TABLE>...</TABLE>** — These tags make the enclosed text into a table.

  - **<TABLE BORDER=#>** — This table attribute tag sets the width of the border around table cells.

  - **<TABLE CELLSPACING=#>** — This table attribute tag sets the amount of space between table cells.

  - **<TABLE CELLPADDING=#>** — This table attribute tag sets the amount of space between a cell's border and its contents.

  - **<TABLE WIDTH=?>** — This table attribute tag sets the width of the table in pixels or as a percentage of the document width.

- **<TH>...</TH>** — These tags set off the table header (a normal cell with bold, centered text).

- **<TR>...</TR>** — These tags set off each row in a table.

  - **<TR ALIGN=?>** — This attribute sets alignment for cell(s) (left, center or right).

  - **<TR VALIGN=?>** — This attribute sets the vertical alignment for cell rows (top, middle or bottom)

- **<TD>...</TD>** — These tags set off each cell in a row.

  - **<TD ALIGN=?>** — This attribute sets the alignment for cell(s) (left, center, or right).

  - **<TD VALIGN=?>** — This attribute sets the vertical alignment for cell(s) (top, middle or bottom).

  - **<TD COLSPAN=#>** — This attribute sets the number of columns a cell should span.

  - **<TD ROWSPAN=#>** — This attribute sets the number of rows a cell should span (default=1).

  - **<TD NOWRAP>** — This attribute prevents the lines within a cell from being broken to fit.

Frame Tags

The base frames document that controls the layout of the frames in a Web page does not hold the page content, but only describes the frames and the HTML documents that will initially fill those frames.

- **<FRAMESET>...</FRAMESET>** — These are the tags in a frames document; they can also be nested in other framesets.

  - **<FRAMESET ROWS= "value,value">** — This attribute defines the rows within a frameset, using a number in pixels or a percentage of the width.

  - **<FRAMESET COLS= "value,value">** — This attribute defines the columns within a frameset, using a number in pixels or a percentage of the width.

- **<FRAME>** — This tag defines a single frame or region within a frameset.

- **<NOFRAMES>...</NOFRAMES>** — These tags define what will appear on browsers that don't support frames. Sometimes this is just a notice that this page is designed with frames and the browser being used does not support frames.

  - **<FRAME SRC= "URL">** — This attribute specifies which HTML document should be displayed.

  - **<FRAME NAME= "NAME">** — This attribute names the frame or region so it may be targeted by other frames.

  - **<FRAME MARGINWIDTH=#>** — This attribute defines the left and right margins for the frame; they must be equal to or greater than 1.

  - **<FRAME MARGINHEIGHT=#>** — This attribute defines the top and bottom margins for the frame; they must be equal to or greater than 1.

  - **<FRAME SCROLLING=VALUE>** — This attribute sets whether or not the frame has a scrollbar; the value may equal yes, no or auto. The default, as in ordinary documents, is auto.

  - **<FRAME NORESIZE>** — This attribute prevents the user from resizing a frame.

Form Tags

For functional forms, you'll need to run a CGI script. The HTML only affects the appearance of a form. We'll cover this in more detail in Chapter 12.

- **<FORM>...</FORM>** — These tags insert a form.

- **<SELECT MULTIPLE NAME= "NAME" SIZE=?>...</SELECT>** — These tags create a scrolling menu; Size sets the number of menu items to visible before you need to scroll.

- **<OPTION>...</OPTION>** — These tags set off each menu item.

- **<SELECT NAME= "NAME">...</SELECT>** — These tags create a pull-down menu.

- **<TEXTAREA NAME= "NAME" COLS=40 ROWS=8>...</TEXTAREA>** — These tags create a text box area; columns set the width and rows set the height.

- **<INPUT TYPE= "CHECKBOX" NAME= "TEXT">** — This tag creates a checkbox; text follows the tag.

- **<INPUT TYPE= "RADIO" NAME= "TEXT" VALUE= "X">** — This tag creates a Radio button; text follows the tag.

- **<INPUT TYPE=TEXT NAME= "TEXT" SIZE=20>** — This tag creates a one-line text area.; size sets length in characters.
- **<INPUT TYPE= "SUBMIT" VALUE= "TEXT">** — This tag creates a Submit button labeled "text."
- **<INPUT TYPE= "IMAGE" BORDER=0 NAME= " filename " SRC= "filename.GIF">** — This tag creates a Submit button using an image.
- **<INPUT TYPE= "RESET">** — This tag creates a Reset button.

Examining a Sophisticated Web Page

Now that we have worked with a simple Web page, it's time to put our newly developed Web skills into perspective. The Web site that you will examine in the next exercise contains images, tables, JavaScript rollovers, and links to Web sites, email and to Active Server Pages. More on these topics will follow in later chapters.

The <Input> tag is an "empty element" that does not use a closing tag.

View Source

One excellent method of learning how to develop Web pages is to examine the source (text) code for the pages that you encounter as you browse the Web. Your browser gives you the option of examining the underlying HTML code if you right-click on the Web page and select "View Source."

View Web Page Source

1. Open the http://www.againsttheclock.com Web site in your browser. This can be accomplished by typing the complete URL or just "againsttheclock" (without the quotes) into the location or address field of the browser. If you do not have an active connection to the Internet, locate the **ATC_index.html** file in your **RF-Dreamweaver** folder and open it with Dreamweaver.

2. Look at the page. This is a sophisticated design, using JavaScript, rollovers, dynamic pages and other advanced techniques.

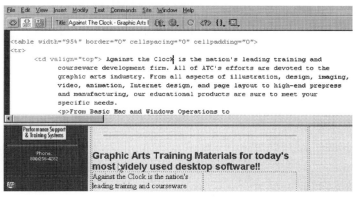

3. Identify the elements of the HTML document: **<HEAD>**, **<TITLE>**, **<SCRIPT>**, **<BODY>**, **<TABLE>**, **<IMG SRC= "?">** (graphics), **<A HREF="?">** (links) and **<FONT>**.
   This is an example of an advanced HTML document, but even this page lacks some elements that may be found in other pages.

4. Close the Source window without saving.

The AOL browser sometimes acts strangely if you don't use the proper URL. For example, typing the site name without using "www." may not work properly.

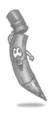

Many Web sites can be reached by typing just the domain name without the protocol (http://) or the domain extension (.com). For example, try typing "Sony" (without the quotation marks), and press Enter.

If the document you are browsing is a Frames page, the source will show only the frame structure, not the content. Use the Shortcut menu (Right-click for Windows and Click for Macintosh) to open the frame in a separate window, and then examine the source code.

Online HTML Resources

Use your favorite search engine (Yahoo!, Excite, Lycos, Alta Vista, HotBot, Snap) to locate HTML resources. There are a number of professional sites that offer regular articles with great information and techniques.

Built-in Reference Tools

Dreamweaver provides an excellent built-in HTML resource library — the complete O'Reilly reference guides. The O'Reilly guides are the standard reference work among professional HTML programmers, offering a complete listing of current HTML codes and covering just about every condition you might encounter. There are actually three different books contained in the reference system: one for CSS (cascading style sheets), one for Java and one for HTML. You can access the panel from the Window>Reference menu or by using Command/Control-Shift-F1. The F1 key is the standardHelp key, and additional modifiers evoke the Reference panel.

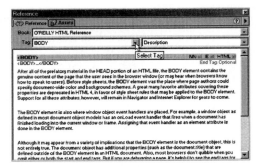

The top of the Reference panel provides several pop-up menus from which you can select the reference book, the tag, and the content of the window.

Chapter Summary

In chapter 2 we discussed the basic code and structure of HTML. You learned how to display the code and design of a Web page in the Dreamweaver window, you learned how to make changes to either the HTML or the design of the page and view the changes in either view. You've reviewed a list of basic HTML commands, and you learned how to access the built-in reference tools provided by O'Reilly in cooperation with Macromedia.

3 The Authoring Environment

Chapter Objective:

In Chapter 3, we move from concept to practice — and learn about the Dreamweaver authoring environment. To become comfortable with the many tools, panels, and inspectors available to you, in Chapter 3 you will:

- Understand the use of Dreamweaver's three primary views: Design (or Document) View, Code View, and Code and Design Views.

- Explore the Document Window, where most of your work takes place.

- Learn about the Objects panel – the most important panel in the Dreamweaver interface.

- Learn about Common objects – the most widely used tools in the program. These include the Insert Image, Draw Layer, Insert Table, and Insert Horizontal Rule objects.

- Begin to learn about other Object panels, including Form Objects, Character Objects, Frame Objects, and others.

- Explore the Site View – a graphical representation of your site, including pages and links.

- Learn to hide, show, and manage panels and inspectors.

- Work with several of the program's preference panels – where you can customize the way Dreamweaver works.

- Learn to set up your Preview browsers, which let you check the way your pages function under various viewing conditions.

Projects to be Completed:

- Cosmic Pets (A)

- Tropiflora Order Form (B)

- Diehard Digital (C)

- Mr. BlockHead's Challenge (D)

The Authoring Environment

Dreamweaver was specifically created to provide Web designers a method by which they could develop their sites (and the individual pages that comprise them) in a visual environment. The program supplies an abundance of tools, panels (also known as inspectors or dialogs), menus and other methods to create and modify pages.

The first step in learning how to use Dreamweaver to develop your page is to become familiar with the interface, and that's what we're going to cover in this chapter.

The Dreamweaver Interface

Dreamweaver provides a *graphic user interface*, or GUI, which allows you to select most tools and commands from the appropriate panel or menu. But, you're always free to code directly in HTML, although you'll probably agree with the majority of designers that many — if not all — commands are easier to apply with using the visual tools available to you.

When you're working in Design, Code and Design, or Code view, you're only looking at a single page. The second view you can employ is the entire site named, appropriately, Site view.

Document View

Document view displays individual Web pages in a full-screen authoring environment, where you can import objects, enter or import text, assign attributes to objects, create links, position individual elements relative to each other and generally construct your pages. Document view starts out as a blank page upon which you execute and develop your page designs.

There are a number of redundancies in the Dreamweaver interface; you'll often find more than one way to accomplish the same task. When this does occur, we'll attempt to point it out. Ultimately, you'll develop your own personal style and favorite ways of performing tasks.

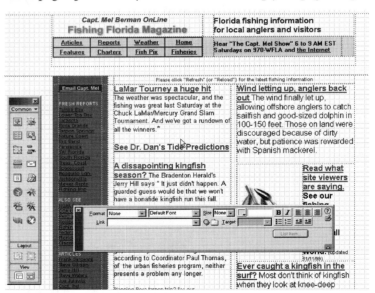

Document view allows you to work on individual Web pages.

Working on local and remote sites isn't funda-mentally different. When you learn about site management, you'll see how to make changes to local pages and then automatically upload them to your "live" site. Live sites are those that people access over the Internet.

Site View

The second view available to you while you're developing your projects is the Site view.

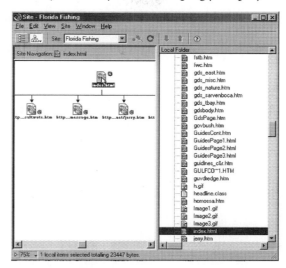

Site view offers several options. As you can see in the image, the window is split into two panes. On the left side you're seeing the site map — a visual flowchart that shows each page on the site and their relationship to one another. It's similar to an organizational chart, except that it's showing the relationships between individual pages instead of who reports to whom.

Alternately, you can display the contents of a remote site in the left pane and the local site (the working copy that you update) on the right pane. We'll talk more about accessing and updating remote sites in a later chapter. For now, we're going to be working on local sites — ones that reside on your hard drive. We feel that it's a good idea for you to learn how to build sites before you learn how to publish and manage them on the Internet.

Throughout the book you'll be working in both Document and Site views, so it's a good idea to familiarize yourself with them now. We'll open several files during the exercises in this chapter so that you'll have something to work with.

Document Window

When you first launch Dreamweaver you'll see a blank page. As is the case in all applications, there's a Menu bar at the top of the screen, and a few panels, or inspectors.

Although you'll routinely switch to Site view and work with the site map, most of your actual development time will be spent in the Document window.

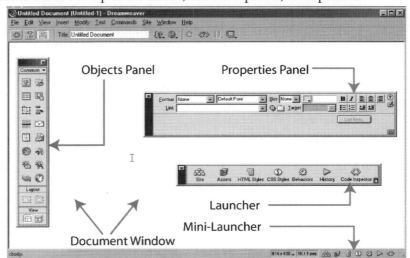

Objects Panels

The first item to look at is the Objects panel. When selected, the Objects panel first appears on the left side of the Document window. There are actually seven different Objects panels — each providing a specific and related collection of commands. The Objects panel contains seven different categories, each with its own selection of tools providing a specific and related collection of commands.

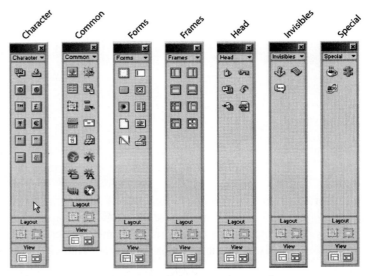

From left to right: Character, Common, Forms, Frames, Head, Invisibles and Special Objects panels.

Each category of the Objects panels is available from the pop-up menu at the top of the panel. The position of the pop-up remains constant, regardless of which panel is active at any given time. A bullet appears to the left of the currently active panel.

By the time you've finished the book, you'll have used all of these Objects panels. For now, let's look at each one and get a basic idea of how they work and what they do.

Objects Categories

The following section is a list of the seven Objects categories, each of which can be displayed in the Objects panel.

Character: The Character Objects panel gives you access to special characters, such as the Copyright "©" symbol, Trademark "™" symbol, and others that aren't normally accessible from the keyboard. In the next chapter, you'll learn to use this panel when creating text elements.

Common: The Common Objects panel contains the commands to insert images, tables, horizontal lines, dates, email links, Flash type and movies, Shockwave content and other common elements. You'll spend more time working with these commands than with all the other commands combined.

Insert Image	Insert Rollover Image
Insert Table	Insert Tabular Data
Draw Layer	Insert Navigation Bar
Insert Horizontal Rule	Insert Email Link
Insert Date	Insert Server-Side Include
Insert Fireworks HTML	Insert Flash
Insert Flash Button	Insert Flash Text
Insert Shockwave	Insert Generator
Draw Layout Cell (Disabled)	Draw Layout Table (Disabled)
Standard View	Layout View

Forms: A critical component of many high-end Web sites, Dreamweaver provides a powerful but simple-to-use collection of form tools. You'll learn how to use them in chapter 12, "Creating Web Forms."

Frames: Although frames aren't nearly as popular as they were in the past, they're still used for certain types of applications — particularly those that contain variable amounts of copy and require scroll bars. Examples are newsletters, and sites where articles of varying lengths are displayed in a rectangular space. If the length of the article exceeds the available space, then a scrolling frame ensures that the reader has access to all the text.

Head: A page's head contains information specific to that page and the site. Items include Meta data, descriptions, keywords (used by search engines to determine if your site matches a surfer's search criteria), links and other information. You'll build your own heads later in this book.

Invisibles: Most pages contain items that aren't visible when viewed in a browser window. The most common ones are comments (written by the designer to help them remember information about specific objects, commands and development notes). Others include scripts, anchors and other items that you'll learn to use as we move forward.

Special: Special commands include graphic support objects such as ActiveX, scripts (such as JavaScript), and plugins. An examples of a plugin is the Flash Player plugin, which is required for the user to view Flash movies. We'll create pages that require plugins toward the end of this book. These are somewhat advanced features that are best left until you have a solid feel for the basics.

Menu Access

You can access the available panels using the Window menu. Those panels and inspectors that allow for keyboard access display the appropriate key combinations to the right of the menu command.

Two of the more useful commands are found near the bottom of the Window menu. The first is Arrange Panels. There will be times when you have a number of panels open at once, and your monitor can become quite cluttered. In the following image the panels we're using are scattered randomly around the monitor.

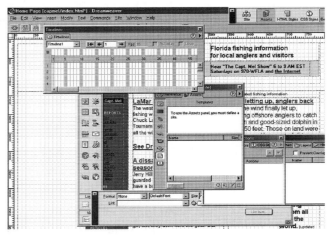

Using the Arrange command causes all panels to automatically snap to the edges of the monitor, leaving somewhat more room than before.

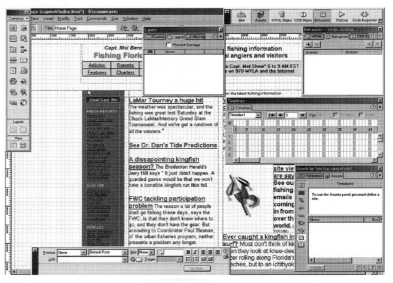

Whenever you quit Dreamweaver, the program remembers which panels were active and where they were positioned. The next time you start the application, it puts them back where they were when the program last quit.

It's a good idea to put plenty of comments on your pages. That way, if you're temporarily unable to manage the site, someone else can read them and gain some insight into what you were thinking when you built it.

You should always try to learn the keyboard equivalents for accessing panels — it's much faster and more efficient than using the Menu bar. Over a long-term period, you'll be surprised at how much time you can save. Even a few hours a year can really add up.

Another helpful command is Hide and Show Panels (F4). If they're showing, the command hides them; if they're hidden, pressing it makes them appear.

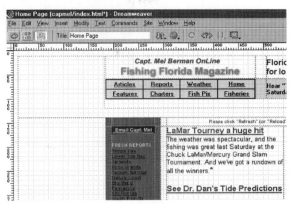

Hiding panels lets you work without having to move panels out of the way.

Launcher Panel

Remember when we said there were some redundancies in the Dreamweaver interface? The Launcher and Mini-launcher panel are examples. Take a look at the panel and the lower-right corner of the Document window and you'll see what we mean.

The Launcher panel provides access to the Site views, Assets (defined objects utilized in the design of a site), HTML Styles, CSS Styles (Cascading Style Sheets), Behaviors (how objects act when triggered by certain actions), History (basically a recording of what you've been doing) and the Code inspector.

Property Inspector

The Property inspector is an important component of the Dreamweaver interface. Depending on the object that you have selected at any given time, it provides a way to edit and modify its attributes.

In the following example, we selected one of the links from the left side of the Florida Fishing home page. You can see the formatting and link information (in addition to a great many more attributes) displayed in the Property inspector:

The small diamond in the lower right of the Property Inspector expands and minimizes the panel.

When we select an image, the options change:

Selecting the graphic displays a completely different set of properties than those we had when we had a link selected. A thumbnail of the selected object appears in the upper-left corner of the panel; tools to create an image map appear in the lower-left, and a variety of other tools and modifiers become available.

Notice the "Edit" button in the lower-right? It launches Fireworks, Macromedia's excellent Web image editor.

Other Panels

There are a number of other panels that provide controls over a wide range of Dreamweaver commands and functions. These include site-management tools (such as the one that displays all the assets — or objects — that make up your site). Others include layers, the reference books that we mentioned in a previous chapter, HTML styles, and others. By the end of this book, you'll have worked with all of them.

Managing Panels

We've seen how to use Arrange Panels and Hide Panels to organize our Document window. In addition to these commands, you can also use Dreamweaver's docking feature to combine, separate and create custom panels that match the way you work — or the specific project that you're working on at the time.

Some panels are already docked — an example is the Assets panel, which is docked with the Reference panel. You can separate any docked panels by grabbing their tabs and dragging them onto the Document window.

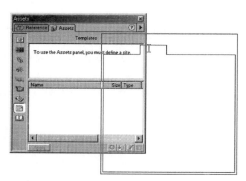

If you have multiple documents open at the same time, their names will be displayed at the bottom of the Window menu. Selecting one will bring that document to the top of the stack.

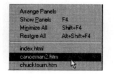

You can customize the Launcher and Minilauncher panels using the Preferences dialog box.

To combine several panels, grab one panel's tab and drag it onto another panel; they'll combine into a single panel with their tabs displayed across the top. To select one, simply click its tab to bring it to the front of the stack. It then becomes the active panel.

You can combine any of Dreamweaver's panels. Again, once you become more comfortable with using the program in the real world, you'll develop your own style of organizing your workspace.

Preferences

The Preferences command (Edit>Preferences) provides even more ways to customize your working environment — down to which browser you use, what application is used to edit content (such as bitmap images, sounds and movies), what colors are used in HTML coding and much more. Many of these settings are somewhat advanced, and will be covered in detail later in the book — but some of them are quite simple, and should be understood early in the learning process.

Using the Preferences Dialog Box

1. Launch Dreamweaver. A blank, untitled document will appear. Select Edit> Preferences to activate the Preferences dialog box. On the left side of the dialog box you'll see a list of categories. Select the first option — the General preferences.

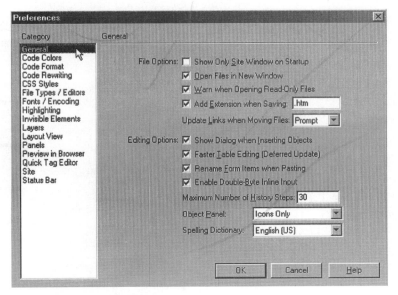

Fireworks is part of the commercially-available Dreamweaver 4 suite. In certain situations, educational institutions purchase special editions of Dreamweaver that don't have the Fireworks application "bundled" as part of the package. Check to make certain that you have Fireworks installed on your system.

If you don't, you can download a trial version from http:// www.macromedia.com. It only works for 30 days or so.

2. On the lower-right side of the dialog box is a pop-up menu that allows you to change the way in which the Objects panels are displayed. You can choose Icons Only (which is the default setting) and two other options. Click on the menu and select Icons and Text. Click OK to apply the changes.

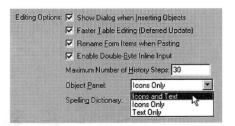

3. Take a look at the Objects panel. The icons are now accompanied by descriptive text — not a bad idea when you're first learning the program.

The Objects panel can be resized, which may explain why the one you see is different than the one we're showing.

4. Activate the Preferences panel by pressing Command/Control-U. Select the Panels dialog box from the list.

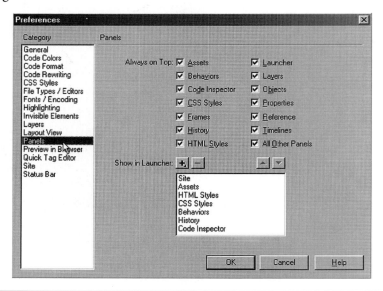

The keyboard command for activating the Preferences dialog box is Command/ Control-U. You can change the keyboard shortcuts for any commands by selecting Edit>Keyboard Preferences.

5. From this dialog box, you can control which panels appear on top of the Document window. It's a good idea to keep them all turned on so that they don't get lost on a cluttered monitor. On the bottom right is a list of the items that currently appear in the Launcher panel. Select History and click the Remove (-) button. Click OK to apply the changes, and look at the Launcher panel.

6. Open the Preferences dialog box again, activate the Panels dialog box, and put the History icon back in the Launcher window using the Add (+) button. Pick History from the pop-up list.

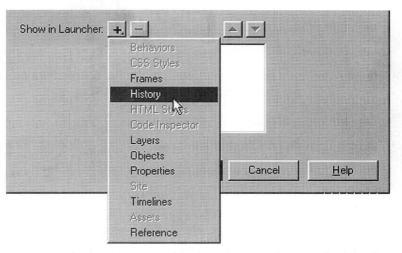

7. Click OK to apply the changes, and look at the Launcher panel. It's back to normal.

8. Close the file without saving.

Page Size Preferences

In the lower-right corner of the Document window — near the Mini-Launcher — is a pop-up menu that lets you select the size of the page that you're working on. Clicking on it brings up a collection of predetermined page sizes.

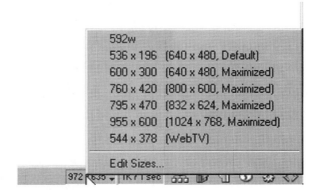

You'll notice an "Edit Sizes..." selection at the bottom of the menu. Selecting this option provides a dialog box that allows you to add additional presets, or modify the ones that are already there. The dialog box is actually one of the Preferences dialog boxes.

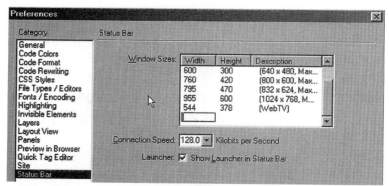

You can also set the Connection Speed from this dialog box. Dreamweaver uses this figure to estimate download times for your pages. It's a good idea to keep it at 28 or 56k — the most common modem speeds in use today.

Editor Preferences

Building Web pages — especially complex, compelling Web pages — requires the use of many different components. It's not uncommon for a site to contain copy, images, animations, sounds and even movie clips.

Although Dreamweaver is a powerful tool for combining elements and developing complex pages, in most cases it's not well-suited to the actual creation of the components that you'll need. External applications — called editors — are the most effective way to create and modify page objects.

In most cases you can launch external editors from within Dreamweaver. To ensure that the correct application is selected when you edit an object, you should check the Editor Preferences. From there you can add or remove external editors, and Dreamweaver will use them from that point forward.

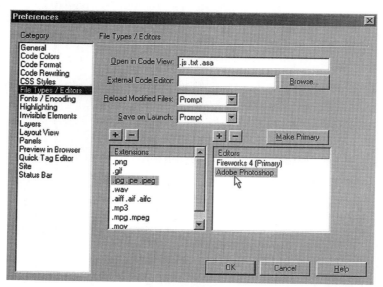

In the above image, we clicked the Add (+) button and selected Adobe Photoshop as an editor for JPG images.

Many users — particularly those that do a lot of coding directly in HTML — add the reference books to the Launcher panel so that they can access them quickly.

You can have more than one editor for any file type. When you do, Dreamweaver will prompt you to determine which one you want to use.

To edit an image with an external editor, select it and press Command/Control-E. You can also select Edit>Edit with External Editor from the Menu bar.

You'll often be editing text, JavaScript and other HTML files directly in Dreamweaver using the Code view. If you prefer to use another editor for these file types, use the Browse button to the right of the External Code Editor field, and locate the application.

When editing a page object, Dreamweaver will update it automatically, or prompt you before it does. These settings are available from the pop-up menus on this same dialog box.

Browser Preferences

A majority of the people viewing your pages will be using one of two different browsers: Microsoft's Internet Explorer or Netscape Navigator. It's a good idea to use them both when you're previewing your pages. You can add, remove or rename your preview browsers from the Preferences>Preview in Browser dialog box.

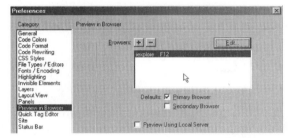

If you're running server software on a PC, you can also choose to preview local files in the browser by checking the box on the lower portion of the dialog box. This option doesn't work on the Macintosh platform.

Chapter Summary

In chapter 3 you learned about the Dreamweaver interface. You're familiar with the Objects panels, and have seen how you can manage the many panels and dialog boxes available in the Document window. You've worked with the Preferences dialog box, and learned how to make changes to several of the default preferences, including external editors, preview browsers and the appearance of the Objects panels.

Notes:

4 Introduction to Site Design

Chapter Objective:

In chapter 4 we build our first site to provide you with an overview of the many techniques and commands you'll learn in subsequent chapters. To build a strong foundation working with Dreamweaver, in chapter 4 you will:

- Learn about the concept of a root folder – a critically important aspect of building and maintaining a Web site.

- Explore the concept of nested folders, which can reside inside the root (or parent) folder to help with organizing the many objects that are used to build a typical Web site.

- Come to fully understand the concept of a home page.

- Build a simple but functional Web site.

- Create and save an index.htm file to act as a home page.

- Enter text and Import images onto your pages.

- Create links between pages on your site.

- Learn to position elements on your pages using simple alignment techniques.

- Learn to map your site, and use the map to move around while developing the site.

- Create a button that links to the home page.

Projects to be Completed:

- Cosmic Pets (A)

- Tropiflora Order Form (B)

- Diehard Digital (C)

- Mr. BlockHead's Challenge (D)

Objects such as images, sounds, animations and movies aren't embedded in an HTML document — they're linked to the original file and downloaded along with the page. A good analogy is when you place an image in a QuarkXPress or PageMaker document.

If you're using common objects (such as buttons, images or logos) in a number of different sites, you can end up with many copies of the same file. This isn't necessarily bad, because it keeps each site you build complete within its root folder. It also allows you to easily update multiple sites.

Introduction to Site Design

In this chapter, we're going to build a few simple pages, and combine them into a small site. For all intents and purposes, the process is the same whether you're building a site that contains thousands of pages or one that only has four or five. Once you've experienced putting a simple site together, the more complex discussions and exercises using type, images, animations, tables, behaviors, layers and other functions of Dreamweaver will be easier to understand.

File and Folder Management

Except for the most elementary of Web sites, most require some degree of organization. If your site has four or five pages, ten or so images, and no complex media (such as animations, sound or video), then you could probably keep everything in one folder. Add a few hundred pages, 10,000 images and some rich media (such as animations, sounds and movies), and managing the site takes on a whole new dimension. Without folders to help you organize your work — particularly if you need to make changes later (and you will), managing your site will prove very difficult.

The Root Folder

All Dreamweaver sites begin their lives in a single "root" folder. The root folder is an important component of your projects. It's in the root folder that Dreamweaver begins looking for links, graphics, objects and pages. Nothing contained in your site can be any higher (outside of) than the root folder. If it is, the browser will fail to find it when the user clicks on the related button. In the case of images or media, they simply won't appear where they should.

You can import elements into a Dreamweaver page from anywhere on your hard drive or network devices. When you do, the program will ask you if you want to create a copy of the object inside of the root folder (or inside of a nested folder within the root folder). This lets you keep common objects anywhere you want, without the need to move an object from its normal location into the root folder of your site.

Nested Folders

You can create as many folders as you want within the root folder. If the project calls for it, you can even create folders within folders; it simply depends on how you want to organize your work. As long as you respect the root folder — making certain that all files you need for the site are within that folder — you can organize the site's resources any way you want.

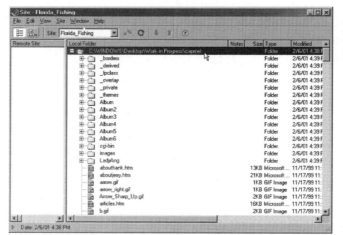

At the top of the list you can see the root folder – it's called capmel, and it's inside of the Work In Progress folder on our desktop. Notice that there are a number of folders within the root folder.

Throughout the book we'll be using the .htm and .html extension. There is no difference between the extensions — they date back to a time when the Macintosh OS used .html and Windows used .htm. They're interchangeable today, and work equally well on both machines. We should caution you that some older servers still require 8.3 naming conventions — so check with your ISP about file naming conventions.

Navigation refers to how the viewer moves through your Web sites. They start at the home page, and then use links or buttons to move deeper into the site. You must make sure that the interface, or navigation strategy, keeps the user from getting confused. Far too many sites have a confusing navigation scheme. Try to minimize the amount of clicking the user has to do.

The Home Page and File Organization

All sites must have a "home" page. It's the starting point for the viewer's experience and the focal point of all navigation schemes.

When you're designing a site, you must tell Dreamweaver what file represents the home page. They're almost never called "home." Most servers require that the home page is named either index.htm or default.htm. Home pages might also be small programs, or scripts (in the case of complex sites), and therefore might be called default.asp (ASP stands for Active Server Page) or index.asp. For now, we're going to be working with .htm files as home pages. Later, we'll discuss the use of Active Server Pages.

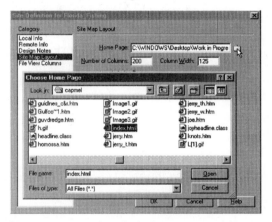

When you're defining a site, you identify the home page so that Dreamweaver can build a site map. All sites have home pages — normally called index.htm or default.htm.

Building a Site

There are several ways in which you can go about building a site.

- You can create the root folder and any nested folders, and then create the pages that will become the site.
- You can create the pages first, and then create the appropriate folders when saving the files.

Either method works fine. As we mentioned before, you don't have to start out with all your images and other page objects in place within the site's folders. When you import the elements onto your pages, Dreamweaver will copy the objects from their original location into the root or nested folder for your new site.

In the following series of exercises, we're going to build a small site. We're not going to try to build a complete, functioning Web site — all we're trying to do is give you a feel for the basic workflow involved in site construction.

Creating a Document

As we just stated, you can either create all the folders you'll need before you start creating any pages, or you can begin creating the pages and create the folders as you go along. We're going to use the second method starting with creating the home page for our site.

On the Windows platform, closing all documents quits the application — on the Macintosh, the program remains active even if all of the documents have been closed.

To create a new document, all you have to do is start Dreamweaver. The document that appears is a new, untitled document.

Creating a Page

1. Launch Dreamweaver. You'll see a blank Untitled Document. Select File>Save. Navigate to your **Work in Progress** folder (which should be on your desktop). Click the New Folder icon (Windows) or the New Folder button (Mac) and create a new folder named "Tropiflora". This will become the root folder for our exercises.

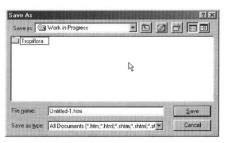

2. Save the file as "index.htm" in the folder you just created. This is going to be the home page for our site.

3. Keep the file open for the next exercise.

Setting Document Properties

Each document or page in your site has a set of properties to which it is attached. These properties define the background color or image, the color of text and a host of other attributes. The exact order in which you determine or set the properties of your pages isn't critical — you can drop all items onto a page and then set the properties, or you can set the properties before you import and/or create the page objects.

Editing Page Properties

1. If the **index.htm** document isn't open, open it now. Select Modify>Page Properties. The first change you should make is to the title of the document. In the Title field at the top of the window, enter "Welcome to Tropiflora".

The page title appears in the Title bar when the page is viewed in a browser window. The file's name and the page title aren't connected in any way.

You should be aware that search engines pay more attention to the title of a page than to its meta tags. Consider this when titling your pages — use titles that will help visitors find your site.

2. Set the background of the page to black, using the pop-up color swatches palette. Black's identification number is #000000. Set the Text color to a blue color — in this case we used #0066FF. Click OK to close the dialog box.

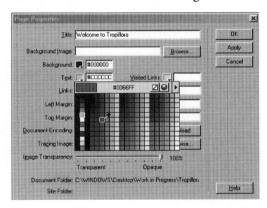

3. Save the file, then enter the following copy onto the page. Press Return after every line: "Tropiflora" <Return>, "Exotic Plants from Around the World" <3 Returns> and then the navigation line. Use a space, the "|" character and another space to separate the following words on one line: "About Tropiflora", "Location", "Products", "Contact Information".

Hexadecimal notation dates back to the early days of computers when programming was often done in a language called "Machine Language." Hexidecimal notation is a method of counting (or assigning unique identification numbers to) objects such as colors.

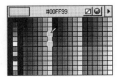

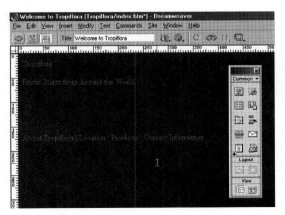

The Pipe character (|) is above the backslash (\) character on your keyboard.

4. Keep this file open and create a new page (File>New). Select Modify>Page Properties, and set the page title to About Tropiflora, the background to black, and the text to blue — just like on the home page.

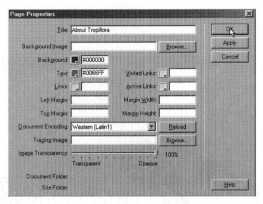

The line of text at the bottom of the Document window is going to be broken out as a series of links. We used the Pipe (|) key to separate the navigation text. It's on the upper-right side of your keyboard, over the top of the Backslash (\) key.

5. At the top of the new page, enter the words "About Tropiflora". Press the Return or Enter key three times and enter the phrase "Back to the Home Page".

6. Save the page inside of the Tropiflora root folder. Name it "about.htm".

7. Create three more new files. One should be titled "Location" and named "location.htm", one should be titled "Products" and named "products.htm", and the last one should be titled "Contact" and named "contact.htm". When you're done, there should be five files in the root folder. Type the title at the top of each page and add the "Back to Home Page" text at the bottom.

Once you create the last file, contact.htm, you'll have all the files you'll need for your site.

You can color the type and backgrounds for these pages the same as the home page, or you can select your own colors — they'll have no impact on how the site works.

These initial exercises are purposely designed to be simple in nature — this will allow you to easily grasp the concepts being taught. Later, as the projects become more complex, they'll get much more attractive as well.

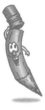

Links work the same way whether you're using text, images or parts of an image. They're essentially pointers that take the browser to another file. Links can point to discrete URLs, which can be an entirely different site.

You can control whether or not the new site opens in its own browser window or replaces the contents of the current window.

8. Keep all the files open as you work. Return to the index.htm (home) page. Click the Show Code and Design Views button at the top left of the Document window. Scroll to the top of the HTML code and examine the title and color settings. These standard HTML codes were taken directly from the Page Properties dialog box. When you're done, switch back to Design view. No need to spend a lot of time looking at HTML right now.

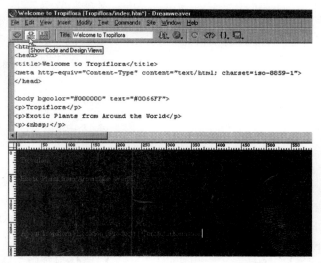

9. Double-check all your work, and make certain that all the files are properly saved. Keep them open for the following exercises.

Linking to Other Pages

We now have five pages — one (index.htm) which will serve as the home page, and four more that will provide the viewer with additional information about our company. Before we move on to using images and formatting to make the site more attractive, let's create the links between the home page the content pages, and back to the home page. That will allow the viewer to "hit" the home page, and move from there to the meat of the site.

Links can be as simple as a line of text or as complex as a complete menu system, with drop-down menus, keyboard equivalents, images or even parts of images. As we move through this book, you'll gain experience with all the different types of links that you're likely to encounter. First we're going to create simple text links, and later in the exercise we'll use a graphic as a link.

Creating Simple Links

1. If the files you created earlier aren't open, open them now. Check the bottom of the Window menu to make certain that they're all there.

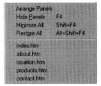

2. Switch back to Design View. Select **index.htm** from the list at the bottom of the Window menu to bring it to the front. Highlight the words "About Tropiflora". If the Property inspector isn't visible on your monitor, activate it by pressing Command/Control-F3. Look to the right of the Link field. There's a folder icon, which is the Browse for File button. Click it.

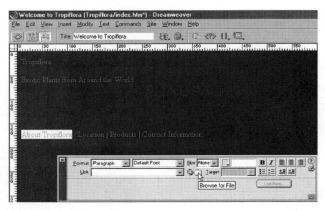

3. The Select File dialog box will appear. If necessary, navigate back to your Tropiflora folder. Click on the **about.htm file** and click Select. You can also double-click the file name and bypass the Select button.

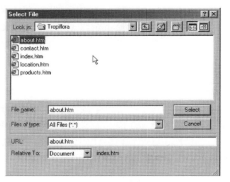

4. See the link? It's now underlined and is a slightly darker shade of blue than the rest of the copy. Look at the Property inspector. The link you selected is now visible in the Link field.

5. Activate the about.htm page. Highlight the "Back to Home Page" text and click the Browse for File button on the Properties dialog box. Link the text to the index.htm (home) page, as you did in steps 3 and 4.

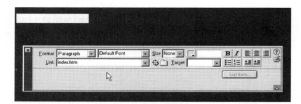

Dreamweaver can maintain a "cache" for your sites, which is a small file that contains index information about links, images, assets in use, and other information. It's a good idea to keep this checkbox selected for all of your sites — it dramatically speeds up certain operations. Whenever you define a site, you'll see the below message. You can check the "Don't show me ..." box to suppress it. Just make certain that you click OK to close it and move on.

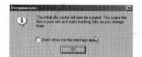

6. While the copy is still selected, press Command/Control-C to copy it (and its link information) to the clipboard. Activate the pages one by one and paste the text over the text that's already there. This will duplicate the link that returns the viewer to the home page.

7. Save all the pages but keep them open for the next exercise.

Defining and Mapping Your Site

When you define a site, Dreamweaver collects all the link information and creates the relationships between the root folder, the links and the individual pages contained in the site. Later, as you add and delete pages, update links, rename files, import additional graphics and generally work on your project, the program keeps track of all your changes and continuously updates the site maps and internal links. It's a wonderful way to build a site, because you don't have spend a lot of time tracking elements.

Using Define Site

1. Select New Site from the Site menu. On the Local Info dialog box, enter the name "Tropiflora Web Site" into the Site Name field. You may also have to browse to locate the correct local root folder.

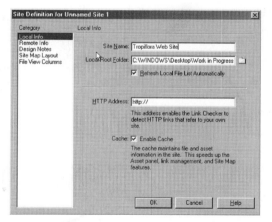

2. Click OK to have Dreamweaver create the site cache. Select the Site Map Layout category from the Site Definition dialog box. Click the Browse for File button next to the Home Page field. When the Select File dialog box appears, select index.htm as the home page. This nearly completes the definition of this simple site. Click Done.

3. In the Site window, click on the Site Map icon. Examine your site. This view shows the graphic representation of the site on the left, and the file list on the right.

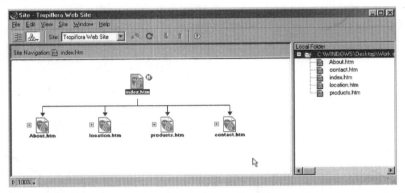

Double-clicking any page icon in the site map will open or activate that page in the Document window. The small icon next to the index.htm indicates that it's active.

4. Take a moment to examine the site map. A small circular icon appears next to the currently active page. In the image above, it's just to the right of the index.htm (home) page.

5. Some of the pages shows a plus (+) sign next to them (the currently active page displays a small target), indicating that they contain links to other pages. In this case, each page contains only one link — the one that takes the viewer back to the home page. Click the plus sign next to the location.htm page. The page it links to — index.htm — is displayed.

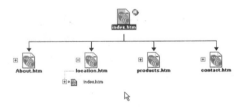

Any page that has links displays them in the site map — that's why there's a plus sign next to several of the pages.

6. Save all the pages and keep them open.

Inserting Images

No Web site would be complete without images — it was the ability to mix images and type and have the pages interpreted by a Web browser that gave birth to the Internet as we know it today. While the Web has come a long way since its humble beginnings, it still relies heavily on graphic objects. As we continue with our discussion, we're going to use some images in the simple site we've been building.

There's a lot to know about images: size, color, file formats, editing, rollovers and buttons are just a few issues that we'll discuss in depth in the appropriate chapters. For now we're just going to see what it's like to place an image onto our pages — and examine how they're handled by Dreamweaver as a component of a defined site.

You can use the List icon to show files on both sides of the window. This is particularly useful when you're working on remote sites (ones stored on a remote server) and you want to drag files back and forth to update your site.

If you wrote your entire site in HTML, you wouldn't have any site management or file management tools available to you — you would have to keep separate notes, pictures and other references to know how the site was built.

Inserting Graphic Objects

1. If the Tropiflora site isn't open, open it now. Activate the **index.htm** (home) page.

2. Position the text cursor in front of the word Tropiflora and press the Return/Enter key. This will insert some space before the word.

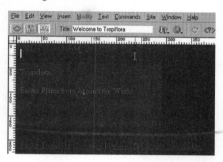

3. Put the cursor back at the top of the page and click the Insert Image icon on the Common Objects panel.

4. Navigate to the **RF-Dreamweaver/Tropiflora_Objects** folder and double-click the **masthead.jpg** file. As soon as you do, you'll receive a message stating that the image doesn't reside in the root folder, and asking you if you would like to copy the file there now. Click Yes.

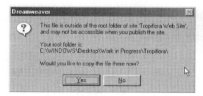

5. The Save dialog box will appear. Again, you'll have the option of creating a new folder. Create one and name it "Images". Once you've finished, double-click to open it and save the masthead.jpg file inside of the new folder.

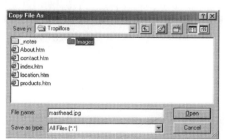

Whenever you want to take a break, instructions to save the page and keep them open for the next exercise present the perfect opportunity. Save everything and close the files. Before you begin the next exercise, open all the files and begin where you left off.

6. Examine the index.htm page. The image will appear at the top.

7. Activate about.htm. Position the text cursor underneath the page title, and import the **Cathcarts.jpg** image from the **RF-Dreamweaver/Tropiflora_Objects** folder. Make certain that you copy the file into the Images folder, just as you did for the masthead.jpg image.

8. Go to the location.htm page. Insert the **tfloramap.jpg** image from the **RF-Dreamweaver/Tropiflora_Objects** folder, following the same steps as before. Make certain that you let Dreamweaver copy the image into the Images folder.

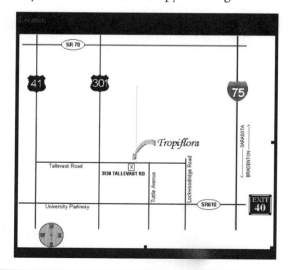

9. Insert the **orchid_1.jpg** image into the products.htm page. Follow the same steps as before to place the image.

10. Save all the files and keep them open for the next exercise.

Aligning Page Objects

There are many different ways to lay out your Web pages, and to align the objects that are used to construct them. For now, we just want to center everything on the page so that everything isn't stuck on the left side.

Positioning Page Elements

1. Go to the index.htm page. Select the Masthead image.

2. Activate the Property inspector. Click the Align Center icon.

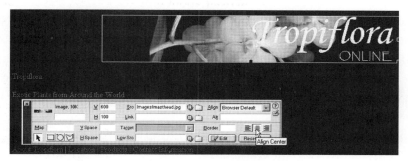

You'll notice a folder inside the Tropiflora root folder named _notes. This is a folder used by Dreamweaver to hold notes and comments that you might add to your site as you're developing the pages.

3. Select all the type by dragging over it with the text cursor. Center align it by clicking the Align Center button in the Property inspector.

4. Center all of the objects on all of the pages.

5. Go to the about.htm page. Underneath the picture of the Cathcarts, insert the **Homebutton.jpg** file from the **RF-Dreamweaver/Tropiflora_Objects** folder. Save the copy into the Images folder as before.

6. The button will appear underneath the image. Select the object and use the Property inspector to link it to index.htm. Delete the text link that you previously created. Repeat the process with all the pages. You have now created your first home button.

7. Save the file but keep it open. We're almost done.

Previewing Pages in a Browser Window

No matter how complex a Web site might be, it all comes down to the same process — the one we just completed. As you learn more about Dreamweaver, you'll be able to create far more compelling and effective pages than this simple project, but the concepts will remain the same.

The last task you have to perform for this project (or any other that you might create in the future) is to test it in a browser window.

To test your projects, simply open the index.htm file and click the Preview/Debug in Browser button at the top of the Document window.

Selecting the Preview/Debug in Browser option in the File menu will launch the primary browser selected in your Preferences>Preview in Browser dialog box. In the following image, we're using Microsoft Internet Explorer (IE) to preview the Tropiflora project.

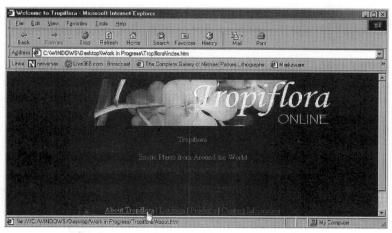

If you look in the Address bar at the top of the browser, you'll see the path and file name of the Tropiflora site we just constructed.

Many sites use a small, low-resolution image as a pointer to a larger version of the graphic. With an image selected, you can select an "alt" file in the Property inspector to link to a high-resolution alternative image for any graphic on your pages.

Chapter Summary

In chapter 4 we learned the basic methods used to construct a Web site, and learned that no matter how complex a site might be, the construction methods are the same. You now understand that all sites are contained within a root folder, which can contain as many folders, objects and files as needed by the site.

Next, you learned how to create a simple site, starting with the creation of a home page, whose properties (such as background and text colors, link colors and sizes) can be controlled with the Page Properties dialog box. We learned how to create simple links from one page to another (and back), and learned how to map these links using the Site Map tools. You inserted graphic images, learned to align objects on a page and created graphic links, or simple buttons. Finally, you previewed your site in your primary browser.

Notes:

5 Working with Type

Chapter Objective:

In chapter 5 we learn about using text and text objects. To build your skills in putting type on your Dreamweaver pages, in chapter 5 you will:

- Learn the difference between live text and graphic objects that appear to be text, but aren't.

- Work with formatting the size of type on your pages, and about relative vs. absolute type size attributes.

- Experiment with importing text into your documents in a variety of ways.

- Learn to input text directly onto your pages.

- Understand how to use formatting attributes such as bold, italics, underline, strikethrough and more.

- Work with using special characters, such as the copyright symbol ©, registration ® mark and others.

- Explore ways to keep your pages readable and uncluttered.

- Learn to use Spell Checking and Search and Replace functions to ensure the accuracy of your documents.

Projects to be Completed:

- Cosmic Pets (A)

- Tropiflora Order Form (B)

- Diehard Digital (C)

- Mr. BlockHead's Challenge (D)

Working with Type

From the standpoint of high-quality typography, the Web is still in its infancy compared to the printed page. All you have to do is look at magazines such as *Esquire, Wired* or *Smithsonian,* and compare the quality of the typesetting to your average Web page.

Until recently, the number of different typefaces available to the Dreamweaver designer was limited. As we proceed through this chapter, however, you will learn about several effective ways to expand your options.

We've already put some simple type onto Web pages, but there's considerably more to learn about how Dreamweaver and Web browsers handle type.

Live Text vs. Graphic Elements

There are two ways to put text on your pages. The first is called "live text." *Live text* is copy that can be selected, copied and pasted, and edited in the Document window. If you have access to the site, you can change live text.

The second text element you can put on your pages is in the form of a graphic. Until recently, you could only use bitmap images as type graphics; with Dreamweaver, you can actually add type from Flash, which allows you to use any font on your system and embed it into your Web pages. If you later need to edit the text, you can still access it on your system. This option is known as using Flash Text.

You can use graphics from a wide number of third-party applications as text elements, although we'll cover specific file formats in chapter 8, "Images." In this chapter we'll discuss live text: how to enter it, edit it, format it and use it in your pages.

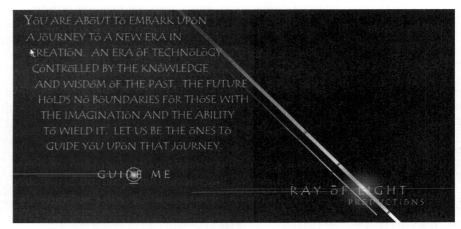

*The type on this beautiful Web page is actually not type at all —
there are a number of different graphics used to display the copy.*

The primary difference between live type and graphic type is its ability to wrap within a specific region of the page. Think about type in a word processor or a page layout program. Within the margins that you establish, type wraps when the cursor reaches the end of the line. If you need to resize the page, or reshape the region where the type is positioned, live text will rewrap. If you're using graphics as type elements, they have to be edited within the original application, and won't automatically fit redesigned pages.

One of the biggest problems with typeface selection is that you never know what fonts the viewers have installed on their systems. If you use a font that they don't have, the page will default to the standard fonts — causing problems with spacing, positioning and line breaks.

Los Angeles artist Yasuto Suga — who works in both electronic and traditional media — designed the Ray of Light site that we use for examples in this book. His work is widely recognized by publishers, artists and designers around the world as being outstanding both visually and technically. His biography and examples of his work can be seen at http://www.rayoflight.net. We strongly suggest you make a visit.

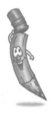

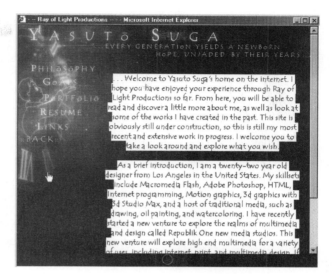

The type on Yasuto's bio page is live. You can tell because it can be selected from within the browser window, and can be copied and pasted into another page.

Fonts and Typefaces

You never know which fonts a user might have available in their system when they happen to be surfing your site.

For items such as mastheads, buttons, icons, maps and other page objects, the user's fonts aren't really an issue. Since you'll be designing and creating these types of elements as graphics, you can use any font you want, and they'll display exactly as you expect. When there's lots of type, such as type on stories on a news site, lists of information or tables of numbers, then they must be constructed from live text. Doing everything as a graphic simply isn't always an available option. You have to consider how you're going to handle the text on your sites.

Viewing Text on Other Systems

There are a number of different font formats in today's graphic design community. The first, and at this point the most prolific, is known as "Type 1." These were originally developed by Adobe Systems for inclusion in PostScript laser printers and for retail sale as individual font packages. The second type, developed by Microsoft, is called TrueType. Recently, a third type of font format known as OpenType has been developed as part of a joint project between Adobe and Microsoft. It's anticipated that this third format will eventually become the standard font format, essentially replacing TrueType and Type 1 fonts.

The primary difference between the two font formats is the manner in which they're built. Truetype fonts are contained in a single file, which both displays the individual glyphs on your monitor as well as imaging them to a laser, inkjet or other type of output device.

Type1 fonts come in two parts — one is used to display the font on the screen, and the other is used to image the font to a printing device. Generally speaking, we're talking about TrueType fonts when we're discussing typefaces in this book. While Postscript fonts are arguably superior for printing purposes, Truetype fonts perform more reliably for Web applications.

Again, for someone to be able to see the fonts that you used on your Web page, they must have the fonts installed. If they're not installed, Dreamweaver will use the default font being used by the viewer's browser application.

Font Categories

Fortunately, most systems today come with a fairly extensive collection of fonts, so there's a decent chance that if you want to use a font such as Bookman, for example, as a heading, and Helvetica, or Arial Bold as a heading font, or Copperplate as a title font, that it will display properly. Falling back to default fonts isn't necessarily bad, though, because most people are used to seeing Arial/Helvetica and Times/Times New Roman when they're surfing the Web.

There are three categories of fonts used by a browser, and standard to contemporary HTML coding conventions:

Serif: Serif typefaces, normally used for body text, display small ornaments at the edges of each character. The body type used in this book — Minion Regular — is an example of a serif typeface. The most commonly used serif face on the Web is Times (Macintosh) or Times Roman (Windows).

Sans Serif: Sans serif typefaces are usually used for headings, and are differentiated from serif typefaces by their lack of rounded or molded ornamentations (serifs) at the corners and ends of each character. The most common sans serif typefaces in today's Internet environment are Arial (Windows) or Helvetica (Macintosh). With Times and Times Roman characters, the only difference in these two fonts is in their names — the character sets are identical.

Monospaced: Monospaced characters are usually used in tables, and to display HTML or other programming code.

Proportional and Monospaced Typefaces

Both serif and sans serif typefaces are said to be proportional — meaning that the amount of space between each character varies from character to character, and within the allocated space where it appears on the page. Each character takes up a different amount of horizontal space — an "i" takes far less room than a "w" or a capital "M."

In monospaced typefaces — Courier New on the PC and Courier on Mac systems — all characters occupy the same amount of horizontal space on the line.

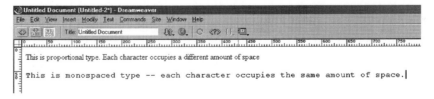

Font Lists

One of the issues you'll always be dealing with is someone on a Macintosh platform viewing pages you've created on a Windows platform, or vice versa. If you designate a font as Times Roman, and they have Times, how can you be sure they'll see the right font? If that one's not found, which one will be next in the list of fonts that they will see?

Fortunately, Dreamweaver includes a powerful feature designed to address the issue of what font will be used next if the one you selected isn't on the viewer's machine; and if this is the case, which font will be substituted.

If you look at the Text>Font menu, you'll see that there are a number of font combinations, or font lists, already built into the program.

You can build a font list in Dreamweaver that lists display fonts in order. If the first font in the list isn't on the viewer's system, you can select the next one that the user's browser will look for.

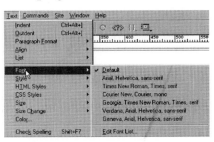

At the top of the list is the Default font. This is the default font that you've selected for the machine on which you're working (in your browser or Internet preferences). Under that, you'll see additional sets. Take a moment to examine them.

The first is a sans serif combination, using Arial (the default Windows sans serif) and Helvetica, the equivalent font on the Macintosh platform. Times New Roman/Times is the serif combination. After that, you will see the mono fonts, Courier New (Windows) and Courier (Mac).

The fourth combination shows an alternative serif combination, starting with Georgia. If this font combo was used on your page, and a viewer had Georgia (a nice serif font found on many PCs), that would be used. If Georgia wasn't available, the browser would use either use Times New Roman (for the Windows user) or Times (for the Macintosh user). The same applies to the list with Verdana and Geneva.

Editing Font Lists

You can edit font lists, and add new ones to the choices available. Simply select Edit Font List from the same menu. A dialog box appears that provides a way to build lists of your own.

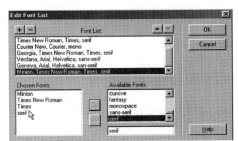

The Edit Font List dialog box lets you design custom font lists for use on your sites.

The dialog box shows you all the lists that already exist, and you can delete them using the Minus (-) key or add new ones with the Plus (+) key. To add fonts to a new list, simply select them from the list of available fonts on your system, and either double-click them or click the Copy (<<) button. You can remove a single font from a list by moving it back to the Available Fonts list (>>). To add a font that's not installed on your system, type its name in the field below Available Fonts and click the Add button. This helps if you're on a Mac and want to specify PC fonts and vice versa.

Entering Text

In the real world, it's likely that you'll be working as part of a team; some people are responsible for writing copy, others are working on the images, still others are putting together numerical or tabular information and you're building the site. While you might wear more than one hat, or even be responsible for every component throughout the site, there will be times when you receive the copy elements from someone else. Your job is to use them during the construction process.

You'll notice that at the bottom of the Available Fonts list are generic titles, including serif, sans serif, monospace, cursive and fantasy. These generic fonts represent the default in each of these categories. Cursive and fantasy are two additional default fonts supported by newer browsers. They extend the three basic defaults — serif, sans and mono. You should always place a generic font at the end of your lists in case the viewers have changed their defaults from Times, Courier or Helvetica.

You've already entered text onto a blank Dreamweaver page. There are several other methods of getting text into your documents.

- The first method is to use the clipboard. Simply open the program where the desired text was created, select it, and use the Copy command (Command/Control-C) to move it to the clipboard. Select the Dreamweaver page where you want to use it, click to create an insertion point and paste it in (Command/Control-V). To remove the copy from the source file, use Cut (Command/Control-X) instead of Copy. Pasting is the same whether the copy was copied or cut.

- The other method is to save the text in HTML format from your word processor and import it into your Dreamweaver page. All major applications offer this option. We use MS Word, and its files come over perfectly on both platforms.

Dreamweaver's text editor includes most basic word processing functions, including spell checking. It's not, however, a full-featured application like MS Word. For long text elements, or for building all the copy for a site, it's probably more effective to create the copy in another application and import it.

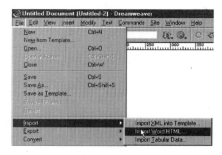

You can also import tabular data from programs such as Microsoft Excel, or from database applications.

When you paste text into your Dreamweaver documents, it loses its formatting. If you want to preserve tabs, spaces and other formatting, choose an insertion point and select Text>Paragraph Format>Preformatted Text. This is particularly useful if someone formatted the text with lots of spaces, tabs and other normally invisible characters. Without this option, extra spaces and tabs are stripped out when the file is imported.

Using Formatting Effectively

Even though Dreamweaver doesn't provide the finest typographic controls for designing Web pages, you should still remember that people need to read the content you're presenting. Using too many typefaces or applying formatting haphazardly can result in the copy being less "readable." Readability is the measure of how easy it is for someone to actually read what you've posted. Use a font that's too small, and some people won't spend the time trying to decipher it; use a font that's too big and it's equally hard on the eyes.

Mixing too many types of fonts is also inadvisable. It's a strain to continuously have to interpret what the viewer is attempting to read.

Many beginning designers think that the more fonts and styles they use, the better their work. To the contrary, stylish design often relies on a minimal number of fonts and styles. That's not to say that some treatments don't call for shocking fonts or dozens of fonts — it's just not always appropriate.

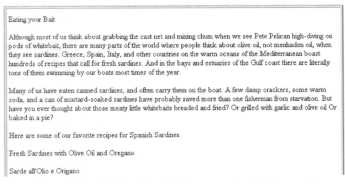

Use too many fonts and styles, and you'll end up making your text too difficult to read. When in doubt, lean to the conservative side — at least until you've determined the general feel for your site. If you want to get creative, do it in headlines and in graphic type elements.

Selecting Fonts and Type Sizes

1. Open the file **sardinescopy.htm** from your **RF-Dreamweaver** folder. It's at the root level of the folder. We aren't going to be working with site construction in this exercise, so just save the file to the root level of your **Work in Progress** folder. The file contains an article about cooking fresh sardines.

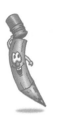

Although you can use word processors to create HTML pages, the code that they produce is, well, horrible. Build your pages in Dreamweaver; copy and paste text from your word processing programs.

Eating your Bait

Although most of us think about grabbing the cast net and mixing chum when we see Pete Pelican high-diving on pods of whitebait, there are many parts of the world where people think about olive oil, not menhaden oil, when they see sardines. Greece, Spain, Italy, and other countries on the warm oceans of the Mediterranean boast hundreds of recipes that call for fresh sardines. And in the bays and estuaries of the Gulf coast there are literally tons of them swimming by our boats most times of the year.

Many of us have eaten canned sardines, and often carry them on the boat. A few damp crackers, some warm soda, and a can of mustard-soaked sardines have probably saved more than one fisherman from starvation. But have you ever thought about those meaty little whitebaits breaded and fried? Or grilled with garlic and olive oil Or baked in a pie?

Here are some of our favorite recipes for Spanish Sardines.

Fresh Sardines with Olive Oil and Oregano

Sarde all'Olio e Origano

This article, published in a fishing magazine, is about using baitfish for dinner — a great idea if you didn't catch any fish all day.

2. Highlight the title — Eating Your Bait. If the Property inspector isn't open, activate it using Windows>Properties. To the right of the Format field (which should now say Paragraph) is a font list. Use the pop-up menu to select the font combination that starts with Verdana.

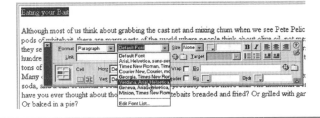

Relative font sizes help you make certain that the overall balance of your pages remains constant — even if viewers have changed the default font size for their browsers. Someone with weak eyesight, for example, might use 14 or even 18 point as the default font, while another user with better visual acuity might use 9 or 10 point as the default. Relative font sizes always use the default font size as the starting point for determining the display size.

3. To the right of the Font field is the Size field. Right now it says None. Click on the menu and look at the choices for a moment. You'll notice numbers 1 through 7, and then two additional groups of numbers from +1 to +7 and sizes from -1 to -7. For now, select the regular number 1.

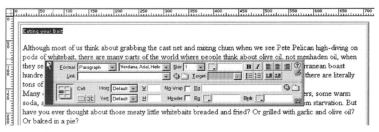

4. The whole, or regular numbers — those without a plus (+) or minus (-) sign — are text sizes. They'll remain the same size regardless of the default font size on the user's system. The sizes represented by the (+) numbers and the (-) numbers are displayed relative to the default font size selected by the individual user. Set the size back to None — you're now looking at the default font size on your system.

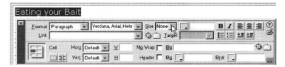

5. Try changing the font size to +1. If your default font size was 12, the size will change to 14. Font sizes generally go from 12 to 14, 18, 24, 36, 48 and so forth, depending on the fonts installed on the viewer's machine.

6. Try applying a few of the (+) sizes. At +7, you've reached the largest of the relative font sizes.

7. Try a few of the (-) relative font sizes. At -7 you've reached the minimum relative font size.

8. Change the title back to normal, or regular size 5.

9. Highlight the title (if it's not already). Click the Show Code and Design Views icon in the upper-left corner of the Document window. Notice the "size=5" code? That's what Dreamweaver inserted when size was applied from the Property inspector.

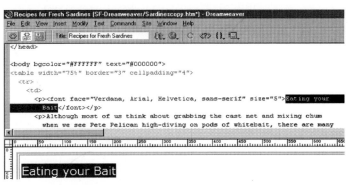

You can also see the coding that was inserted when you selected the font category for the title — it's the <font face ="Verdana...> code. The size command is included.

10. Switch back to Show Design view. Save the file but keep it open for the next exercise.

Physical vs. Logical Styles

So far we've made changes directly to the size of the page title, and viewed the effect of both normal and relative font size attributes. There are a number of other characteristics that you can apply to type. Some of them fall into the Physical category and others fall into the Logical, or Virtual category.

Physical Styles: Physical styles are styles that are applied directly to the text, and aren't a function of how the browser interprets the formatting. Examples of physical styles or attributes include bold, bold italic, underline, strikethrough and super-script/subscript.

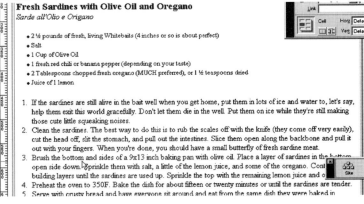

Several physical styles are seen here in this formatted version of the student file we used in the last exercise.

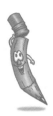

The basefont, or default font size, can be controlled from your Dreamweaver pages. Open the HTML inspector, find the <body> tag, and insert a return after it. Enter the <basefont="x"> code, and use a number from 1 to 7 for the x variable. The standard default basefont is 3. Using a smaller or larger number changes the size. You won't see the size change on the Dreamweaver page, however: it doesn't directly support the HTML code. To see the change, preview your page in any new browser.

Logical Styles: Logical styles are styles that are entered as HTML code and interpreted by the browser. Examples include <strong>, which most browsers display as bold, and <em> (for emphasis), which is usually seen as italic. Others include <code> — used for displaying HTML code — normally in the monospaced (Courier New/Courier) default font.

There are several others, such as <citation>, <definition> and <sample> that aren't often used. Most date back to the earlier days of the Web, when the Internet was primarily the domain of the academia, who used it to publish their scholarly works on weird old terminals with green type on black screens.

Some styles, such as bold and italic, can be applied directly to type by using the B and I buttons in the Property inspector. Others, such as strikethrough, underlining, or superscript and subscript, must be previewed in the browser. To achieve them you have to enter the HTML code. Fortunately, Dreamweaver provides several simple ways to insert code, or to "wrap" code commands around an object. We'll see that happen when we continue with the next exercise.

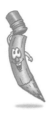

Use the Character Objects panel whenever you need to use quotes, otherwise you will end up with inch marks. Inch marks are a sign of an amateur designer.

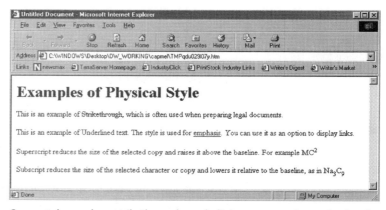

Some styles, such as strikethrough, underlining, superscript and subscript must be previewed in a browser and are achieved through the use of HTML code.

Using Special Characters

As you develop pages, you'll find yourself needing to include special characters in your documents. These include the copyright "©" symbol, the Trademark "™" symbol and others. Dreamweaver has a Character panel that makes insertion of these glyphs simple.

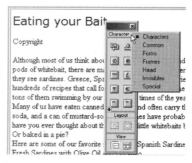

To insert any of these special characters, simply activate the panel. Either click an insertion point at the spot where you want the symbol and click the icon, or drag the icon to the point where you want to insert the character. Either way works fine. Dreamweaver will automatically create the symbol and enter the appropriate HTML.

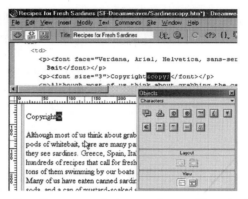

You can see the <©> code that was inserted into the font code.

Formatting and Editing Copy

Even with all the HTML coding going on behind the scenes, Dreamweaver's text-editing functions are similar to those found in other word processors.

Common examples of these similarities include:

You should try to avoid using underlining — it's commonly used by browsers to indicate that a word or string of text is linked to something else. Using underlining on copy that's not a link will confuse your viewers.

- Selecting a word by double-clicking it.
- Moving from one word to another using Command/Control-right arrow or Command/Control-left arrow.
- Moving between paragraphs by using Command/Control-up or down arrow.
- Highlighting text by dragging over it with the cursor.
- Inserting text by clicking to create an insertion point and beginning to type (or pasting in copy from the clipboard).
- Replacing text by highlighting it and typing in the new copy (or pasting in the replacement copy from the clipboard).

Editing and Formatting Copy Elements

1. If the **sardinescopy.htm** file isn't open, open it now. Let's remove the first sentence to make the article somewhat more general. Drag the cursor over the text to select it. Once it's highlighted, delete it, using the Backspace or Delete key.

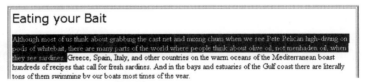

2. Highlight the first two paragraphs and enter a "2" in the Size field of the Property inspector.

A glyph is a term applied to single characters — the letter "a" for example or the © symbol.

3. Select the title of the first recipe. Set the Size to 4 and click the B and I icons to apply bold and italic styles. Make the color a deep red — select it from the Swatch pop-up menu or enter the hex value (#990000).

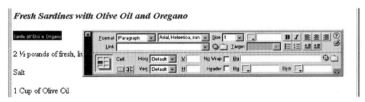

4. Highlight the Italian recipe name and make its size normal 1.

5. Save the file.

Search and Replace

One of the more useful commands found in word processors, and fortunately provided in Dreamweaver, is Search and Replace. With it you can find some or all occurrences of a word or phrase and replace them with other words or phrases. To find and replace words or phrases, select Edit>Find and Replace. The dialog box that appears provides a number of different options for finding and replacing words or phrases.

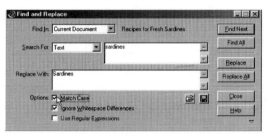

In this example we're going to capitalize all the occurrences of the word "sardine." To do so, we enter the lowercase word "sardine" in the Search For field, turn on the Match Case option, and type in the capped word in the Replace With dialog box. When the Find Next button is clicked, the program will find the next lowercase word and ask if you want to change it.

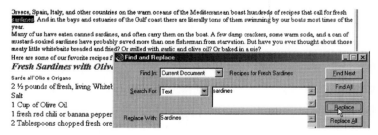

Clicking the Replace button will change that one occurrence. To change all the occurrences in the document, simply use the Replace All button.

You can add dates to your documents using the Insert Date command (Insert>Date). This command does not provide the viewer with the current date, however, it only dates the file at the time it's inserted. You can choose to automatically update the date field whenever you save the file.

There are several ways to apply the command — in the current document, in the HTML code or across the entire site. This latter option allows you to easily make global copy changes — even if your site contains hundreds of pages.

As you can see, the built-in text-editing capabilities of Dreamweaver are fairly strong. Again, if you're working on long documents or in a work group, it's perfectly OK for you to gather your text from other sources.

One of the easiest ways to bring text in is to import it from Microsoft Word. To import files from this popular word processing program, simply save the files as HTML by selecting File>Save as Web.

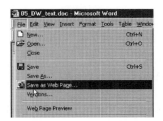

Microsoft Word lets you save your documents as HTML. This is a good option for bringing in copy from other people. Formatting and style sheets come across as well.

Chapter Summary

In chapter 5 you learned about using text in Dreamweaver documents. Starting with the difference between live text and graphic objects that appear to be text (but aren't), you learned how to control the size, formatting and importation of text objects. You worked with entering text directly into a Dreamweaver document and learned how to effectively use formatting without cluttering the pages. You learned how to access special characters such as the copyright or trademark or symbols. Finally, you learned how to edit text in a Dreamweaver document, and how to use the Search and Replace function to make global changes to long text documents.

You could actually use MS Word to lay out pages, and then bring them into Dreamweaver. Word supports the creation of Web pages directly in the software. In our opinion, Word shouldn't be used for page design — not when Dreamweaver exists. It's probably more efficient to use Word solely to get the copy into the system. Once there, bring it into Dreamweaver — that's what it's designed for.

Notes:

⑥ Paragraphs and Styles

Chapter Objective:

In chapter 6 we build on the text techniques you learned in chapter 5, moving on to the formatting of paragraphs and the use of styles. To learn about paragraph formatting and management, in chapter 6 you will:

- Learn how paragraphs are created, and the difference between a return and a non-breaking space.

- Work with basic paragraph alignment, including left, centered, right and full justification.

- Explore indents and margins, which control the first line of a paragraph, and the measure — or width — of a paragraph.

- Create and format both numbered and bulleted lists – a common and important element of professional Web pages.

- Learn about HTML styles, which let you quickly apply formatting to a single word, a paragraph or to a range of text on your pages.

- Work with Cascading Style Sheets (CSS), which expand on the concept of HTML styles and let you make global changes to objects in one or more sites at once.

- Learn about style sheets, which let you use the formatting of one site to build another.

Projects to be Completed:

- Cosmic Pets (A)

- Tropiflora Order Form (B)

- Diehard Digital (C)

- Mr. BlockHead's Challenge (D)

Paragraphs and Styles

So far, we've worked with formatting characters — changing fonts, applying attributes such as bold and italic and re-sizing text. The second step in learning to format text in the Dreamweaver environment is understanding how the program treats paragraph formatting.

Paragraphs

A paragraph is created whenever you reach the end of a line, sentence or group of sentences and press the Return key. This inserts an invisible character at the end of that line. In some cases, you might want to break a line without creating a new paragraph. To do so, use the Insert Line Break command (Shift-Enter).

Using Line Breaks

1. If the **sardinescopy.htm** file isn't open, open it now. Normally, when you press the Return/Enter key, a considerable amount of space is put between the lines. You can see this in the list of ingredients below.

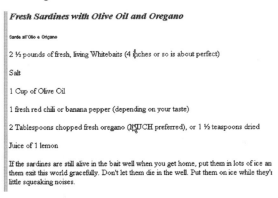

Fresh Sardines with Olive Oil and Oregano

Sarde all'Olio e Origano

2 ½ pounds of fresh, living Whitebaits (4 inches or so is about perfect)

Salt

1 Cup of Olive Oil

1 fresh red chili or banana pepper (depending on your taste)

2 Tablespoons chopped fresh oregano (MUCH preferred), or 1 ½ teaspoons dried

Juice of 1 lemon

If the sardines are still alive in the bait well when you get home, put them in lots of ice an them exit this world gracefully. Don't let them die in the well. Put them on ice while they'r little squeaking noises.

2. Put the cursor in front of the word "Salt" in the second paragraph. Press the Backspace key and the word will pull back and become part of the first paragraph.

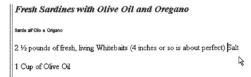

Fresh Sardines with Olive Oil and Oregano

Sarde all'Olio e Origano

2 ½ pounds of fresh, living Whitebaits (4 inches or so is about perfect) Salt

1 Cup of Olive Oil

3. Holding down the Shift key, press Return. This inserts a line break — the two elements are on separate lines, but they're still the same paragraph.

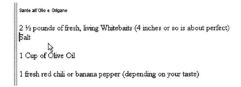

Sarde all'Olio e Origano

2 ½ pounds of fresh, living Whitebaits (4 inches or so is about perfect)
Salt

1 Cup of Olive Oil

1 fresh red chili or banana pepper (depending on your taste)

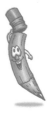

If you enter more than one space after a line, HTML will normally ignore the space. Dreamweaver inserts a non-breaking space to preserve your formatting.

4. Repeat this action: Move the cursor to the end of the word Salt and press Delete/ Backspace and then Shift-Return. The olive oil line is now separated by an invisible line break instead of an invisible paragraph marker.

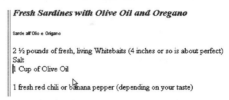

You can also put the cursor at the beginning of a line and press the Backspace key to combine a paragraph with the one immediately above it.

5. Continue combining the ingredients until they're all separated by a line break.

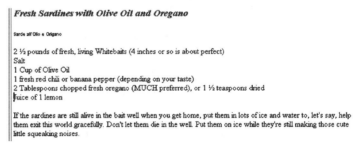

6. The ingredients are all together now, and the instructional paragraphs follow. Save the file. You can close it for now, or keep it open.

You can add horizontal rules to your pages to help further delineate one subject or section from another. For example, if you want to separate the recipes, you can place the cursor at the position where you want the rule to appear and click the Insert Horizontal Rule icon on the Common Objects panel.

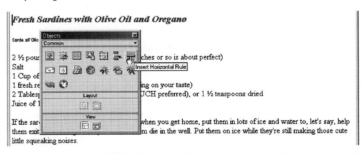

The rule will appear where you click the insertion point, maintaining its position even if you add or remove copy above or below it.

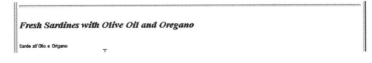

Your Objects panel might look different than ours — we normally resize panels so that they make better screen captures. By default, Dreamweaver displays the Objects panel tall and thin, with two columns of icons.

Alignment

You can align both copy and image objects in several ways. To do so, select the object and click one of the alignment icons on the Property inspector. In this example, we selected the recipe's name, the Italian title and the ingredients, and then clicked the Center Align icon.

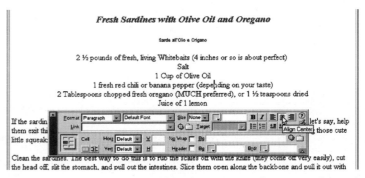

You can also align objects to the right side of the browser window using the Right Align icon.

Indents and Margins

You can indent the margins of any paragraph by using the Indent icon on the Property inspector. Simply select the paragraph in question, and click the icon as many times as you want — each click will indent the paragraph one more time.

To the right of the Indent icon is the Outdent icon — it moves the indent of a paragraph or group of paragraphs to the left.

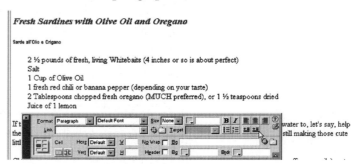

Lists

HTML and Dreamweaver both support two types of standard lists: Bulleted lists and Numbered lists. Bulleted lists are paragraphs formatted with a bullet symbol (•) to the left of the copy. Numbered lists are exactly what they sound like — each paragraph has a number. If you add or delete any paragraphs in the list, the numbers adjust themselves accordingly.

Dreamweaver contains a third type of list that's not used very often called the Definition list. There are two components to the list: the terms and the definitions. By default, they're formatted in pairs: the term is italicized, and the description (the following paragraph) is not. You can change these defaults when you learn to modify HTML styles.

Using Alignment and List Functions

1. If it's not open, open **sardinescopy.htm**.

2. Place your cursor inside the first line of the ingredients list — the list where we inserted the line breaks. Click the Indent button in the Property inspector. The list will move to the right.

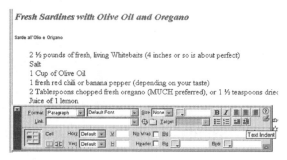

3. Highlight the paragraphs that comprise the instructions for the recipe. Click the Unordered List button in the Property inspector. Notice what happens: Dreamweaver puts the bullets in place, and slightly indents the copy at the same time.

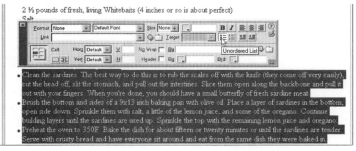

To remove list attributes from a paragraph, simply click the icon again in the Property inspector. These attributes turn on and off easily.

4. While they're still selected, click the Ordered List icon to the right of the Unordered List button. Dreamweaver numbers the paragraphs.

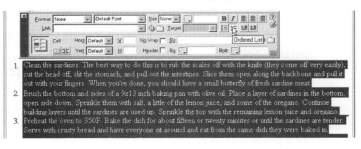

When you learn about tables, you'll find that you have many more layout options than are available using only paragraph formats. You can align copy within table cells, for example, to achieve complex page designs.

5. Experiment with indenting the text.

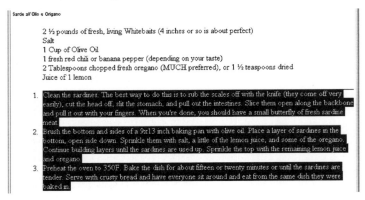

6. Save the file. You can either close it or keep it open for the following exercises.

Styles

Thus far, we've been using the term "style" to refer to attributes applied either to individual characters, words, phrases or paragraphs. Unfortunately, the use of the term style can lead to confusion — especially when you're new to Dreamweaver or to HTML editing in general.

There are styles, and then there are styles. The term "styles" as it relates to formatting, such as bold or italic, predates Web development, and originated in the early days of typesetting.

Recently, as word processing and page layout programs appeared and began to evolve, the term "style" began to take on a new meaning. The term "style sheets" began to appear. *Style sheets* are formatting instructions that take into consideration character formatting, paragraph formatting, positioning, page break information and more.

Think about how documents are structured — particularly lengthy documents. The recipe copy we've been working with is an example — this Dreamweaver book is another.

Longer documents — and Web pages certainly fall into this category — are organized into "editorial priority." In the case of this book, there's a primary heading, which is the name of the chapter. Underneath that main heading, there are secondary headings, which break the chapter into logical chunks.

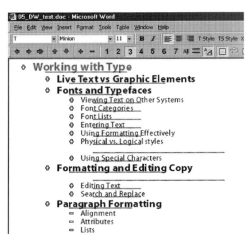

Images and content in tables can also be justified vertically. We'll learn more about that in later chapters.

When you selected the Ingredients list and applied the indent, every line followed suit. That's because the lines aren't separate paragraphs — they're only one paragraph, and the lines are created using line breaks, not the Return key.

Many of the secondary headings have headings underneath them, and in some cases there's actually a fourth heading. These headings are named, appropriately, Heading 1 (title), Heading 2 (second level heads), Heading 3 and Heading 4. Each heading has a specific format applied — font, size, color, space before and after, and page break information. For example, you'll never find a heading alone at the bottom of the page — each heading contains instructions stating that it shouldn't be separated from the copy that follows.

Each of these headings is assigned a style sheet which contains all the formatting attributes we defined before we started writing this book. HTML treats headings the same way that we treated them in this outline, by defining and structuring the content being introduced.

Editing Text
Common examples of these similarities include:

- Selecting a word by double-clicking it.
- Moving from one word to another using Command/Control-right arrow or Command/Control left arrow.
- Moving from one pararagaph to another using Command/Control-up or down arrow.
- Highlighting text by dragging over it with the cursor.
- Inserting text by clicking to create an insertion point and beginning to type (or Pasting in copy from the clipboard).
- Replacing text by highlighting it and typing in the new copy (or Pasting in the replacement copy from the clipboard).

Editing and Formatting Copy Elements

1. If the Sardinescopy.htm file isn't open, open it now. Let's remove the first sentence to make the article a little more general. Drag the cursor over the text to select it. Once it's highlighted, delete it using the Backspace or Delete key.

Each paragraph and copy element in the ATC books is assigned a style sheet. This ensures their consistency and allows us to make global changes to any style in the document.

Headings aren't the only elements in the ATC book that are assigned a style sheet. Each element — body text, exercise headings, the numbered steps that comprise the hands-on activities, bulleted lists, unnumbered lists, captions and sidebar text — is assigned a style sheet.

Types of Styles

There are two types of style sheets in use today. The first is known as HTML styles and the second is Cascading Style Sheets, or CSS. Both allow you to combine formatting attributes to create and identify a style. Once this style has been defined, it can be applied to any text object with a single click.

> **HTML Styles:** HTML styles are older, and they're not as robust as CSS style sheets. You can use character and paragraph attributes to build an HTML style, and apply it manually to any text, but changing the style doesn't change every item to which it was already attached. Nor does modifying an existing HTML style change incidences of that style throughout your site. When you save a style sheet, HTML styles are stored in your root folder under the name Styles.xml. You can load this file into another document if you want to use the same styles in another document.

> **Cascading Style Sheets, or CSS:** A newer form of style sheets, CSS also contains and defines character and paragraph attributes, but offers a marked difference: when you change a CSS, any text to which it was assigned changes to reflect the new attributes. This can be done on the page or throughout an entire site. This is a more flexible technique, and can save considerable time when compared to HTML styles. CSS styles can be independent of a single site — the same set of styles can be used by multiple sites, and can allow global changes to those sites through the modification of the shared styles.

There are two types of style sheets we'll be talking about: the first is known as HTML styles, and the second is called CSS, or Cascading Style Sheets. HTML styles are more limited than Cascading Style Sheets, but are supported by all browsers.

Defining HTML Styles

The real power of HTML styles is in their ability to define the structure of your site — not just the type style, size, color or alignment. Heading styles (Heading 1, Heading 2, Heading 3 and so forth) serve to define the order in which information is organized. Paragraph styles (body and lists, for example) provide the information contained under each heading.

Creating HTML Styles

1. Open the **sardinescopy.htm** file if it's not already open. Activate the HTML Styles panel by clicking on its icon in the Launcher panel.

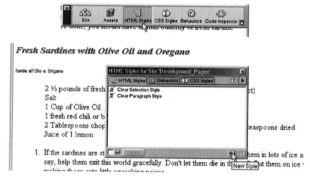

2. In the first line of the ingredients, highlight the words "Fresh Sardines" and select Edit>Copy. Click the New Style (+) icon at the bottom of the Define HTML Style panel. Name the style "Recipe", click the Apply to Paragraph button, and click OK.

3. Look at the HTML Styles panel. Your new style appears in the list. You can see by the icon to the left that it's a paragraph style. You can also create character styles that affect only characters, while leaving the paragraph intact.

4. Move down in the document to the next recipe title. Click the insertion point in the line of text and click the Recipe style in the HTML Styles panel. The paragraph will assume the same style.

5. Save your changes, and close the file.

HTML 4.0 specifications state that you shouldn't use HTML styles, but that you should lean toward the use of Cascading Style Sheets. While more powerful, CSS aren't supported by earlier browsers.

If you are using CSS in your site designs, be certain to adhere to standard HTML naming conventions such as Heading 1 through 5, body, paragraph, lists and so forth. This will ensure that if a person is viewing your site with a browser that doesn't support CSS, the visual structure of your pages will remain intact.

In this recipe example, the English term is referred to as the title.

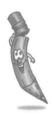

In the previous exercise, we worked with paragraph styles. You can also create styles that only effect single words, called character styles. They're great for applying multiple attributes such as size, color and font style to individual words within the copy. When you create a character style, you can see that it has a different icon — a lowercase "a" instead of the paragraph icon that we created when we made the Recipe style.

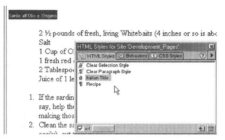

If you want to experiment with styles, use the Recipe file. You might consider using rules to separate recipes, and assigning styles to everything in the document until it's completely formatted and structured to your taste. And you might try the recipes — they're great!

Cascading Style Sheets

As we mentioned before, the major difference between HTML style sheets and CSS, or Cascading Style Sheets, is that CSS styles can span multiple sites, making a change to the style sheet updates and applying the changes to every occurrence of the style on the site or sites using the sheet, making them dramatic timesavers.

In addition to their ability to store formatting information such as font, size, color and alignment, CSS styles can contain even more complex information and attributes, including special effects, rollovers (which we'll discuss in a later chapter) and even link information.

When you create a new CSS style, the options far exceed those available for HTML styles. To create a new style, copy or delete existing styles, or edit ones that are already there, use the CSS Styles panel. You can activate it from the Windows menu, from the Launcher panel or by pressing Shift-F11.

Clicking the New Style icon displays the New Style dialog box.

Custom Classes

The first component to examine in the New Style dialog box is the Type category. There are three different types of CSS styles, and they all act differently.

> **Make Custom Style (Class):** Custom styles are like regular styles, except that they apply equally to both paragraphs and text — there's no apparent difference between them. When you define a custom style, Dreamweaver inserts the <class> tag. If you create a style named "Ingredients", and apply it to a list, the code will read <ul class="Ingredients"> where <ul> represents unnumbered list, and "Ingredients" represents the named CSS tag or class.

Redefine HTML Tag: This selection allows you to redefine all the normal HTML tags. For example, if you create a CSS tag named Heading 1 or H1, and select this option, all regular HTML styles will become CSS styles as well, and be subject to global change if you modify the CSS style.

Use CSS Selector: These tags allow you to modify particular combinations of existing tags. For example, if you want to change only those occurrences of a style found in tables on your site while leaving other non-tabular data alone, use this command. For example, if you use <td Ingredients=x>, only recipe names contained in tables will be affected by the definition of x.

Once you create a new CSS style, Dreamweaver prompts you for the name of the style sheet to which you wish to add the style; if there are none open, you're prompted to create one. If the page you're working on is part of a site (i.e., contained in a defined root folder containing a defined site), you can choose to save it there. If not, you're asked to create a new style sheet. This file, with the .css extension, can then be loaded and accessed from any site.

Once you save the style sheet, you're presented with the Style Definition dialog box, which contains a number of different attribute categories.

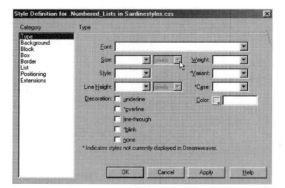

You'll notice that this dialog box offers a number of style attributes — such as Variant (small caps, and so forth), Case (upper, lower, capitalize), overline (a rule over the copy) and blink (just what it sounds like, and very annoying) that are identified as not being supported by Dreamweaver. To see what the style looks like, you'll have to preview it in a browser.

Another way of creating a new style is to copy an existing style and modify it. This is convenient if you already have a style and want something similar. You can copy that style, and use it to create another one, while avoiding having to reapply the existing attributes.

Take a moment to examine some of the CSS categories; you'll notice that there are many available attributes.

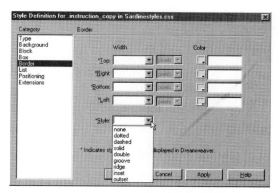

The List category allows you to easily substitute graphics for the bullets in bulleted lists — a task that's not easy to accomplish if you're coding directly in HTML.

As we move forward through the book, you'll be presented with more opportunities to work with CCS and HTML styles — particularly as you develop the projects and project assignments. It is important to remember that styles offer you an easy way to ensure that similar elements are formatted the same way throughout your pages and across your sites.

Chapter Summary

In chapter 6 you continued to build on your knowledge of text management in Dreamweaver with a discussion of paragraphs and styles. Beginning with the way in which paragraphs are created, you learned to align them, how to control indents and margins, and how to format lists — such as numbered and bulleted lists. These are common elements on many Web pages, and understanding how to format them is a key skill for you to learn.

You learned about working with styles , which are collections of attributes that can automatically be applied to a single word, paragraph or range of text. You learned the difference between HTML and CSS (Cascading Style Sheets) and how to create both types.

The keyboard command for activating the CSS Style panel is Shift-F11 on both Windows and Macintosh platforms.

Notes:

7 Links

Chapter Objective:

In chapter 7 we begin an in-depth exploration of links — how they work, how to manage them and how to use them effectively. To build a solid understanding of links and their role in navigation design, in chapter 7 you will:

- Learn the definition of a link, and the role that they play in building a navigation strategy.

- Create Named Anchors — the most basic type of link, which work within a single page to position the page within the browser window.

- Learn about relative links, which are used to navigate within the confines of a specific site.

- Learn about absolute links, which are normally used to direct the user to another site or a page outside the site they're currently viewing.

- Learn about root-relative links, which look up to the root folder of the site to locate the target link.

- Learn about updating links when you make changes to your site.

- Explore identifying and fixing broken links — ones which point to pages that Dreamweaver cannot locate.

- Create email links which automatically launch the user's mail client and address the message.

Projects to be Completed:

- Cosmic Pets (A)

- Tropiflora Order Form (B)

- Diehard Digital (C)

- Mr. BlockHead's Challenge (D)

Links

Links are the fundamental building block of the Internet. They provide the viewer with the ability to move from one page to another, from one part of a page to another or from the current Web site to a completely different address, or URL. Links are often referred to as hyperlinks, a term we mentioned in chapter 1.

Links can take many forms: they can be a single word, a phrase, an icon, a picture or even a part of a picture. When the user moves the arrow pointer over a link, the arrow normally turns into a little pointing finger.

You can see the Finger icon hovering over the "Message Boards" link in this popular fishing site. Clicking it will take the viewer to a different page within the site.

Dreamweaver offers a variety of tools and methods for creating links within your pages. Before we continue our discussion on the different categories of links and how to create and manage them, it's important that we first explore how Dreamweaver manages Web sites.

While it might seem premature to discuss managing an entire Web site — whether it's on someone else's server (such as an Internet Service Provider), or on your own machine — site management and links are closely related. If you want your links to work properly, and not send the user into Internet limbo, then you need to know about site management, file organization and a host of other issues.

Pages and Sites

It's conceivable that one could build an entire Web site on a single page. As long as you didn't use any graphics or external objects (such as movies and sounds), you wouldn't need anything but that one page — it would provide all the content that the user wanted. Even in this simple example, however, there would still be a site to manage.

On the other hand, almost all sites today are built of dozens, even hundreds, of pages. Each page often contains graphics, and many of them even make use of external objects such as Flash movies, animations, sound files, download areas, forms and more. If a page is to display properly, the resources that were used during its construction must be available when the users load the page in their browser.

During the loading process, the browser looks around to see if it can find the objects and resources it needs to display the page. And it doesn't look very far. If it can't find what it needs to properly display the page, it loads what it can and leaves the rest out. In some extreme cases, it simply shows the user an error message and stops dead in its tracks.

You can use pictures in some inventive ways to provide links and navigation tools to the viewer. This technique is called using "image maps"; we'll discuss the concept later.

File Naming Conventions

All programming languages, including Dreamweaver, must follow fairly restrictive file naming conventions.

Illegal Characters: You shouldn't use periods or dots (.) except to separate file extensions. Examples of proper usage include .jpg, .htm, .gif, .swf (Flash movies) or .png (Fireworks graphics). Slashes (\, /) are out — they're used by HTML to identify paths. The forward slash (/) identifies folder paths, and the backslash (\) is an illegal character on Windows NT servers. Don't use colons (:); they're used to identify folder paths on the Mac platform as well as in many scripting languages, and can confuse the browser. Lastly, avoid question and exclamation marks (? or !); they're used to identify comments, and can also make the browser act strangely.

Spaces: Although most operating systems allow you to use spaces in your file names, they don't work with HTML. We could name a file Against The Clock.doc on our desktops, but the Web site must be named againsttheclock.com. Many site developers use underscores (_) or dashes (-) instead of spaces to separate words.

Upper and lowercase: UNIX servers are case-sensitive — they identify GardenFoods.htm as being different than gardenfoods.htm or Gardenfoods.htm. This can cause links to fail if a file name isn't entered correctly. To minimize problems, use only lowercase file names.

Folder Organization

A simple site could conceivably be built inside of just one folder, with all its pages and accompanying graphics residing comfortably on a single level. In the real world, however, this simply isn't practical. Many sites are constructed of hundreds — even thousands — of individual files. Attempting to manage them all in one folder level would be difficult.

Links

There are several types of links available for constructing your site: named anchors, relative (folder and site) links, absolute links, email links and links that target a specific area of a framed page — something we'll cover in a later chapter.

There are a number of names that are "internal" — meaning that they are used only by Dreamweaver and not by the browser being used to display the pages. These internal names don't have to conform to HTML file-naming conventions, so you can use any name you want. You'll see several examples in this book.

Named Anchors

Named anchors are links used to navigate within long pages — ones that won't fit in a single screen. Imagine a long page containing row after row of product images and descriptions. You could create an alphabetical directory at the top of the page linked to Named Anchors where each category began. Clicking the link would reposition the page, automatically scrolling down until the anchor was positioned in the upper-left corner of the browser window.

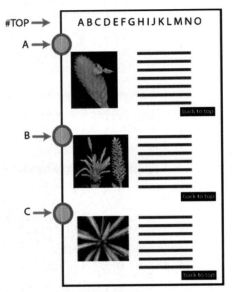

A "Back to Top" command can be used to take the user back to the top of the page. Simply create an anchor at the top (usually named "top"), and create a link to the anchor.

Creating Named Anchors

1. Open the file **Products.htm** from your **RF-Dreamweaver** folder. Save it into the Tropiflora Site folder that you created before. A file named Products.htm already exists in the Tropiflora folder. When saving, replace the old file with the new one.

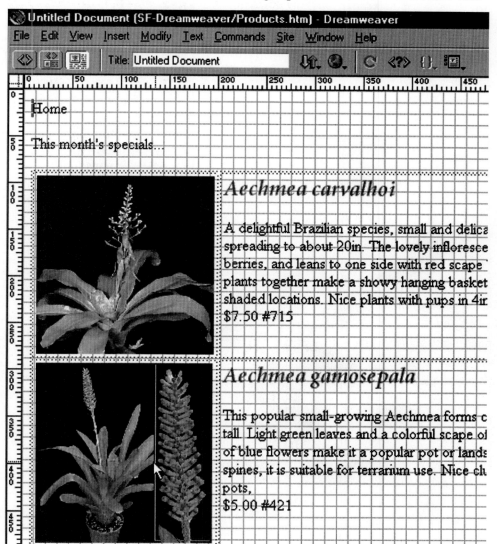

2. Choose Site>Open Site and select the Tropiflora site.

3. Position the cursor at the end of the last line and press Return. Type the word "Aloe", press Return, "Jewel Orchid" (Return) and "Zamia" (Return).

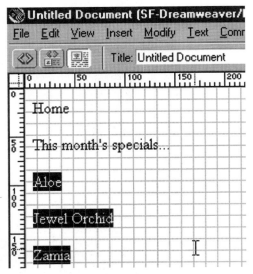

You can also insert named anchors in front of words or phrases.

You can turn on Invisible Anchors and move them around manually if they're getting in the way of anything on the page.

The keyboard shortcut for inserting a named anchor is Command-Option-A (Macintosh) and Control-Alt-A (Windows). It's a useful keyboard equivalent when you're working on a long page with a lot of anchors.

4. Select the list and use Text>List>Unordered List to turn them into a bulleted list. They're going to be turned into links in a few minutes.

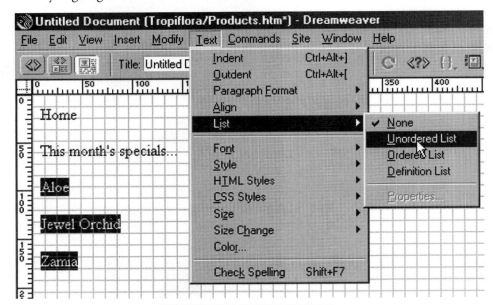

5. Scroll down the page until you see the line drawing and text description for *Aloe conifera*. Select the image, and select Insert>Invisible Tags>Named Anchor. This action will assign an anchor to that image.

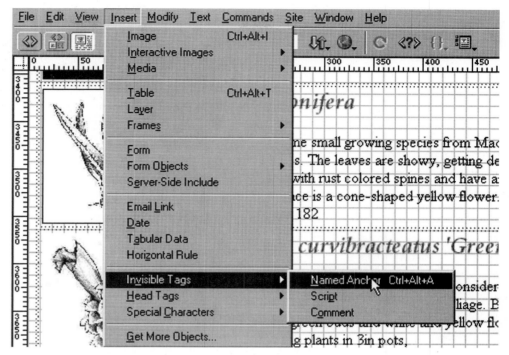

If you've turned off Named Anchors (keeping them hidden) in the Preferences dialog box, Dreamweaver will warn you that you can't see them whenever you create a new one. You can turn off this warning if desired. After a while, you'll remember they're invisible.

The page we're working with uses the Dreamweaver Tables feature — something we'll cover in depth in chapter 9, "Tables." Tables are a powerful feature that give you a good deal of control over page layout and design.

6. As soon as you release the mouse, a dialog box will appear that lets you name the anchor. Name it "Aloe".

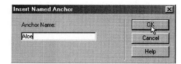

7. Find the "Ludisia" image and create an anchor named "Jewel". The Zamia image is at the bottom of the page. Find it and create an anchor for it as well (you can call it Zamia). You now have three anchors.

8. Your preferences settings control whether or not you can see the anchors (they'll be invisible in the previewed page). Under Edit>Preferences>Invisible Elements, try checking and unchecking the Named Anchors box — you can either leave them on or hide them.

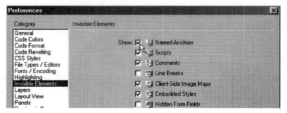

9. If the anchors are visible, they seem to knock the images around. Don't worry, though; when the page is previewed it will display correctly.

10. Select the Zamia anchor. Look at the Property inspector. You can rename a link in the Name field if you want to. Don't do that right now, though, or the exercise won't work.

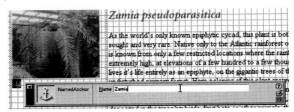

11. Go to the top of the page and select the word Aloe. In the Property inspector, in the Link field, type "#Aloe". The text will become underlined — indicating that it's now a link. You can also highlight the object and use the Point to File icon (the small target to the left of the folder and drag the pointer to the anchor to create the link.

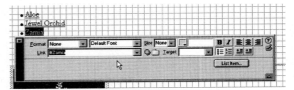

12. Repeat the process for the next two items. For Jewel Orchid, type the anchor's Link name as "#Jewel", and "#Zamia" for Zamia. The # sign is identified by HTML as a link to a named anchor.

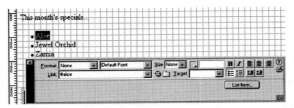

13. Preview the page in your browser window. Click the Aloe link. The page will immediately scroll down so that the Aloe anchor is at the top of the window.

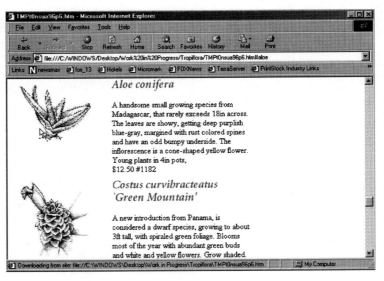

14. Use the scroll bars to return to the top of the page and click the Jewel link. The same thing will happen; the Jewel Orchid image will be at the top of the window.

15. The problem is that we have to scroll back to the top of the page to use the other links. We need to add a way to navigate back to the top of the page. Close the preview browser, and position your cursor at the top of the document page. Insert an anchor named "top".

16. Go to the Jewel Orchid entry. Position the cursor after the last price and press Return. Type "RETURN TO TOP". Center it, increase its point size, and color it.

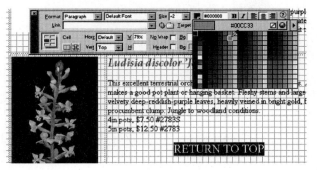

17. In the Property inspector, type "#top" in the Link field.

18. Preview the page again. Try the Jewel Orchid link. When you get there, the Return to Top link will pop you back to the top of the page. You could "wire" (hook up) the other links, but it's not necessary.

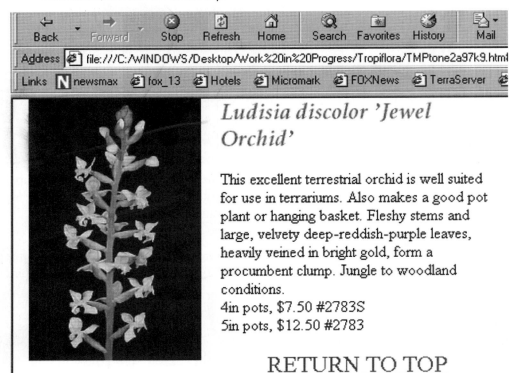

Any anchor without a specific destination will automatically default to the top of the page.

19. Save and close the file.

Once you've created the RETURN TO TOP link at the bottom of the Jewel Orchid copy, you could save steps by copying and pasting it into all the other items. Later, when we examine the concept of "libraries and templates," you'll see how you can store common items such as Return to Top and Home buttons, and use them repeatedly when designing new sites.

Relative Links

Relative links are links that take you from one page to another within the same site. When we created the Tropiflora site, we created a root folder, which contained the index.htm (or home) page, as well as the pages that represented other content (such as about us and products). You might say that the home page is the "parent" and the other pages are the "children." This parent/child relationship is important to consider when you're building your sites; the home page is the patriarch — the topmost parent. Other pages below that level — while children to the home page — can certainly have their own children (pages linked from that page).

There's no limit to the number of links you can build on your site, but you should remember that the less clicking and searching visitors have to do to find what they're looking for, the better. Visitors are fickle and impatient — they want what they want and they want it now.

Relative links come in several forms. Imagine that you had a page at the root level, and wanted to link to another page on the same level. You don't need to specify anything but the other file's name — since it's on the same (root) folder level.

Take a look at this diagram.

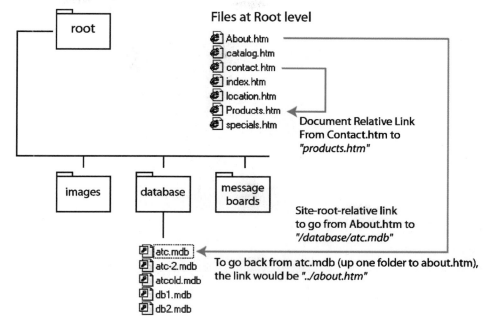

Files at Root level

- About.htm
- catalog.htm
- contact.htm
- index.htm
- location.htm
- Products.htm
- specials.htm

Document Relative Link
From Contact.htm to
"products.htm"

images database message boards

Site-root-relative link
to go from About.htm to
"/database/atc.mdb"

- atc.mdb
- atc-2.mdb
- atcold.mdb
- db1.mdb
- db2.mdb

To go back from atc.mdb (up one folder to about.htm),
the link would be *"../about.htm"*

You can create a visual link using the Point to File icon in the Property inspector. To use it, select the object or text you want to use as the link, and click and drag the icon — an arrow will appear that lets you point to any file in the site file list.

Imagine that you wanted to create a link between two pages at the root level — from "contact.htm" to "Products.htm." On the contact page, you could select the type or graphic you wanted to use as the link, and type "Products.htm" in the Link field. Since they're both on the same level, this relative link will work just fine.

If you wanted to link from a page on the root level (for example, the "about.htm" page) to one inside of a folder (the "atc.mdb" database file), you would have to tell the program to look down into the Database folder. To do this, you would use the slash (/) character, the folder name and the file name as the link (/database/atc.mdb).

To move up from one folder to another, or to the root, you would use the (../) code. This tells browsers to move up one or more folders to find the link. For example, to go back up to the root level from the atc.mdb file, you would use (../About.htm).

When to use Document-relative Links vs Site-relative Links

When you use a file name as a link without the (/) symbol, the link is said to be "document relative" — indicating that the browser looks in the folder that the parent page is in. It therefore uses the current location of the document as the point from which to start looking. That's fine, as long as you don't move pages around too much.

If you're developing a complex site where pages may routinely be moved around, then it's probably better to use the site-relative link preceded by the (/) symbol. The problem with this technique is that it relies on the server where the site is located. If you're hosting a site on multiple servers, or hosting multiple sites on the same server, then they're fine to use. If you're in doubt, or just beginning to develop sites, use document-relative links.

Absolute Path Links

Absolute links are links that point to pages that are on different sites or different servers. They require a real address — something like http://www.againsttheclock.com. Clicking them takes a person to another site.

A good example of the use of absolute links can be found on any page of links — something that many sites utilize as a resource for their viewers.

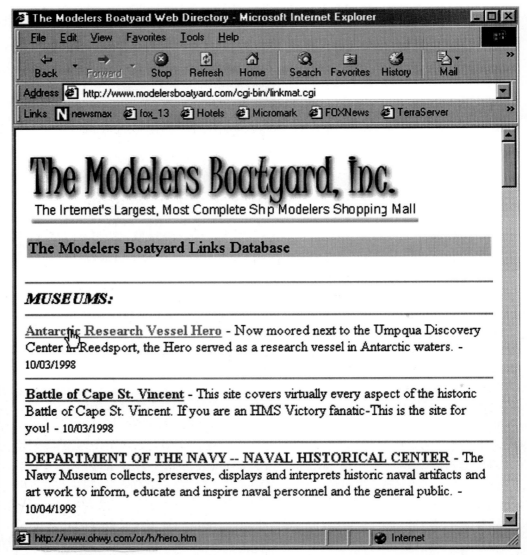

Use absolute links when linking to external sites. Although you can certainly use full path names for the files in your own site, this will severely limit your ability to edit your site. Moving a file, for example, requires that you locate all the absolute links and change them to make sure that they still work. Again, document-relative links are the most versatile and simple to use.

Of course, document-relative, site-relative and absolute links can be used in your navigation strategies and in so-called "navbars".

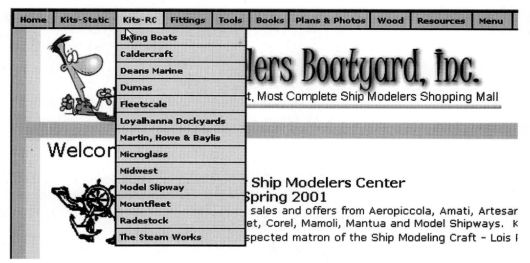

Navigation bars — or "navbars," as they're often called — are an integral way of taking advantage of Dreamweaver's linking capabilities. Since they're primarily graphic treatments requiring the use of imaging capabilities, it's better if we cover them in depth in chapter 8, "Images."

Updating Links

Without question, one of Dreamweaver's strongest features is its ability to update links and fix links that — for one reason or another — get broken.

The first step in managing links is to identify the current state of your links. Selecting Site>Check Links Sitewide will cause Dreamweaver to check every link on the site and produce a report telling you which ones are broken and which ones are working properly.

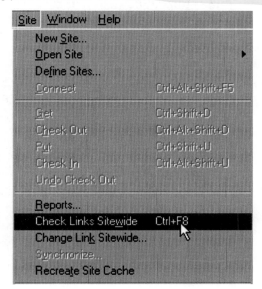

When you issue the command, the program produces a report that categorizes all of the links on the site, letting you know which ones need attention.

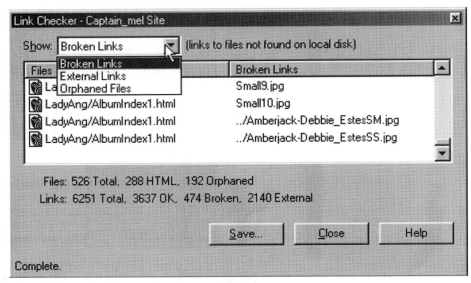

You can write the results of this report into a tab-delimited text file. Just click the Save button and select a place where you want to save the file. Use the .txt extension to ensure that it works properly, regardless of the platform. You can also create a Web page with a table — which we'll cover in a subsequent chapter — to display the exported report.

You can choose to look at broken links, external links or orphaned files — those that exist in the site but aren't linked to from any of the site's active pages.

You can also change a link sitewide — which can be useful if you're moving a site from one place to another (from a server to your local drive, for example). This is common when you're performing a complete site overhaul. You could put up a few temporary pages, drag the entire site down to your hard drive, reconstruct it and put it back again.

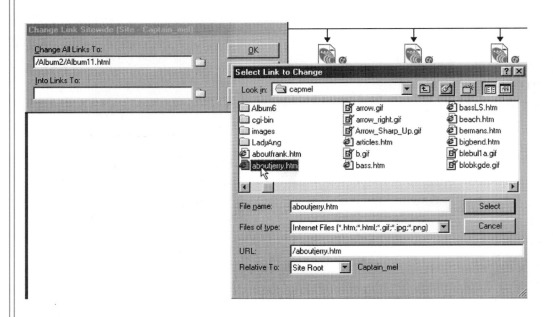

Using the Change Link Sitewide dialog box allows you to fix broken or modified links across your entire site. The folder icons to the right of the name fields let you browse for the links you want to change, as well as the new, or changed links.

Creating Email Links

Email links are a specific and unique category of links that automatically launch the person's default mail program, depending on the browser that they're using and their mail client.

To create an email link, select Insert>Email Link. A dialog box will appear that lets you enter the text for the link (which will appear in the subject line of the email, and the email address that you want the link to connect to.

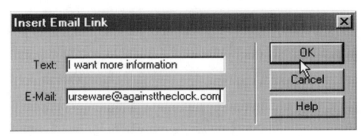

You can also select text and use Insert>Email. Dreamweaver will automatically make the selected text an email link and format it accordingly.

Clicking the link opens a blank, pre-addressed email window that the user can fill in with whatever message they like. The following image shows our default mail client, Microsoft Outlook Express.

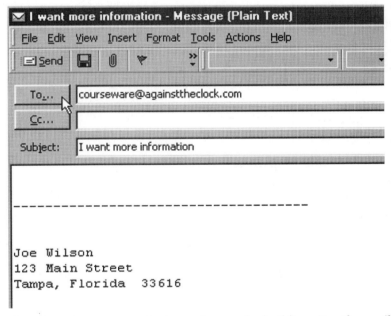

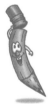

Some of our technical editors experienced problems with the text message appearing in the Subject line of their email messages when using Netscape Messenger. Except for this problem, the function still works. Make sure you check a few different email programs to make sure they work as expected.

Since linking is such an important technique when you're building sites, there will be more opportunity to discuss and use linking methods as we continue through this book. For example, linking using images, image maps, navigation bars and buttons will be covered in chapter 8, "Images."

Chapter Summary

In chapter 7 you began learning about links, and how they're used to let the viewer move from page to page within a site, or across several different sites. You learned about the basic types of links, including document-relative, site-relative and absolute links. You learned about checking links and fixing broken links, and how to change a link sitewide. Lastly, you learned how to create an automatic email link that will open the viewer's email client software and automatically insert an email address and a subject line.

Notes:

8 *Images*

Chapter Objective:

In chapter 8 we work with images — arguably the most important component of the World Wide Web and an important part of your development efforts. To learn about importing and managing images, in chapter 8 you will:

- Learn to use the Insert Image object on the Common Objects panel to insert images onto your pages.

- Create borders for your images directly inside of Dreamweaver.

- Learn to resize images for design purposes, and understand why it's important to size the final versions using an external image-editor — not in Dreamweaver.

- Work with the Image Property inspector, which provides a wide range of control over images on your pages.

- Create graphical navigation bars, using images created in an external image-editor combined with Dreamweaver's powerful Insert Navigation Bar feature.

- Learn the four states of a button: up, over, down and over while down.

- Experiment with creating image maps — a popular and powerful way to create navigation strategies using images.

- Understand how to create rollovers — images that change when the users move their mouse into the area they occupy on the page.

Projects to be Completed:

- Cosmic Pets (A)
- Tropiflora Order Form (B)
- Diehard Digital (C)
- Mr. BlockHead's Challenge (D)

Images

There was a time, not so long ago, when images and computing didn't coexist. The earliest incarnations of the machines we use day in and day out operated in a text-only world — and even that was green type on a black background. Putting images onto computer screens is a relatively recent advance; seeing images on Web pages even more so.

When images began to appear on Web pages — most notably in a browser called Mosaic — the Internet was on its way to becoming part of almost everyone's lives. Pictures are, indeed, worth a thousand words, and without the rich content we've grown accustomed to, the Web would be a much more full, and arguably less popular, place to be.

Entire Web sites can be built using only images. As we mentioned earlier in chapter 5, "Working with Type," many of the most compelling Web pages you see on the Internet can built with mostly graphics and very little, if any, use of type.

Two problems are associated with using only images to build your site. First, they're not accessible to people surfing without having their browsers downloading images; second, images are not text and can't be located by search engines.

The only real text on Dwayne Ferguson's Diehardstudio.com Web site is the disclaimer at the bottom that says the site is constantly being updated.

The one caveat about using only images to build your sites is that they "weigh" more — that is, it takes longer to download an image (or collection of images) than it does type. A page containing only text comes up much faster for someone with a slow connection. There are, however, ways to optimize your images to ensure the quickest possible access speed. We will cover these methods later in this chapter.

Image Formats

There are several formats that are commonly used to build Web sites — and there are dozens and dozens of common file formats that can't be used on an Internet site without conversion to a compatible format. Most popular illustration and imaging programs — Macromedia Fireworks, Adobe Illustrator, Macromedia Freehand, Adobe Photoshop and others — provide methods to accomplish these conversions, so your options for creating artwork aren't all that limited.

Image formats for the Web fall into two broad categories — bitmap images, which are comprised of individual pixels containing a specific color or tone value, and vector graphics, which are built of lines, fills and shapes. The use of vector graphics on the Web is relatively new, and includes Flash movies — one of the most popular and powerful animation programs available to the designer. In this chapter we'll cover the use of both types of images.

Bitmap Images

There are several common bitmap formats available today.

PNG files were originally developed as a native format for Macromedia's Fireworks image editor, which was specifically engineered to create Web graphics. We're confident that the improved functionality of the file format will eventually lead to widespread acceptance and support by the major browsers.

GIF: Pronounced GIF with a hard "G" or GIF with a soft "G" (as in Jif), GIF files are the most common image format used in the construction of Web pages. The term is an acronym for Graphic Interchange Format. The format is best used for graphics with large areas of solid (also called "flat") color such as navigation bars, button elements and images containing transparent regions. Sequential GIF files can be displayed one after another, simulating movement or simple animation. This technique creates what are known as animated GIFs. They can contain a maximum of 256 colors, can contain transparent backgrounds and can be made to load in a series of steps — each step making the graphic appear sharper until the final quality is reached.

JPEG: Also referred to as JPG; the format was developed by the Joint Photographic Experts Group — hence the name. JPEG format is the clear choice for images that contain many subtle colors, such as photographs or gradients. The file format supports anywhere from a few colors to millions — also called high-color images. JPEG is a compression technique, and the higher the quality of the image, the larger it is and the longer it will take to download. Experimentation will provide you with some insight into attaining a balance between the size of the file and the quality you want to achieve.

PNG: Developed by Macromedia, PNG (Portable Network Group) is a relative newcomer to the Web graphics scene, and isn't supported by many browsers. Even those that do support PNG only support certain features of the format.

Vector Images

Vector images are images comprised of mathematically described lines and shapes. As previously mentioned, they're relatively new, and largely associated with either Macromedia's Flash or Adobe's LiveMotion animation programs. They allow for quick downloads, and have the ability to create dramatic animations. For more information about Flash and to learn how to create elements that can be used in your Dreamweaver sites, refer to the ATC book *Macromedia Flash: Animating for the Web*.

You can see how the circle is being stretched in the Flash vector animation application.

As we proceed through this chapter, you'll be presented with the opportunity to use Flash objects in your pages. Dreamweaver allows you to create Flash objects — such as animated buttons — directly in the program, even if you don't own Flash.

Inserting Images

Inserting images is quick and easy with Dreamweaver. You've already imported images onto a page using several of the methods available to you. Additional methods to import images onto a page include:

- Dragging an image from the desktop, or from the site folder, directly onto the spot where you want the image to appear. This avoids having to see the Insert Image dialog box.

- Dragging the Insert Image icon from the Common category of the Objects panel directly onto the page. This displays the Insert Image dialog box, where you can browse your hard drive to locate the file.

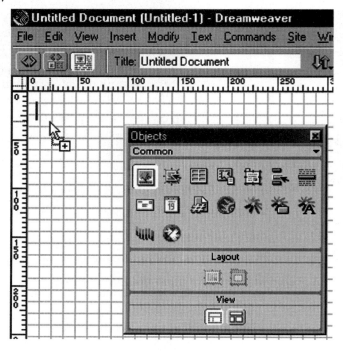

We strongly recommend that any design studio be equipped with both Flash and the Dreamweaver/ Fireworks applications. This combination of animation tools, vector drawing (Flash), vector and bitmap editing (Fireworks), as well as site design and management (Dreamweaver) is hard to beat.

Remember, we often resize our Objects panel to make our screen captures fit the page. Yours is probably tall and thin by default. We also keep our grids turned on. Don't let these two facts confuse you; they don't have any effect on the exercises.

By default the F11 key will activate the Assets panel.

Dreamweaver's companion program, Fireworks, is a powerful editor for the creation of Web graphics. It normally comes bundled with Dreamweaver, and provides a seamless method of creating graphics and editing them once they are in place on your pages.

- Dragging an image from the Assets panel directly onto the page. The Assets panel can be accessed from the Mini-Launcher or Launcher, as well as from the Window menu. Any files you copy into your root folder or a child file within the root are available. This is an extremely useful way to use elements on more than one page of your site.

Image Properties

Once you've inserted an image onto your page, Dreamweaver provides several fundamental techniques for modifying them. While the program doesn't really offer any graphic-editing functions, it does provide the ability to add borders, as well as methods for resizing images once they've been inserted. You should be aware, however, that using HTML to resize an image isn't very efficient. Create the image at the correct size in an image editing program so that you don't have to resize it. The only exception to this is if you're using the same image several different times at its normal size somewhere else on the site.

The following exercise will provide some experience using the Image Property inspector.

Working with Images

1. Create a folder inside of your **Work in Progress** folder and name it "Images_Site". It's going to serve as the root folder for a new site.

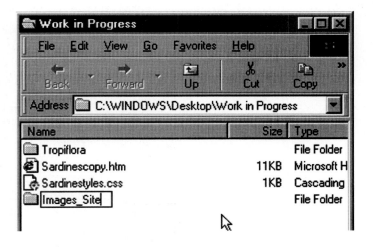

2. Start Dreamweaver. A blank, Untitled Document will be created. Save it into the folder we just created as "index.htm". Select Site>New Site, and select the new folder as the local root folder. Title the site "Images_Site".

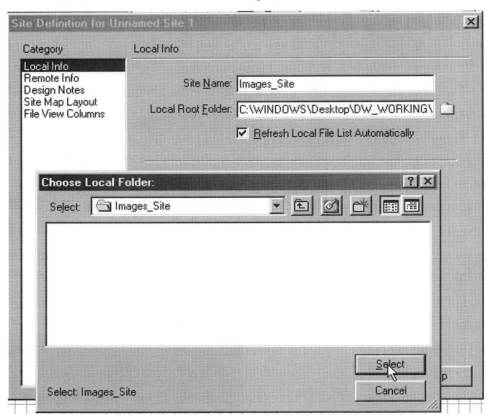

3. Enter a title for the page: "Working with Images". Press Return to insert another line, and position the cursor back in the title. Set the style of the title to Heading 1.

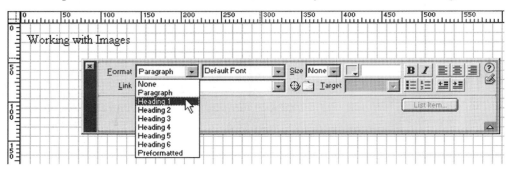

4. Choose Site>Define site, and select the index.htm file as the home page. We'll use this small site as we work through this chapter.

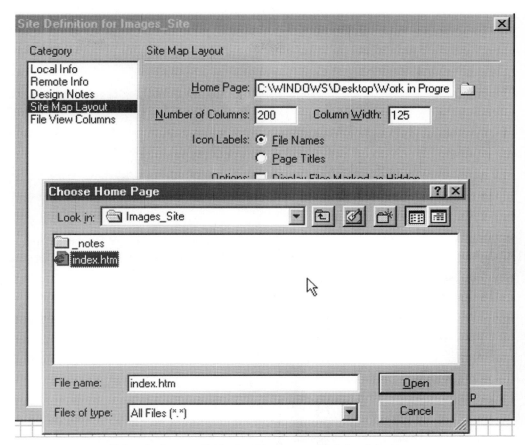

Using the Browse (folder icon) button to the right of the Home Page field makes it easy to locate and select your home page.

5. From the Common Objects panel, drag the Insert Image icon underneath the page title. The Select Image Source dialog box will appear.

6. Inside the **RF-Dreamweaver** folder is another folder named **ATC_Icons**. Navigate into that folder, and click once on the image **graduate.gif**. When you select it, notice that at the bottom of the dialog box you're warned that the image isn't currently inside of the site root folder.

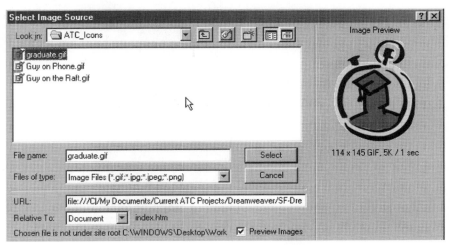

7. Click the Select button. Dreamweaver will ask you if you want to copy the image to your site. Click Yes.

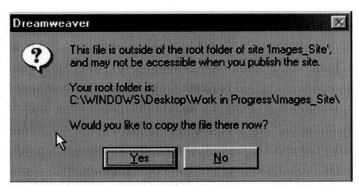

8. Usually we don't want all the images for the site just lying around in the root folder. Once you click Yes, use the New Folder icon to create a new folder inside of the root folder. Name the new folder "Images". Open the folder, and then click the Save button.

9. The image will appear underneath the title.

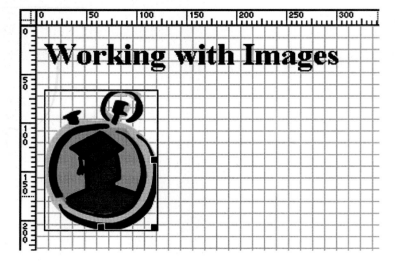

10. Activate the Property inspector (if it's not already visible) by selecting Window> Properties or by pressing Command/Control-F3. If you'll look to the right of the image icon, you'll see a name field. Name the image "graduate". This name is an image property used by Dreamweaver when you're creating JavaScript behaviors, something you'll learn about in a later chapter (and in one of the projects).

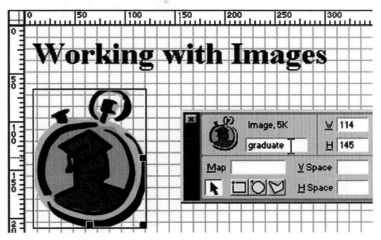

The grid size we're using is 10 × 10 pixels. You can activate your grid by selecting View>Grid>Show Grid, or by using Command-Option-G on the Mac or Control-Alt-G on the PC.

11. You can add borders to any image by entering a value in the Border field on the Property inspector dialog box. Try adding a 3 pixel border to the image by typing 3 in the field. You may need to click the More Options button to see additional attributes.

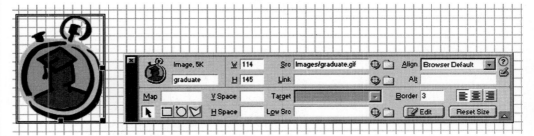

12. When the border is selected, it shows as double lines. When you deselect the image, the border shows in its true thickness.

When you're creating images for use in your Web site, try to use proper naming conventions. Don't use spaces (use underscores instead), and try to use logical names. Even though you can see a preview of an image before you insert it, it can become quite confusing if you don't establish some sort of standardized naming strategies.

13. To visually resize an image — a useful function when you're first designing a site and aren't totally sure of the final image size — simply select the image and pull its handles. Try that now. Notice that as you resize the image, the W and H fields change dynamically. Make the image slightly wider than it is tall.

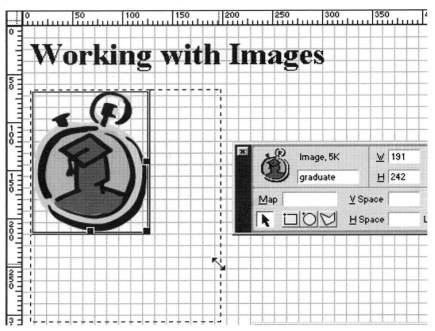

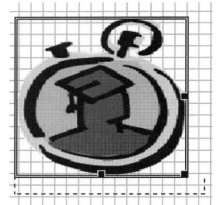

14. Undo the resize by pressing Command/Control-Z. The image will revert back to its original size. This time hold down the Shift key while resizing the image. This technique constrains the scaling — thereby protecting the image's original proportions.

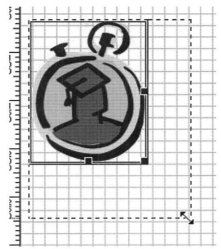

We want to emphasize that this technique of manually resizing an image is only effective when you're first designing your site — once you're sure of the size of the final object, go back to your image editor and change the size and resolution there. Don't let HTML resize your images.

15. Save the file but keep it open for the next exercise.

The Alt Field

There's one field in the Image Property inspector that you should make note of. It's called the Alt field. Alt is short for Alternative, and it's a very important detail that some designers don't bother with. Unfortunately, lack of attention to detail when you're building a Web site can mean the difference between a clean, functional design and one that's amateurish. Attention to detail will show in your work.

The Alt field lets you name and describe all the image on your pages. In this example, we selected the ATC logo at the top of the page and entered a name for the image in the Alt field. This name doesn't have to be the file's name — it can be anything you want.

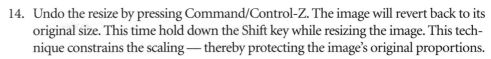

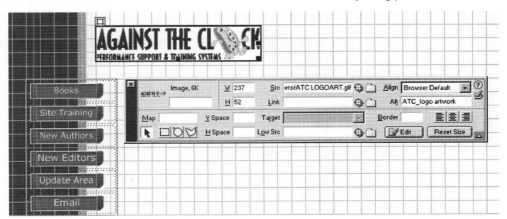

The reason you want to use Alt descriptions for every image on your site is that some people — particularly those with slower connections — turn off images in their Browser preferences to speed up surfing. If they do so, they won't know what picture should be in any spot. If you're thoughtful enough to provide an Alt description, it will appear along with the image icon.

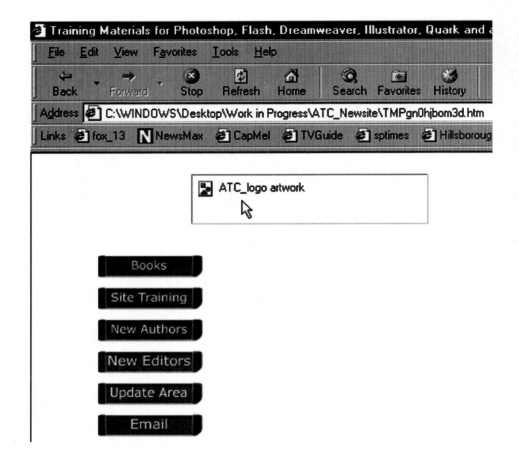

Remember, if you insert an image that's not already inside of your root folder (or a child folder inside of the root folder), Dreamweaver will ask if you want to copy the file into the site's root. You should always do this. If images aren't in the right place, Dreamweaver won't find them when the page downloads to the viewer's system.

Alignment

You've seen how you can add borders to images, and how to resize them. Other appearance issues concern how images align to each other and to surrounding text.

You've already seen simple alignment techniques when we built the primitive Tropiflora site earlier in the book. Using the Property inspector, you can align objects on the left side, in the center or on the right side of the browser window. Alignment commands not only affect the browser preview; they also affect the Design view.

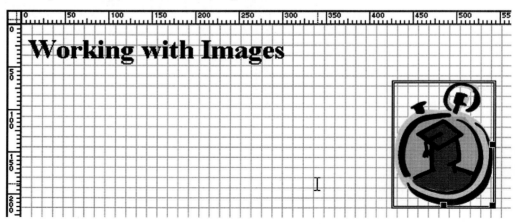

Aligning Text and Images

1. If the **index.htm** file isn't open, open it now.

2. Click the cursor to the right of the graduate image, and type "Our Graduate Program offers amazing benefits for the aspiring student".

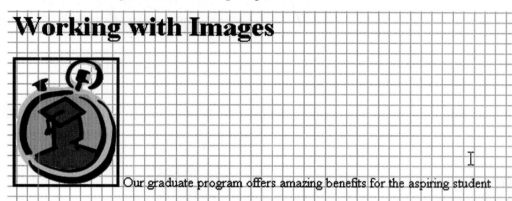

3. At the end of the line, insert the **phoneguy.gif** file from the **RF-Dreamweaver> ATC_Icons** folder. When prompted, copy the file into the site's Images folder.

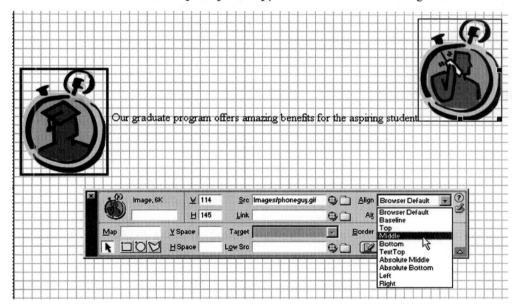

4. In the Property inspector, set the alignment of the left image from Browser Default to Middle. Do the same to the second image.

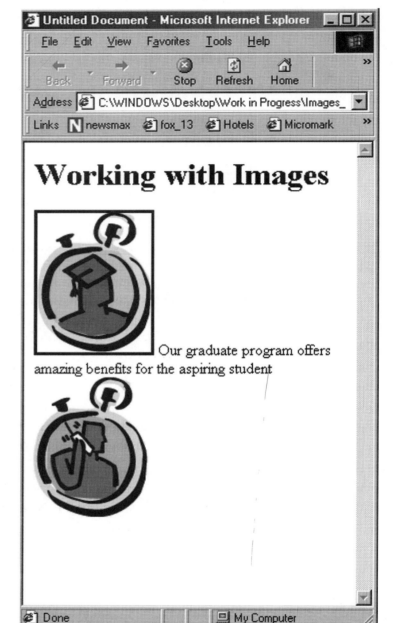

While it's important to know the various alignment options available to you when text and graphics coexist on your pages, using tables, frames and layers offers considerably more control over page elements. We'll be working with them in later chapters.

5. Continue to experiment with the various alignment options. They're logical once you've previewed them in the browser window — which is a good idea, because some options act in mysterious ways.

6. Once you're comfortable with aligning images, save the file and close it.

Navigation Bars and Other Image Links

One of Dreamweaver's most powerful features is its ability to automate the creation of navigation bars. "Navbars," as they're often called, are a common element in all contemporary Web sites. They provide a fixed location on the page that remains the same regardless of the page's content, and make it easy to move from location to location within the site.

There are two separate issues involved when creating navigation bars. The first is creating the links between images and the pages to which they take the viewer. We've already covered the various types of links available to you.

The second consideration when creating navigational elements on your sites is the use of images. Fortunately, Dreamweaver's navbar features let you automatically insert images as you build your interface.

Creating Navigation Bars

Dreamweaver supplies you with options for creating navigation buttons, bars and icons. First, you can import them from Flash or Fireworks. Second, you can create a series of GIF images and automatically insert them into a navigation bar from within Dreamweaver using the Insert Navigation Bar command.

Inserting Navigation Bars

1. Open the Images site. From the **RF-Dreamweaver>Navigation Bars** folder, open the **navbar_page.htm** file. Save it into the root (Images_Site) folder.

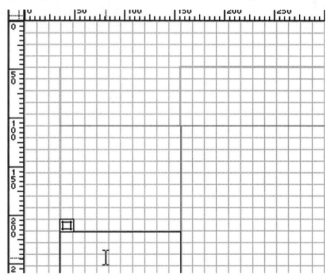

Whenever you're previewing your pages in a browser, be sure to resize the browser window into different shapes to make sure nothing unexpected happens — such as images getting stuck inside of your sentences

2. This page is built with layers to give you a feel for positioning an element such as a navigation bar. We'll learn how to build pages with layers in a later chapter, but for now just click the cursor in the third rectangle from the top left. You'll know you're in the right place if the little Layer icon appears over your cursor.

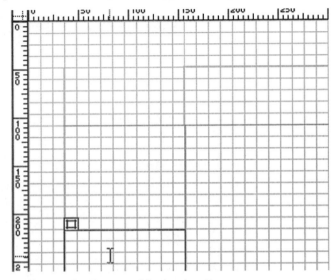

You can resize Flash and other Vector images to your heart's content; resizing bitmap images can result in image degradation. It's best to size the image correctly in the authoring program once you know what size they're supposed to be.

3. Select Insert>Interactive Images>Navigation Bar.

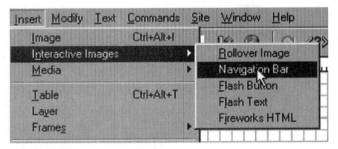

4. The Insert Navigation Bar dialog box appears. While it might look confusing at first glance, it's simple to use, and elegant in its functionality. In the Element Name field, enter the first category — Courses. Press the Tab key to move to the first image field — the one named Up Image.

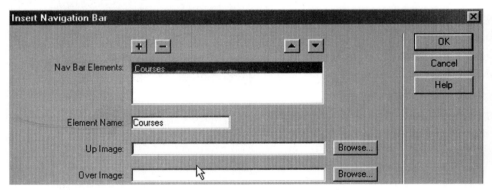

The order in which you create your pages, whether to use imported buttons or create them directly within Dreamweaver, or whether you use image maps to create your pages, is a personal preference. When considered in their totality, the processes you use and the order in which you apply them are referred to as "workflow."

5. Click the Browse button. Inside of the Navigation Bars folder is another folder named **navbarimages**. Open that folder and select the **cwareup.gif** file. This image will serve as the "up" state — the condition of the button when it's just sitting on the page.

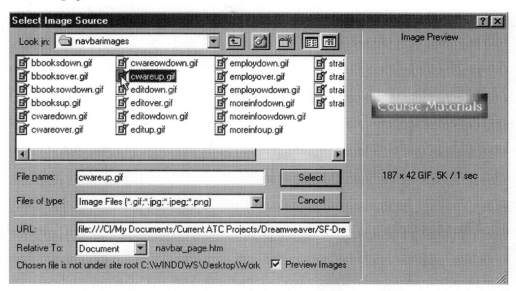

6. Once again, you'll get the warning message that says you need to copy the image into the root folder of your site. Click Yes and save the file into the Images folder within the root folder.

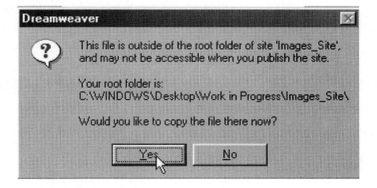

7. In the Down Image field, click the Browse button and find the **cwaredown.gif**. Do the same for Over Image, and Over While Down Image. The file names are **cwareover.gif**,(Over Image) and **cwareowdown.gif** (Over While Down).

8. Click the plus (+) sign to add another element. Name this one "Site_Training". Use the Up, Over, Down, and Over While Down images that start with the word "strain". Copy them into the site's Images folder. When you've finished, you'll have two elements in the navigation bar.

9. Add a third Element Name called "Books". Use the "bbooks" GIF files for the different states. Make sure that the Insert Vertically option is selected.

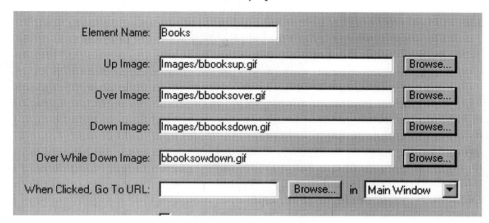

10. Click the OK button. Dreamweaver will use the three buttons we just created to build a navigation bar. Take a look.

11. Save the file and preview it in your browser. Try out your buttons. If everything went well, they should all be working. Notice how they change as you move the mouse over them. If you click one, it will display the Down image; move the mouse over it while it's clicked, and Dreamweaver displays the Over While Down image.

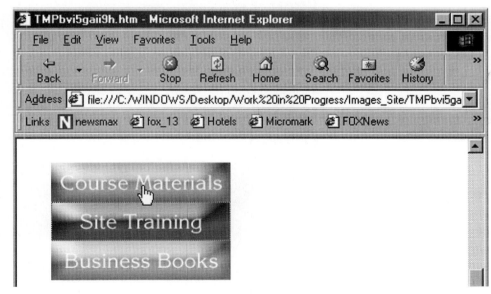

12. Save the file, which will also save the site.

Although it might seem tedious to go through the save warning every time you import a file, it's important to understand that most designers work on their site components in one place and then move them into the root folder (or child folder) after they're completed. Using Dreamweaver to create the copies automatically preserves the original file. That way you can go through the exercise again and have the originals to work with.

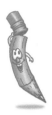

You'll notice that when you're building navigation bars, you can make them vertical or horizontal along the side of your page or at the top or bottom). Select this option from the pop-up menu at the bottom of the Insert Navigation Bar dialog box.

The disadvantage of using image maps is that they're difficult to edit. With a Dreamweaver navigation bar, for example, adding or removing elements isn't difficult at all — simply edit the list of elements in the dialog box. If you build a navigation system out of a bitmap image, you have to edit the image to change the structure. That's not always as easy as it sounds.

You should be aware that you can have only one automatic navigation bar per page — although that certainly doesn't stop you from putting other navigation elements in other places. This limitation only applies to navigation bars created with the built-in command. If you want to edit an existing bar, simply choose the Insert Navigation Bar command again, and you'll receive a warning. Clicking OK will access the bar that's already on the page.

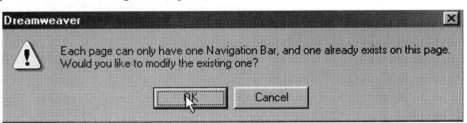

Image Maps

Another way to create graphical navigation systems is with the use of image maps. Many designers use this technique, and it can be used to create some dramatic effects.

An image map is an inserted graphic that contains "hot spots." These hot spots are (usually) invisible links that are created using the image map tools.

Creating an Image Map

1. Create a new file and save it into the root folder (Images_Site) as "imagemap.htm".

2. Insert the **military.jpg** image from the **RF-Dreamweaver** folder. Save it into the site's Images folder.

3. Activate the Property inspector. The tools on the lower-left side of the panel let you create hotspots on an image. Use the Rectangle tool to draw a rectangle around the Opportunities image on the page.

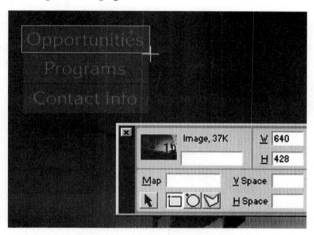

4. Select the rectangle. The Hotspot panel appears. To create a link for the spot, simply enter the URL or browse to locate the linked page.

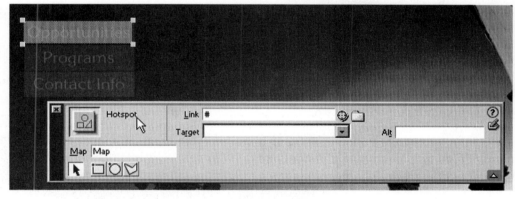

5. Save the file and close it.

As you can see, there are several powerful ways to create graphic interfaces using Dreamweaver. Again, the exact method you select to use when you're building your own sites is up to you. Image maps work well for some applications, and automatic navigation bars work well for others. You could also use both in the same site.

As is often the case, there's almost always more than one way to accomplish the same task. For example, you could use a background image and place a navbar on a page, which could simulate the effect we achieved in the above exercise, while still offering the various button states we saw in the Insert Navigation Bar dialog box.

We haven't actually "wired" any of these buttons while building the navigation bar. We've focused more on building the graphics. To set a link for any of the buttons, simply use the When Clicked, Go to URL field and the Browse button. Locate the desired file and click OK. The button will be linked up. You can also use the Property inspector for the objects to assign an absolute or relative URL to the buttons.

Rollovers

Rollover images are popular in contemporary page design. They work fairly simply: you put an image on the page, and when the user rolls the mouse over the top of the image, a different one appears.

To create rollover images, you simply select Insert>Interactive Images>Rollover Image. The Rollover Image dialog box appears. Name the image, and use the browse buttons to find the original image.

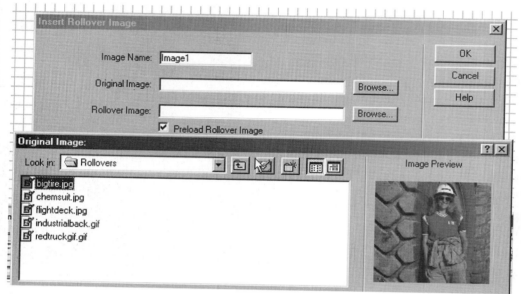

The original image is the one that will appear when the mouse touching it (the default image when the page opens). The rollover image appears if the user touches the image with the mouse. To achieve this, you either type the image's name into the Rollover Image field or use the Browse button to locate it.

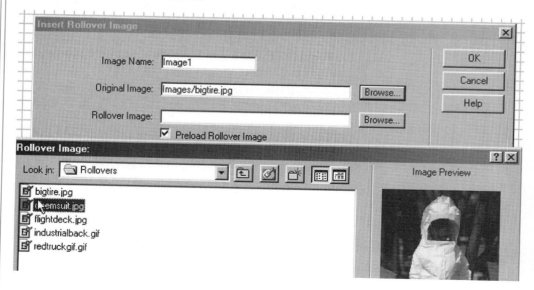

You can use the ALT message line in the Property inspector dialog box to add the title to the page in case the image doesn't load. Even if it does load, the image title is often useful to the viewer. You can turn off autoloading of images in your browser's preferences. Adding titles is good for people who don't have fast connections. They can choose to load an image by clicking on it.

To see the effects of your work, you have to preview the page in the browser. If you keep the Preload Rollover Image box checked (as you always should; there's no advantage to not loading it, since it will cause a delay when the user moves their mouse over the image), the images change instantly when touched.

You're going to have an opportunity to work with Image Rollovers in the project that follows, chapter 9.

Chapter Summary

In chapter 8 you explored some of the options available to you when importing images. You learned how to add borders to your images, and how to position them relative to surrounding text. You learned that you can resize images, and how to work with the Image Property inspector. You learned how to use Dreamweaver's powerful Navigation Bar feature, and created a series of buttons that displayed different "states" depending on the user's actions. You also learned how to create an image map — another popular method of creating a graphical user interface (GUI). Finally, you began to learn how to create rollover images — pictures that swap out whenever the mouse moves over the top of them.

Notes:

(9) *Tables*

Chapter Objective:

In chapter 9 we will work with tables — the most common and predictable way to create design layouts for your pages. To build a solid knowledge of how to create, edit and manage tables in your documents, in chapter 9 you will:

- Learn to use the Insert Table object from the Common category of the Objects panel.

- Understand the difference between rows and columns, and their relationship to the Insert Table dialog box.

- Learn to determine the size of a table using several different positioning techniques.

- Learn to merge cells and build complex tables.

- Work with nested tables — tables inside the cells of other tables.

- Experiment with table attributes such as borders, spacing and padding.

- Learn to apply color to tables to help the user differentiate between different components.

- Work with the Format Table command, which provides a collection of pre-defined tables that you can use on your site.

- Learn about Layout view — a dynamic visual environment where you can draw freeform table objects to develop compelling layouts.

- Understand populating your tables with text, images and media content.

Projects to be Completed:

- Cosmic Pets (A)

- Tropiflora Order Form (B)

- Diehard Digital (C)

- Mr. BlockHead's Challenge (D)

Tables

Tables were originally used to present tabular information. Now, tables are one of the four major techniques that you can use to accomplish complex page designs. The others — CSS Boxes, frames and layers — are covered in their own chapters. For now we're going to concentrate on the use of tables, and the tools that Dreamweaver provides for their creation, editing and management.

In its simplest form, a table is a list of text and/or numbers.

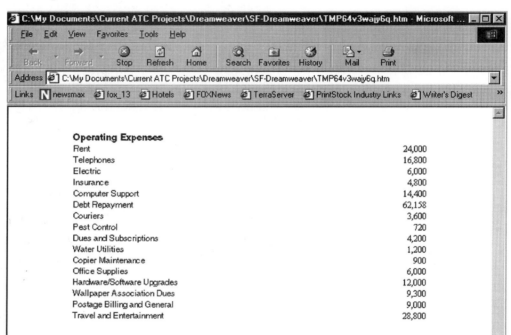

In the above browser window, the table is fairly simple. What's interesting is that the copy on the left side of the table is left justified, while the numbers in the right column appear to be right justified. This was accomplished by the creation of a table — in fact, this data was simply saved from Microsoft Excel as an HTML file and opened directly inside of Dreamweaver. If you look at the same table in the Design view, you'll see that there are a number of individual "cells" that contain the data.

Tables let you design pages that contain fixed regions to contain your images, text, navigation elements and other page components. They're a powerful tool that will dramatically expand your design options.

When you create new pages in this chapter, you can just keep working in the Images_Site folder that you created in the last exercise. That way you won't have to create a new site just for this chapter.

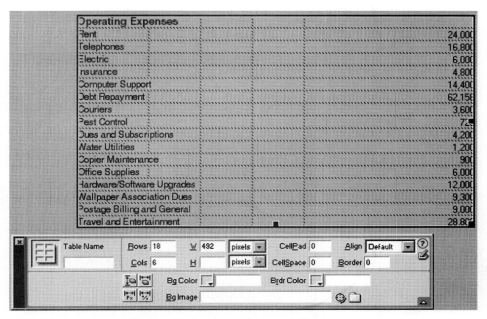

Each table contains a number of attributes common to all tables.

Rows, which run horizontally across the width of the table.

Columns, which separate the table into vertical regions.

Cells, which are created by the intersection of a row and a column. A table can have as little as one row and one column, which would create only one cell. Most tables have more than that.

Data, which, in the case of the example, takes the form of the title (Operating Expenses), the categories on the left (Rent, Telephones and so forth) and the corresponding values for each category.

While tables are certainly appropriate for displaying tabular information, they're even more effective when used as a layout aid. Most Web sites that you see today use tables in one way or another. Using tables, you have almost — not quite, but almost — as much design flexibility as you would have with programs like QuarkXPress, Adobe InDesign or PageMaker.

Here's the home (index.htm) page from Dwayne Ferguson's Diehardstudio.com site. Each of the page elements — the face, text and other images occupy their own cells.

In addition to providing the projects for this book, Ferguson also wrote several of the chapters.

With Dreamweaver's table tools, it's a relatively simple task to build the design into which the page elements would be inserted. In the following example, we selected different background colors for each of the cells, so that you can see them clearly.

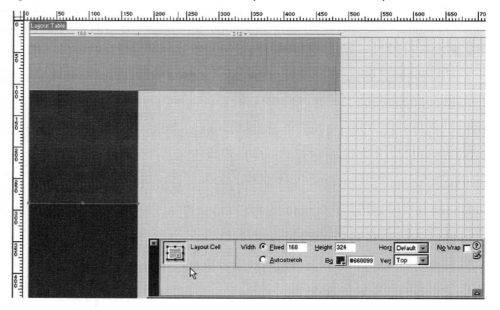

In the case of Dwayne's site, the background color for the page was set to black, and each cell had the same attribute. You can color each cell in a table differently, or keep them all the same — what you choose to do is governed solely by the design you have in mind.

Creating Tables

There are actually several ways to create a table. Two are easy, and one tedious and time-consuming.

Options for Creating Tables

The first way to create tables is to code them in HTML. While some people might think this is a skill critical to one's self-esteem, we don't. Coding tables in HTML is tedious, time-consuming and no fun at all.

The next way to create a table is to use Dreamweaver's Insert Table command. You can access it from a number of different places: from the Insert>Table menu selection, the keyboard or the Common category from the Objects panel.

The keyboard equivalent for inserting a table is Control-Alt-T on Windows platforms and Command-Option-T on the Macintosh.

The Insert Table dialog box provides fields that allow you to select the number of rows and columns, the padding (how much space there is between the object within a cell and the cell's border), spacing, the width of the table relative to the page (or other cells), and borders. We'll cover each of these attributes in this chapter. This method works fine for applications where you have a table that contains a fixed number of rows and columns. To create more complex tables, you'll probably want to use Layout view — the second option.

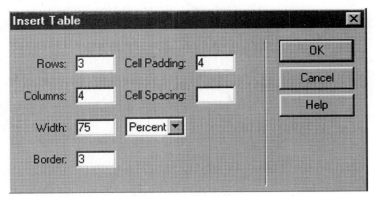

The Width pop-up menu provides a choice between Percent and Pixels, which is a way to fix the width of the table you're creating.

Once you enter the appropriate information in the fields, the table will automatically be created. It appears at the insertion point, or at the location you drag the Insert Table icon from the Common category of the Objects panel.

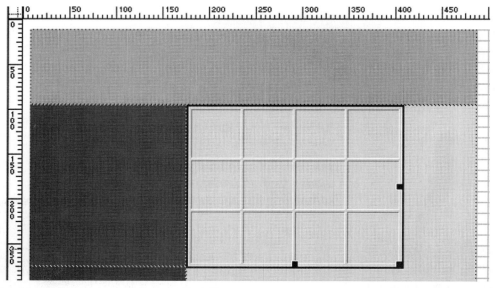

The third way to create tables is probably the one you'll end up using the most — and that's with the Layout view. When you're in Layout view, you can draw cells anywhere on the page, and Dreamweaver will automatically write the complex code it takes to make the page work. In Layout view, Dreamweaver literally becomes a functional layout program for building Web pages.

You can switch to Layout view from the Objects panel. At the bottom of the panel — regardless of which category of objects is active at the time — is an icon that switches from Standard to Layout view.

Designing Tables

Even tables meant to present data require some amount of designing — you have to decide upon the number of rows and columns you'll need, and how you want the data to appear; color, background shading, font size, borders and other factors impact even the simplest of tables. As you move toward using tables to do page design, you'll need to learn how to make tables that contain uneven numbers of rows and columns, and cells of different sizes.

Creating a Simple Data Table

You'll probably notice that we work with the grids and rulers turned on in Design view. It makes it easier for us to position elements. We also keep the Snap-to-Grid feature turned on. They're both available from the View menu.

1. Create a new page. If Dreamweaver isn't running, simply launching the program will start a new page. Save the page as "tables.htm" in your **Work in Progress** folder.

2. Make sure that you're in Standard view — click the left icon on the bottom of the Objects panel.

3. Click the Insert Table icon. The Insert Table dialog box will appear. Create a table with 5 rows and 2 columns. Set Cell Padding and Spacing to 4 and 2 respectively, the Width to 80 Percent, and the Border value to 3.

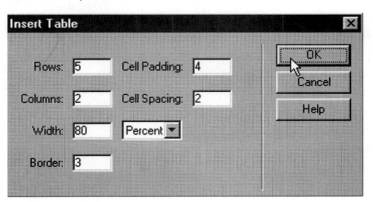

If you don't set values for padding, spacing, and border, they're not automatically set to 0: the defaults are Border 1, Padding 2 and Spacing 2.

You can toggle back and forth between percentage measurements and pixel widths using the buttons on the bottom left of the Table Property inspector. The icons above the measurement icons will clear cell heights or column widths, reducing them to their minimum sizes.

4. The table will appear at the top of the page. If you look at the Property inspector, it now reflects the attributes for the table — with the same variables that were available to you when you created it.

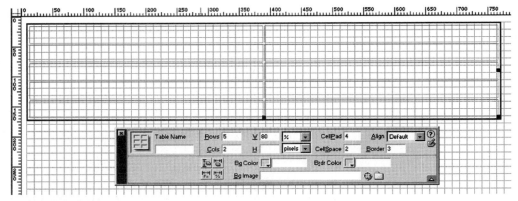

5. Grab the handle on the right side of the table. Reduce the size of the table by dragging it to the left. Watch the percentage value on the Property inspector and change the width of the table to 60%. This value is relative to the width of the browser window.

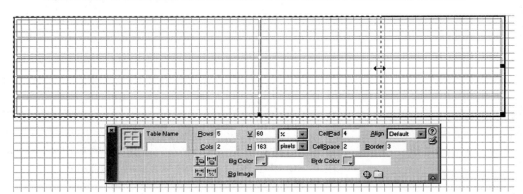

6. Resize the table to make it deeper. Type the number "450" into the H (Height) field. The Height field is measured in pixels, while the width is measured relative to the width of the browser window that the table is being viewed with.

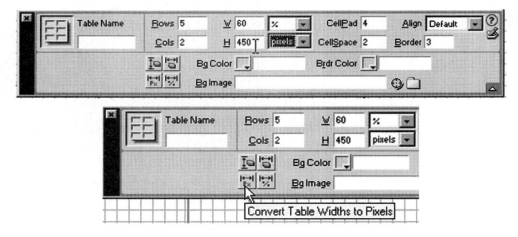

7. Try changing the width of the two cells. Grab the line between the two columns and drag it to the left about half the distance to the edge of the page.

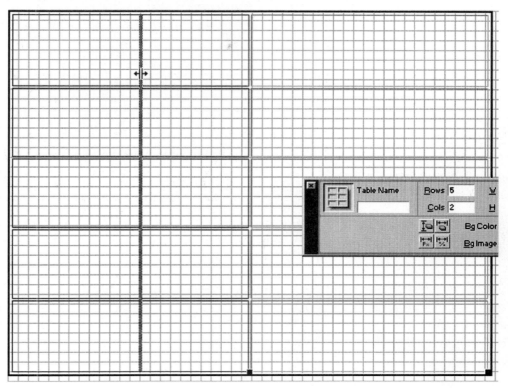

8. You can create more complex layouts by splitting individual cells into rows or columns. Click in the first cell to create an insertion point. Choose Modify>Table>Split Cell, or click the Splits_Cell button in the Property inspector. In the Split Cell dialog box, choose Split Cell Into Rows or Columns.

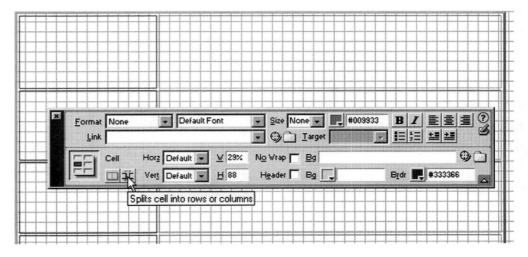

9. Click the Columns radio button and enter "3" for the Number of Columns.

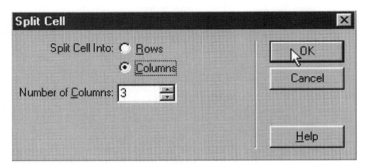

10. Examine the table. The top row is now different than the four at the bottom.

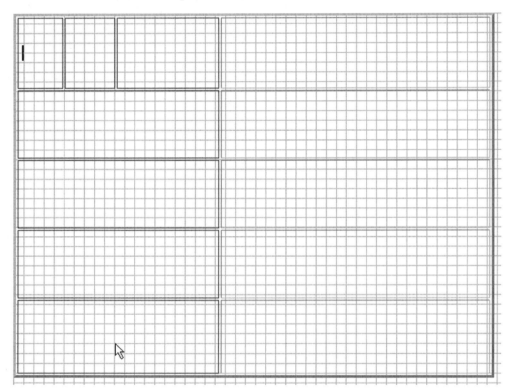

11. You can edit entire columns or rows. Position the pointer over the top of the second column. It will turn into a downward-pointing arrow — click to select the column.

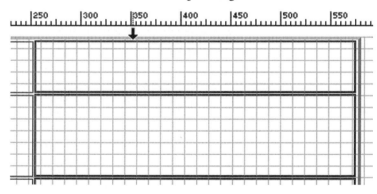

The Hspace and Vspace fields let you determine the amount of space that a browser will provide for your table. Hspace adds space to the left and right sides of your tables, while Vspace does the same at the top and bottom.

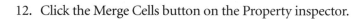

12. Click the Merge Cells button on the Property inspector.

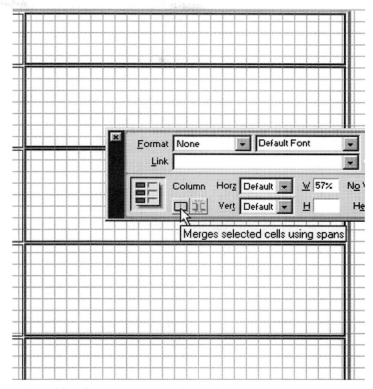

13. Examine the table. It's now a multi-column layout. Remember, you can put any content into any of the cells, as we'll see in a minute.

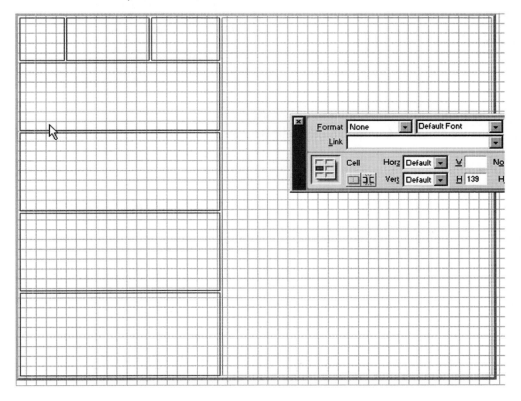

14. Continue experimenting with your options. Try selecting two or more cells while holding the Shift key; this lets you select and merge multiple cells (they have to be contiguous for this to work).

15. When you're comfortable with your ability to create and modify tables with the Insert Table command and the Property inspector, select the entire table with the Pointer tool, and delete it (press Backspace or Delete). Save the file but keep it open. We're going to use it in a little while to do a page layout using Dreamweaver's layout tools to create a freeform table.

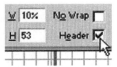

There's another way to edit existing tables, and that's with the Context menu. If you're on a PC, you can access the menu using the right mouse button; if you're on a Macintosh, Control-clicking will accomplish the same thing. The Table menu provides access to all of the features we've used so far.

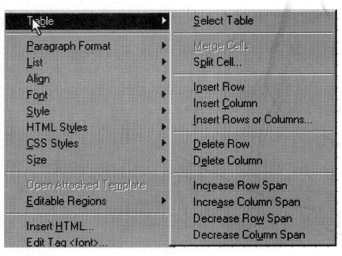

If you're creating a table like the budget example we showed you before, you can select the first cell (the one presumably holding the title of the table) and check the Header attribute in the Property inspector. It also centers the headings and boldfaces the text.

Nested Tables

There's really no limit to the way you format your tables. You can even create what are called nested tables. *Nested tables* are tables that you insert into the cell of an existing table. Just click to create an insertion point and use the same methods to insert a table that we used in the previous exercise.

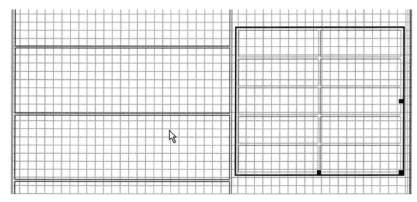

Nested tables can be edited just like any other table — with merged and split cells and rows, and the same ability to contain any type of content.

Coloring Your Tables

Many tables will benefit from the addition of color — and in some cases, images. For example, if you want to create a background image for your site, you can create one large table, set the background image using the Property inspector, and then create tables on top of that one that let the background image show through. You should note, though, that not all browsers will display cell background images — like some versions of Netscape.

If you want to select a table, the Context menu's Select Table option is one of the safest ways. While you can select a table using the Pointer tool, you run the risk of moving it or accidentally resizing a row or column.

The more tables you have on your pages, the longer they take to load — be aware of that and try to design with the minimal amount of tables that you need to accomplish your design. Don't design tables with columns or rows that aren't needed.

Coloring rows and columns is simple. First select the row, column or cell. Then select the color from the Background Color pop-up menu on the Property inspector. You can color both the borders and the individual cells.

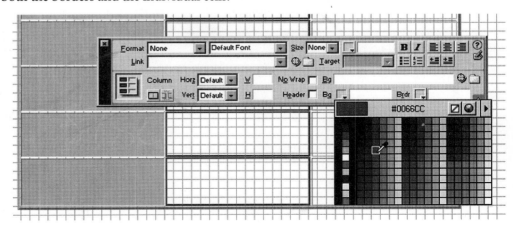

For financial and data tables, the Format Table command provides a collection of pre-defined table color combinations. First create your table, and then select Commands> Format Table. The dialog box that appears lets you create and apply several different color and appearance formats.

You can also use the Point to File icon to point to an image to use as a table's background.

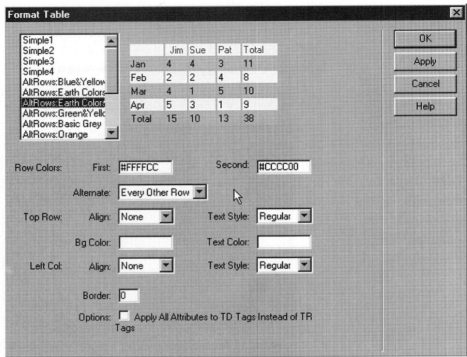

Using Layout View

Layout View, the third way to design your pages using tables, is the easiest and most flexible method. While you can certainly build fairly complex tables using the regular Insert Table commands, using Layout view is more flexible and natural — especially if you have experience using page layout programs like QuarkXPress, Adobe InDesign or Adobe PageMaker.

Make sure to check how different browsers display background images. Your visitors might get unexpected results if you don't.

Designing a Page with Layout View

1. If the blank **table.htm** page we created before isn't open, open it now. Click the Layout View icon in the bottom right of the Common category of the Objects panel. An instructional dialog box will appear.

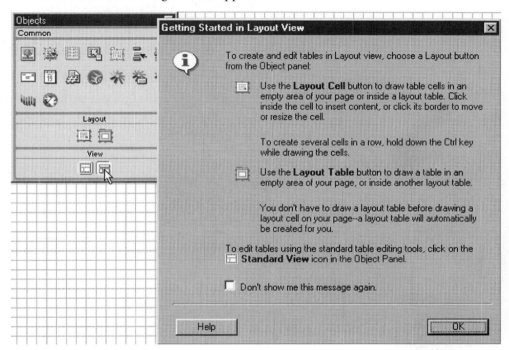

2. Take a moment to look at the instructions. They contain just about everything you need to know to work in Layout view. Notice that it says you don't have to create a layout table before you start using the Layout Cell button.

3. Select the Draw Layout Cell button and draw a cell across the top of the page. Make it 450 pixels wide × 100 pixels high. You can always use the Property inspector to fine-tune the sizes if you can't draw it perfectly.

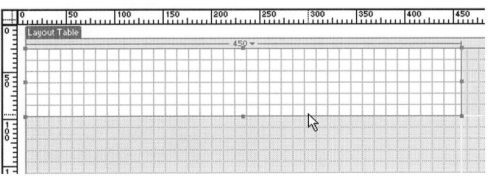

4. Draw another cell below the first one. Let it extend down to about 500 pixels.

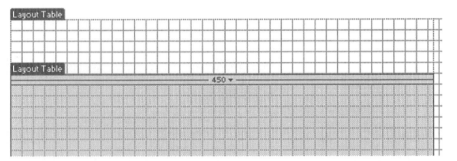

5. Select the Draw Layout Table tool and change to Standard view. Add a long, thin vertical cell on the left side of the window. Click the small triangle at the top of the cell and look at the selections.

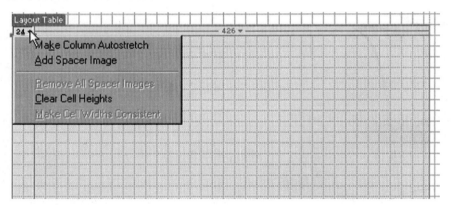

6. A *spacer image* is a null image object that's created solely to keep the spacing accurate in your tables. You need to add spacer images in certain situations, because some browsers ignore empty cells, which might mess up your award-winning designs. Select Add Spacer Image from the menu. You'll see a dialog box that asks you if you want Dreamweaver to create the spacer for you, or if you would like to use one that you already have. Select Create and save the spacer.

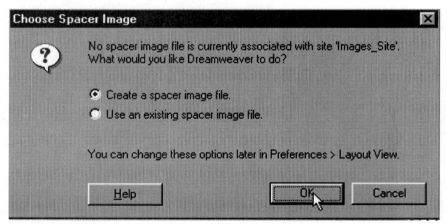

7. Create a small square cell inside the right column and another tall one to the right of that. Your design should look similar to the one below. Make sure it's at least 130 pixels wide.

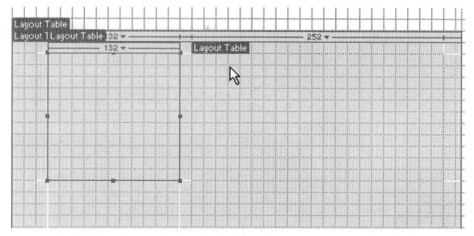

8. Select the table and take a look at your layout. Using simple click and drag techniques, we've designed a fairly complex Web page — one that's ready to be populated.

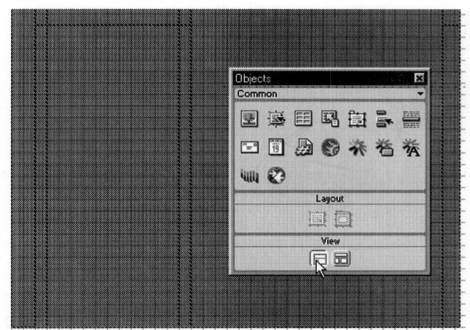

9. Save the file but keep it open for the next exercise.

Populating Your Tables With Content

You can populate the cells of your tables with just about any type of data you have — from Excel spreadsheets to images, text files and interactive objects (such as Flash buttons, Flash Text or navigation bars — like we created in chapter 8, "Images"). All you have to do is click the insertion point, select the images and build your pages.

Inserting Content into a Layout

1. Click in the top cell. Select Insert>Interactive Images>Flash Text. Select a typeface that you like. Color it, and size it at about 30 points. Type the text "Little Dogs".

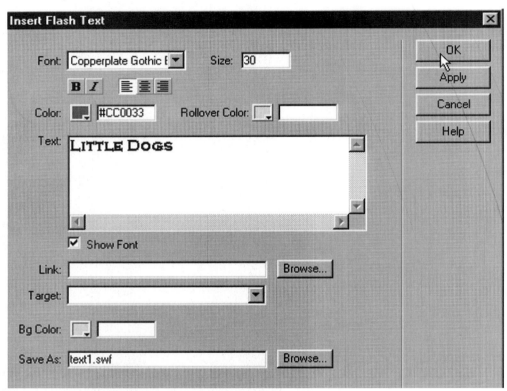

2. Put another Flash Text element underneath the first one. This one should be a little smaller and in a different typeface. It should read "The Shiba Inu". You'll know what one is in a minute.

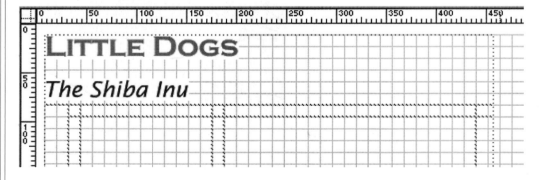

3. In the square cell, insert the image named **chaseman.jpg**. You'll find him in your **RF-Dreamweaver** folder, inside the **Little Dogs** folder. Copy it into the Images folder for your site when prompted to do so.

4. Open the file **description.htm**. Select all the text and copy it to the clipboard (Command/Control-C). In the working document, click the cursor into the right column and paste down the text. Close the **description.htm** file.

5. Open the **history.txt** file from the same folder. Select all the text, copy it to the clipboard. Close the history.txt file. In the working document, put the cursor to the right of his picture and press Return. Paste the text, which will go underneath the picture of Chase.

Using Flash text lets you use any typeface on your system without worrying about whether it will display properly on another person's system. As long as they have the Flash plugin (and most newer browsers have it preinstalled), your type elements will remain intact.

LITTLE DOGS

The Shiba Inu

Shiba Inus have lived with the Japanese people for centuries. Considered the smallest and oldest of Japan's dogs, the Shiba's ability to maneuver steep hills and mountain slopes, together with its keen senses, have repeatedly shown it to be a superb hunting dog. Interestingly, Shiba Inu

With black button nose, little pricked ears and a curly tail, the Shiba enters the world knowing he is a superior being. Whether with intrepid boldness, squinty-eyed cuteness or calm dignity, he is KING.

The Japanese have three words to describe the Shiba temperament. The first word is "kan-i" which is bravery and boldness combined with composure and mental strength. The opposite of "kan-i" is "ryosei" which means good nature with a gentle disposition. One cannot exist without the other. The charming side of the Shiba is "soboku" which is artlessness with a refined and open spirit. They combine to make a personality that Shiba owners can only describe as "irresistible"!

6. Save the page and preview it in your browser window.

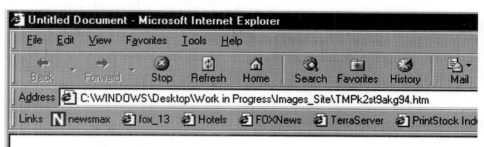

LITTLE DOGS

The Shiba Inu

With black button nose, little pricked ears and a curly tail, the Shiba enters the world knowing he is a superior being. Whether with intrepid boldness, squinty-eyed cuteness or calm dignity, he is KING.

The Japanese have three words to describe the Shiba temperament. The first word is "kan-i" which is bravery and boldness combined with composure and mental strength. The opposite of "kan-i" is "ryosei" which means good nature with a gentle disposition. One

Shiba Inus have lived with the Japanese people for centuries. Considered the smallest and oldest of Japan's

If you get a message that says a file is read only and cannot be changed, choose Make Writeable from the dialog box. This only happens on the PC, not the Macintosh. You can also select all the files, select File>Properties, and un-check the Read Only box. You can only do this after you've moved them to your hard drive — you can't change them on the CD.

7. You probably get the idea. You can continue to format the page — think about adding headings over the articles, changing font sizes and coloring the background or the individual cells. The possibilities are endless. When you're done, save the file — it's your first real layout job with Dreamweaver.

Chapter Summary

In chapter 9 you began to explore how tables can be used to design complex and effective pages, without a lot of tedious coding. First, you learned how to use Dreamweaver's Insert Table command. You learned how to add and remove columns and rows, how to determine the size of a table and how to set such attributes as spacing and padding. You learned how to put borders on tables and how to color cells — both manually and with the Format Table command. Lastly, you learned how to use the Layout view to create dynamic tables, complete with spacers, images and text.

Complete Project A: Cosmic Pets

Notes:

Free-Form Project #1

Assignment

You need to put together a digital resume — complete with samples of your creative, examples of some of the sites that you've worked on, and images from several print campaigns. You can use some of the projects that we've done throughout this book, and you're free to design content specifically for inclusion in this portfolio.

Realize that your personal portfolio will remain a work in progress throughout your career. At this point your assignment is to lay the foundation; as your skills, knowledge and abilities evolve, you'll enhance the site — when and if you have the time, that is.

Applying Your Skills

As you develop your personal portfolio site, you'll need to apply several techniques and methods that you've worked with so far. While you shouldn't be afraid of trying new things, at the very least you should:

* Draw a flow chart that establishes the pages that you'll need to build the basic site. You should have a home page, a page containing your background and experience, and a page containing samples of your work. Use this flow chart to determine how the links will work.

* Draw a basic layout for the pages.

* Create a root folder on your local drive. This folder should contain all the elements and objects that are used to develop the pages that make up the site.

* Create a blank home page. As you've learned, the safest approach is to name it "index.htm."

* Write a brief bio, some background and personal interests.

* Experiment with various text styles until you're satisfied with the headings, body text, lists and paragraph formats. Define HTML or CSS styles for the primary elements.

* Gather graphics and create an assets folder inside the root folder and put the images into the folder.

* Consider using a long page to hold your samples. Create named anchors to position the page properly within the Browser window when the user goes from image-to-image.

Specifications

The home page should download quickly, and fit within a 640 pixel × 480 pixel window. Keep the page small — make sure that it downloads in less than 30 seconds on a 56k modem. Other pages can be as big as 45k, but certainly no larger.

You can use rollovers if you want, but keep the images small – less than 8k each. If necessary, prepare them beforehand in an image-editing program like Photoshop or ImageReady.

Make sure that you only use Web-safe colors.

Create your design using tables. Most browsers can handle tables without any problem.

Publisher's Comments

It's estimated that nearly 100,000 new users log onto the Internet every day. While we think this might be a bit of hyperbole, there's no question that new sites appear every day, and every day someone makes a commitment to putting their company online in the near future.

Besides the opportunity to build new sites, there's also a large demand for good designers and site-developers to redesign existing sites. Considering how many poorly designed sites you come across when you're surfing, it's no surprise that you can make money making poor sites.

If a company, organization or association wants to create or update a site, there's not better way to determine the competency of a prospective contractor than to see the work they did on their own site. Remember, though, that lots of bells and whistles do not make a good site. Think elegant and classy before you think noisy and flashy. That's not to say that you can't let your imagination run wild – just remember that prospective clients represent a wide variety of different people. Sticking to a conservative look and feel is less likely to turn some of them off.

Review #1

Chapters 1 through 9

To evaluate our progress so far, let's review the lessons we've learned. After completing the discussions, exercises and projects, you should:

- Be familiar with how the Internet started, and know about the Web consortium, which determines and publishes the standards by which the web functions. You should have learned about HTML, and how it's interpreted by browser applications. You should know what an ISP is, and understand the role they play in making Web sites available to the surfing public.

- Have a beginning knowledge of the Hypertext Markup Language (HTML), and know what tags are and how they control what appears on your Web pages. You should understand how a tag works, and be able to make simple changes to the HTML that Dreamweaver generates.

- Be comfortable using many of the program's interface features, including panels and inspectors. You should understand how to use the common category of the Objects panel, and know how to manage panels, dialog boxes and inspectors to reduce clutter.

- Be able to build a simple site, insert images, create text and construct a simple interface using links. You should be comfortable with the concept of a root folder, nested folders, and the importance of the home page — commonly named index.htm.

- Know how to work with different forms of text, and be familiar with basic text formatting. You should know to avoid using underlining so that the user doesn't become confused with something that looks like a link. You should have learned about paragraph formatting, and have an understanding of both HTML and CSS styles.

- Know the difference between document-relative, absolute and site-relative links, and be able to create and manage named anchors, which let you move the position of a single page relative to the Browser window in which it's being viewed.

- Understand how to insert images, and control their borders, size and position on the page. You should know how to create image-based navigation bars, and use images as image maps.

- Know how to build pages using tables — a commonly used and widely compatible method of designing complex page designs. You should be able to populate tables with images and text, and use a number of techniques to merge cells, create nested tables and position those tables on the page. You should know how to color tables and how to use the Format Table function to select a table from a collection of pre-defined designs.

10 Frames

Chapter Objective:

In chapter 10 we will learn another way to format and control the content of Web pages — using the Frames feature. To learn the benefits and pitfalls associated with this common technique, in chapter 10 you will:

- Learn why some browsers still cannot support or properly display frame-based pages, and how to determine if they can.

- Learn about the pros and cons of frame-based sites.

- Explore the differences between frames and tables.

- Understand that pages built with frames can display multiple HTML pages in the same place.

- Learn to use frames to build stable navigation strategies.

- Experiment with framesets — special collections of pages and definitions that control the appearance of your frame-based pages.

- Understand how to edit and manage framesets.

- Learn about the Frames panel and the controls it offers.

- Work with populating your frames with text, graphics and other HTML documents.

- Explore targeting — the method by which the user moves from frame-to-frame and page-to-page within your sites.

Projects to be Completed:

- Cosmic Pets (A)

- Tropiflora Order Form (B)

- Diehard Digital (C)

- Mr. BlockHead's Challenge (D)

Frames

Frames allow you to design pages that are split into individual sections. What makes frames unique is that each frame you create on a page is an HTML page. The frameset is the master document that keeps track of the number of frames on a page, the sizes of each frame and the HTML that is contained inside each individual frame. The frameset itself is not displayed in the browser, it remains behind the scenes so the browser knows how the page should look.

The more frames you create, the more actual HTML pages you are opening in one window. As you can imagine, using frames can be both a good and a bad thing.

The frameset can be thought of as a cruise ship with each frame representing a passenger. This parent/child relationship exists in many applications.

This page from Jeff Fox's Buccaneers Magazine was done using frames and tables. Host Rivals.com offers timely and diverse information about a wide range of different sports.

Frames vs. NoFrames

Before your begin using frames, you should determine whether or not you can achieve similar results without them. Frames offer a nice solution to creating an organized Web site, but they come at a price. Not every browser can display them; and the more frames you have, the slower the browser may operate.

One solution to this problem is to use Dreamweaver to insert your HTML in a NoFrames statement that will allow your page to be viewed in text-only and older browsers. If the browser detects frames and cannot support them, the contents of what you place inside the NoFrames statement will be displayed instead.

Using a NoFrames Statement

1. Select Modify>Frameset>Edit NoFrames Content.

2. When the Document window clears, follow one of these options:

   (a) Type your new content or insert your image(s) in the Document window.

   (b) Select Window>HTML Source and type your content or HTML in between the <noFrames> tags.

3. When you have finished entering your information, select Modify>Frameset>Edit NoFrames Content to return to your document.

Browser Considerations

You already know that not all of the features in Dreamweaver can be viewed in all browsers. Many people are still using older, or alternative browsers to the mainstream. Sometimes frames are not supported by these browsers, which means you may have to create two versions of your site.

Pros and Cons of using Frames

Double-check the actual HTML code to make sure all the information you specify has actually been placed in between the NoFrames tags.

Pros: Using frames is similar to using tables, but frames offer more freedom in the choices you can make design-wise. You can split your page into as many frames as you need to neatly place elements. Like tables, your frames stay where you put them, and can ensure that your design is as consistent as possible across the many different browsers that support frames.

Another benefit to using frames is that you can create a portion of the page that will remain static, while other parts of the page change (for example, the corporate logo or a Menu bar that is placed in one of the frames). Someone can click a menu item, and instead of the entire page changing to a new URL, the new page displays on the same page but in a different frame.

Cons: The major drawback to using frames as a design tool is the inherit difficulty of maintaining the frameset. When you use single pages or tables to design your pages, if you need to update the content at a later time, all you need to do is add to or subtract elements from the page and upload your changes to the server.

Not all browsers support frames, and you may potentially lose an important customer. You may have to design two versions of the site, with a button giving the visitor a choice to view a NoFrames version.

Using frames multiplies the work you must do by a factor of the number of frames you use on a page. If you have five frames on a page, you now have to make changes to the individual frames as well as to the frameset. It can quickly become harrowing.

Frames vs. Tables

Another problem is that Search engines cannot properly locate content within frames.

Web pages, like their print counterparts, require pinpoint placement of elements such as text and graphics. Dreamweaver provides solutions to a designer, such as frames and tables.

Both options provide benefits and drawbacks. Tables can give you precise placement of elements in a grid-like structure, but at the expense of making it difficult to design dynamic-looking pages. Tables do not allow the freedom that layers spread about a page can give you.

Framesets contain discrete areas that can each contain a separate and distinct HTML

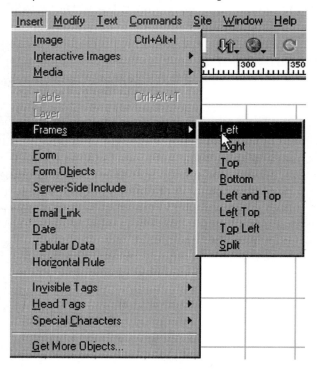

document. Frameset documents define the regions into which the page is divided. They must be available to the page in question or its frames won't display properly.

Frames also give a you another solution to designing precision pages, but the major drawback is that you add download time for each frame you create. Not only that, but maintaining a frames-based site with tens or hundreds of pages is a virtual nightmare.

Framesets

Pages that are built using frames must be accompanied by a corresponding file known as a frameset. You can create and save framesets using Dreamweaver, but you have to make sure you keep track of them and keep them in the proper folders within your site structure.

Once you design a frameset, you can incorporate graphics and text in all the frames you create. The frameset keeps track of what goes where in the document. That's why it's so important to keep the frameset available to the browser.

Creating a Frameset

For the exercises in this book, drag the Frames folder from the **RF-Dreamweaver** folder into your **Work in Progress** folder. Make sure you use Define Site to reset the links — your hard drive is probably named differently than ours.

1. Open the **index.htm** file from the Frames site. It's a blank page.

2. Select the Modify menu, then choose Frameset>Split Frame Left.

To activate the Frames Property panel, click on one of the frames' borders. Otherwise, when you click inside one of the frames, the panel reverts to the normal (Character and Paragraph) Property inspector.

3. Look at the page. It's been split into two different regions.

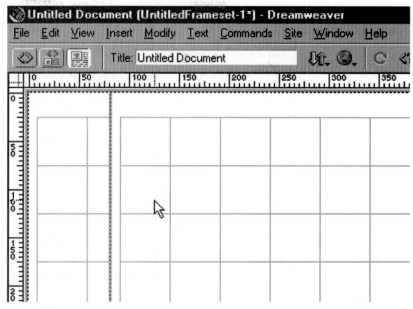

4. Open the Frames panel by choosing Window>Frames. This panel shows a miniature version of your pages as you add frames. This allows you to always know exactly in which frame you're working.

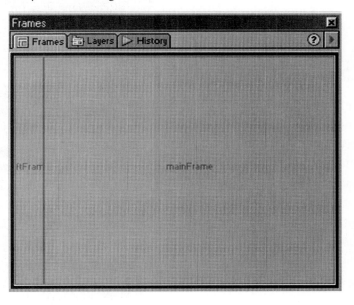

Frames are automatically named on Windows machines. On a Macintosh, there is no name.

5. To add another frame, hold the Option/Alt key and drag the frame border at the top of the Document window. Notice that the page image updates in the Frames panel.

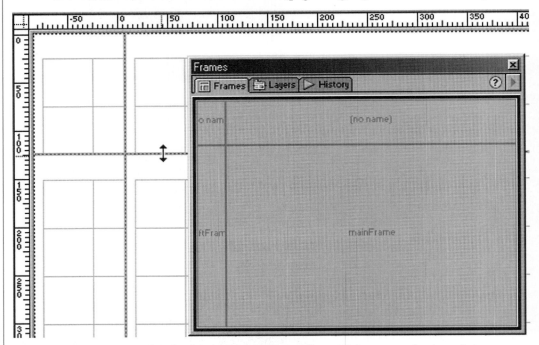

6. Display the ruler by choosing View>Rulers>Show. Make sure a checkmark is next to Pixels in the menu.

7. Drag the new frame borders to the left of the page until the frame is 150 pixels from the left of the Document window and 100 pixels from the top of the Document window.

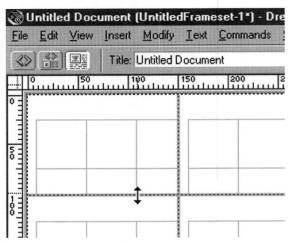

8. Save and keep the document open.

You'll see that we're still working with the grid turned on, and set to 50 pixels. The exact size of the grid that we're using isn't what's important, though; what's important is that we always use the grid for proper alignment.

Reusing Framesets

Whenever you create a frameset, you are dealing with the HTML page that defines all of the associated HTML files located in each frame. We need to save each frame as a separate HTML file and then save the entire frameset.

Saving a Frameset

1. Select File>Save Frameset. Save the file under the name "homepage_frameset.htm". This frameset is the file that keeps track of the contents, targets and other frame-specific information.

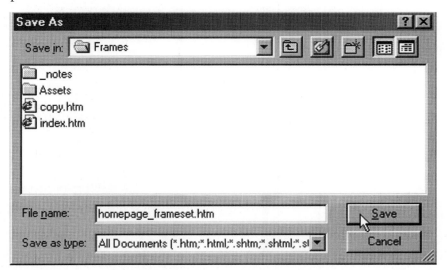

2. To save all open HTML documents select File>Save All Frames. This will save both frame and frameset documents. If you are working on a Macintosh you will have to save the files one at a time.

By default, Dreamweaver will call the framesets "untitled_framesets1.htm" and keep increasing the numbers associated with the file names. You should name your framesets, because it makes it easier to know which set is associated with which file.

Editing Framesets

There are a number of different frame attributes that are important to understand. The easiest way to edit a frame's properties is from the Frames panel.

For example, to name a frame —which is a good idea— select the frame in the Frames panel. This activates the Frames Property panel, where you can enter the name in the Frame Name field.

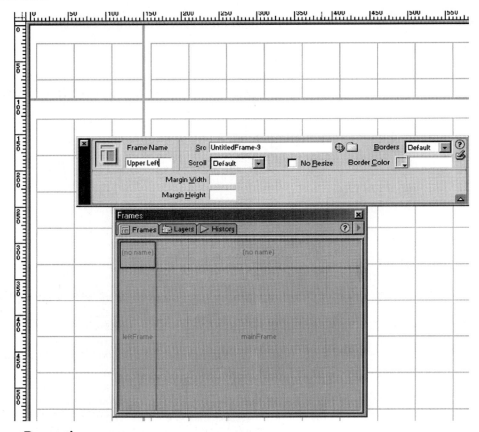

Frame Properties

When you click on a frame in either the Document window or on the Frames inspector, the properties for that frame appear in the Property inspector. Let's take a tour of the options:

File Name: Allows you to input a name for the selected item.

Src: Tells you which HTML document has been assigned to the frame.

Borders: Places a border around the edges of your frames. You may turn Borders off.

Scroll: Allows you to turn scroll bars on or off (on is set by default).

No Resize: Gives you the choice of having the user resize the selected frame.

Border Color: Allows you to choose the color of a border.

Margin Width: Changes the left and right margins for the selected frame.

Margin Height: Changes the left and right margins for the selected frame.

You can delete a frame by dragging its border to the edge of your monitor. Before doing so, it's a good idea to save the page first. Once you delete a frame, you cannot undo the operation, and you may have to revert to the last saved version of your document.

In the previous exercise, we adjusted the width of the left frame and the height of the top frame by dragging the frame borders on the page. You can also adjust frame sizes using the Frame Property inspector. Setting the width or height of a frame mathematically is also a good way to ensure that the sizes are consistent from one page to another. If you couldn't adjust the size visually, try this exercise.

Changing Frame Dimensions

1. Click once inside the frame border to select the frame.

2. Click the expander arrow in the Property inspector.

3. Click the column or row you want to change in the RowCol Selection box.

4. Enter a number in the Value text field and select one of these resizing options:

    (a) Pixels

    (b) Percent

    (c) Relative

Designing with Frames

When frames grew in popularity among Web designers, they quickly became an overused gimmick and were looked down upon due to their poor design. Pages were laden with scroll bars and ten or more frames on a single page.

Use frames to create neat divisions of the elements on your page, avoiding clutter. Leaving empty space lets the eyes relax and enjoy the contents of the page. You can always add more links to new pages and information instead of cramming it all on one page.

One good use of a page with more than two frames is to use one to hold a company logo, and another to hold the navigation bar, while the largest frame is used to display changing content.

Frames are a good choice for pages with animated banners and graphics-heavy navigational systems. With frames, these items need load only once, while new pages are displayed in a separate frame.

Since each frame you create is actually a discrete HTML page, you can apply colors to each frame. This offers a great design device that doesn't take any extra processing power, especially if you choose not to use borders.

Nothing says, "beginning Web designer" better than a page with fifteen or so frames, all with scroll bars and multiple colors all over the page. Try to use the least amount of gimmicks to make the best impression. "Less is more" is a good rule to follow in Web design.

Building a Functional Frames Page

1. Name the four frames on the page: "Rollover" (upper left), "Menu" (lower left), "Logo" (upper right) and "Book" (lower right).

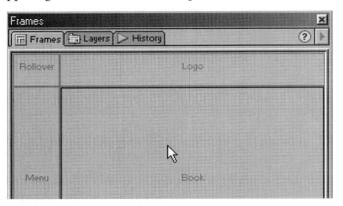

2. Click in the upper-left (Rollover) frame. Select File>Save Frame. This will save the frame as a page.

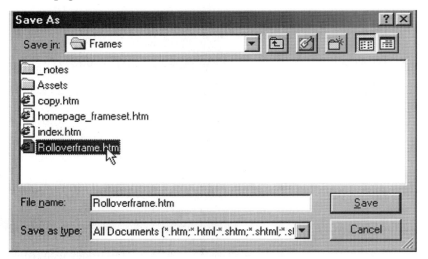

3. Create a rollover image (Insert>Interactive Images>Rollover Image). Select the **graduate.gif** as the original and the **phoneguy.gif** as the rollover image. They're both in the Frames/Assets folder.

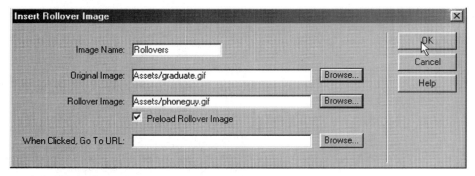

4. Click inside the Menu frame. Select File>Save Frame and save the page as "Menu.htm".

5. Click inside the Menu frame, and select Insert>Interactive Images>Flash Button.

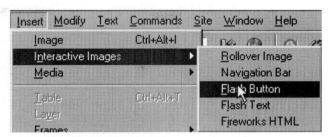

6. In the Insert Flash Button dialog box, select Beveled Rect-Grey and use "Flash" for the text. Don't worry about the link right now.

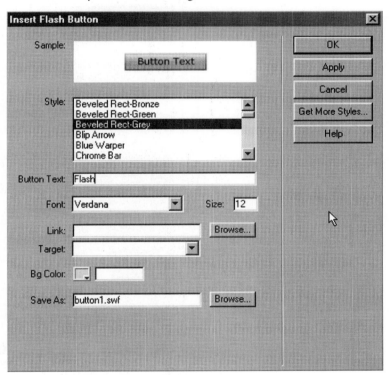

Remember, every frame is a different HTML document; you have to save the documents before you can use them properly. If you're not concerned about the names, simply select Save All Frames from the File menu.

7. Insert another Flash button underneath the first one. Use the word "Photoshop" for the button text.

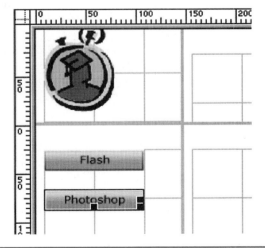

8. Open the file **copy.htm**. Select the text for the Flash book, and copy it to the clipboard.

9. Create a new page. Save it as "Flashbook.htm".

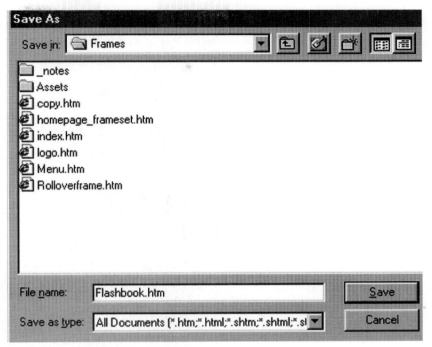

10. Paste the copy into the page. Insert the **flash.gif** image before the copy, and align it left using the Property inspector.

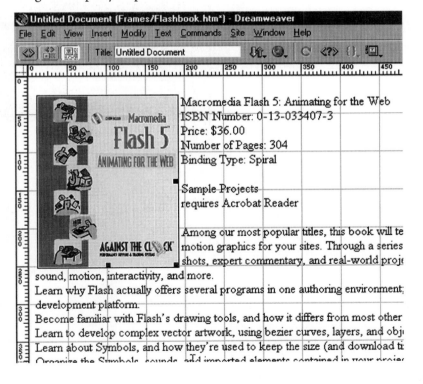

11. Save the page. In the frameset document, double-click the Flash button. Set the Link field to the page we just created (Flashbook.htm). In the Target field, use the pop-up menu to select the Book frame. This will cause the button to link to the Flashbook.htm file and target it (put it) into the Book frame.

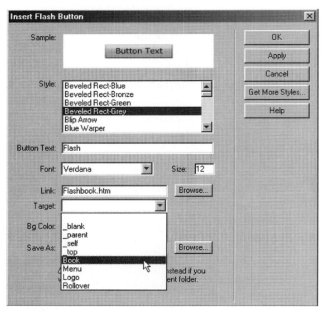

12. Using the same copy and paste techniques, create another page for the Photoshop book. Link it to the Photoshop Flash button and target the Book frame. When you're done, preview the page in your browser.

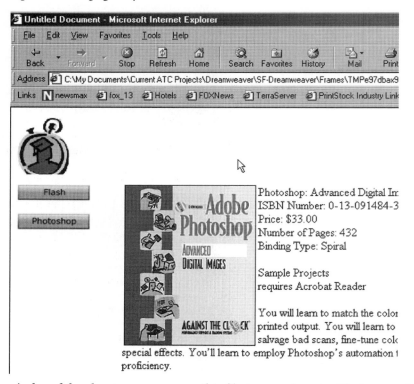

For the remainder of the chapter, you can use this file to experiment with the use of Frames.

Applying Colors to Frames

1. Click once inside the frame to which you'd like to apply a color.
2. Select Modify>Page Properties to open the Page Properties dialogue box.
3. Click the Background color chip and choose a color.
4. Click OK.

Borders

When you create frames, they are surrounded by 3D-like lines called borders. You can reposition borders, color them and even hide them altogether.

Adjusting Frame Borders

1. Click the frame you want to change in the Frame inspector or Option-shift/Alt-click inside the frame you want to change.
2. Choose your options in the Property inspector:

   (a) Decide Yes, for borders, No, to have no borders, and Default, which will show borders automatically.

   (b) Change the color of the border.

Adjusting Frameset Borders

1. Click the frame you want to change in the Frame inspector or Option-shift/Alt-click inside the frame you want to change.
2. Choose your options in the Property inspector:

   (a) Decide Yes, for borders, No, to have no borders, and Default, which will show borders automatically.

   (b) Change the color of the border.

   (c) Enter "0" in the Border Width field to turn them off.

Content

Frames give you the flexibility to create new content in each section in the same manner as a newspaper. You also have the choice of importing pre-existing HTML documents and images into each frame. You can even have one frame act as a conduit into another frame by linking them to each other or to outside URLs.

Linking Within Frames

One of the benefits of using frames is the ability to have both static and dynamic elements in a Document window. This is achieved by having one frame hold a static image such as a menu that links to a new document that opens in another frame within the same document. This is called "targeting a frame."

Linking Frames

1. Choose the image or text that will form the link to the new frame document.

2. Select one of the following methods of creating the link:

   (a) Enter the name of the file to which the image or text will link.

   (b) Click once on the Browse for File folder icon and select a file to link to.

   (c) Drag the Point to File icon to another page or file to link to.

3. Decide which of your frames will act as the target for the document to open. If you named all the frames in the Property inspector, they will appear as potential targets in the Target drop-down list. You have these options to choose from:

   (a) _blank will open the linked document in its own browser window, while keeping the original window open in the background.

   (b) _parent will open the linked document that is the parent in the frameset created.

   (c) _self will open the link in the currently selected frame.

   (d) _top will open the link so that it replaces the content of all frames in the document.

It is a good idea to name all the frames in your document so that you will be able to accurately create a target frame out of one of them.

Seamless Images

Some Web designers use frames to create a graphic that, although comprised of several separate pieces, forms a seamless image in a browser.

Creating Seamless Images

1. Create the image components in an image-editing software application.

2. Slice the image into pieces and insert them into adjacent frames.

3. Turn off borders for the frameset.

4. Set the border width to "0".

Background Images

Frames can have the same options applied to them as do full Web pages, and that means you can fill them with background images.

Applying Background Images in Frames

1. Click once inside the frame in which you'd like to apply a background.

2. Select Modify>Page Properties to open the Page Properties dialog box.

3. Click the Browse button to the right of the Background Image text field.

4. Browse to locate the image with which you wish to fill the background.

5. Click OK.

Frames Objects

You can insert any sort of object in a frame. We've already experimented with putting rollovers and Flash buttons in frames.

Using the Frames Objects Panel

1. Click the Common category on the Objects panel.

2. Select the Frames panel.

3. Select a frameset to use for your document.

4. Drag the icon representing your design choice to the empty Document window.

5. Save the file when you're done.

Chapter Summary

In chapter 10 you explored the use of frames, one of the most powerful tools available to the Web designer. You examined non-frame browsers, and studied the pros and cons of using frames. You compared frames to tables, and created framesets designed to display several HTML documents at the same time. You edited the framesets that you created, learned to reuse them for other projects, and learned how to modify frame properties. You learned how frames can be used as a design tool, and placed content within frames. You learned to link and target frames.

Notes:

11 Using Layers to Design Pages

Chapter Objective:

In chapter 11 we'll work with layers — a powerful and relatively new method of designing pages in a visual environment. To understand how to build pages using layers, and to know when using them is appropriate, in chapter 11 you will:

- Learn to create layers and place content onto a layer.

- Learn the limitations of layers.

- Understand how to use layers during the design process and later convert them to tables.

- Experiment with several display options that affect how much layer content the user can see.

- Learn to convert tables to layers, so that you switch back-and-forth between layout methods while designing and constructing your pages.

- Work with the Layers panel — an interface feature that lets you manage the layers in your documents.

- Come to understand the z-index, which determines the "stacking order" of layers on your Dreamweaver pages.

- Learn to control the position, size and other attributes of layers using the Layers Property inspector.

- Work with clipping images within layers and learn how to ensure proper position of layers and their content.

Projects to be Completed:

- Cosmic Pets (A)

- Tropiflora Order Form (B)

- Diehard Digital (C)

- Mr. BlockHead's Challenge (D)

Using Layers to Design Pages

Layers are a unique and powerful tool for designing compelling and exciting Web pages. Similar in function to layout tables, layers offer additional advantages when doing page layout on your Web sites. Although some care must be taken to ensure that the final HTML will display properly on a fairly broad selection of browsers, they nonetheless offer creative flexibility that's difficult to ignore.

While layers are indeed powerful and flexible, they're only supported by the most current browsers, and even then, some features don't translate well — as is the case with Netscape Navigator, which often positions layers incorrectly. (Beta versions of Navigator version 6 does support the layers standard.) Fortunately you can still use layers as a design tool and let Dreamweaver convert them into more commonly compliant tables.

To use Dreamweaver's animation features, you have to understand layers. We discuss animation techniques in chapter 14, "Animation."

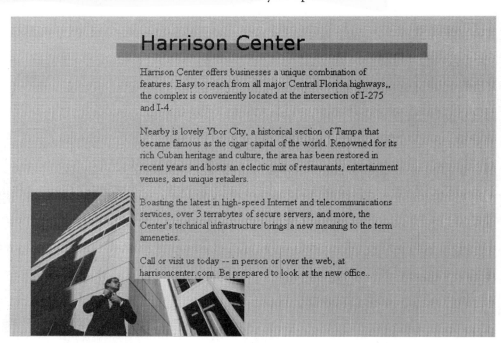

As a design tool, layers are hard to beat; you just have to make sure you use them wisely.

Working with Layers

In some ways, layers in Dreamweaver act the same as layers in other programs; you can control their stacking order, whether or not they're visible or hidden, and their positions. In other ways they're totally unlike their equivalents in other applications. For example, they can be made not to overlap, and they can have behaviors associated with them. They can also be defined as styles.

Adding and Deleting Layers

You can add layers in several ways. First, you can select the Draw Layer button from the Common category of the Objects panel. Once selected, you can draw a layer of any size or shape on the page. The second way to create a layer is to drag and drop the Draw Layer button from the Objects panel onto the page. The layer will appear wherever you drop it.

When you create a layer, you can see it has a small rectangular layers icon in its upper left-hand corner. This icon lets you know a layer is selected.

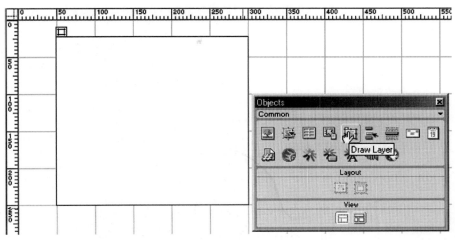

You can draw any number of layers, depending on what they're meant to hold, and depending on how many you need to develop your design.

The third way to add layers to your document is to use the Insert>Layer menu selection. The layer will be inserted at the top of the page, or wherever the insertion is at the time.

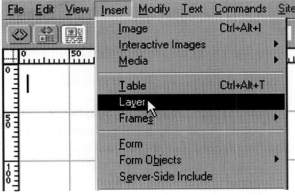

To delete a layer, simply select its layer icon and press the Backspace or Delete key. When you delete a layer, it is also deleted from the Layers panel, which we'll discuss shortly.

If you want to draw several layers at once, just hold down the Command/Control key when you select the Draw Layer button. As long as you keep holding down the key, the cursor will remain as a crosshair, allowing you to draw as many layers as you need to hold the elements destined for your page.

Positioning Layers

The easiest way to position layers is by simply dragging them around the page. When you select a layer (by clicking on its border or its layer icon), you can move it anywhere.

You can drag any layer into position using the Layer icon.

You can also position layers using "absolute" X-Y coordinates by entering the desired values into the appropriate fields in the layer Property inspector. This is referred to as *absolute positioning*. The Layer Property inspector is not the same as the Layers panel, which we'll discuss a little later.

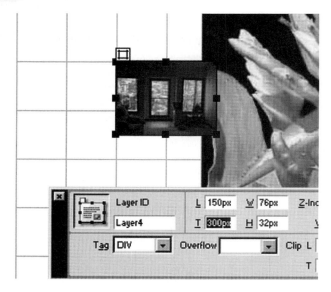

Nested Layers

You can create *nested layers* — that is, layers that are inside of, or children to, other layers. When you create a nested layer, the parent layer can pass its attributes down to the child layers. For example, if you hide the parent layer, the nested layer becomes hidden as well. Alternately, you can show a nested layer and hide the parent, or vice versa. This becomes important when you learn about animations and behaviors — both of which can affect, and be affected by, layers.

Layer Preferences

Dreamweaver provides a central location where you can control many of the default properties for new layers. If you examine the Preferences dialog box (Edit>Preferences), you'll see that there is a specific category for layers in the list on the left side. Selecting Layers will activate the Layer Preferences dialog box.

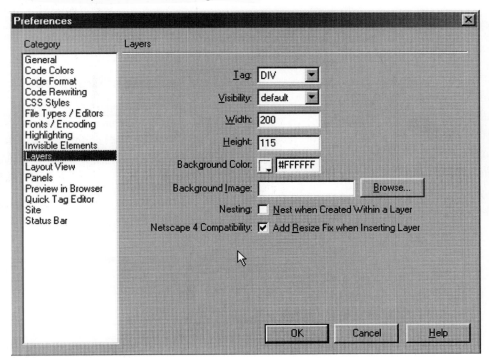

Dreamweaver uses the "div" and "span" tags to identify layers in the HTML code. They work in similar manners, but the div tag allows for regular (from the top of the document down) text flow, while "span" interrupts text flow. The "layer" and "ilayer" tags are used to ensure that layers function properly in Netscape Navigator, which dropped support for layers after version 4.0.

The Layers Panel

The Layers panel — not to be confused with the Layer Property inspector — provides ways to organize and control your layers and their stacking order. *Stacking order* refers to which layer is on top of or underneath other layers on the page.

Creating Layers in Your Documents

1. Open the **Images_site** site that we created in an earlier exercise — it should be in your **Work in Progress** folder. We'll use that site to build the exercises for this chapter. Save the open untitled document into the site folder as "Layers.htm".

If your rulers aren't visible, turn them on using Control-Alt-R if you're on a Windows system, or Command-Option-R if you're on a Macintosh. Make sure they're set to pixels (View>Rulers>Pixels).

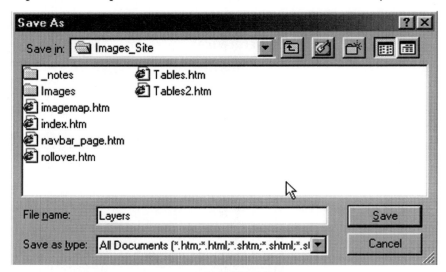

This screen capture was done on our development systems — it probably won't exactly match what you're seeing on your monitor.

2. In the Title field, enter "Working with Layers". We tend to title our documents as soon as we save them, so doing this will ensure that your screen images match the ones you'll see here.

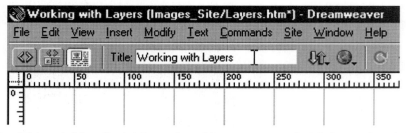

3. Select View>Grid>Edit Grid. Set the grid size to 50 Pixels (if it's not already). We once again used a light blue to represent the grid, but you're free to use any color that you like. You'll have to use View>Grid>Show Grid to make it visible.

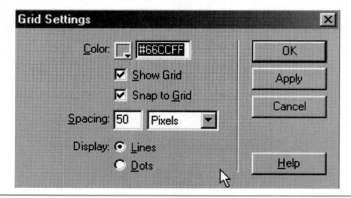

4. Select the Draw Layer object from the Common category of the Objects panel. Use the crosshairs to draw a layer from 100 pixels to 300 pixels on the horizontal (top) ruler, and from 50 pixels to 400 pixels on the side (vertical) ruler.

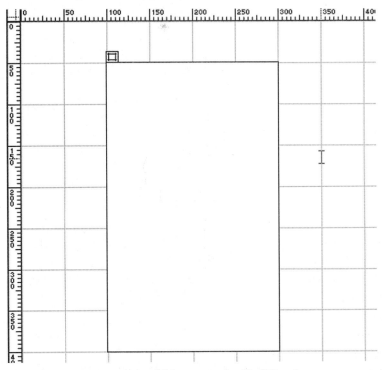

5. Inside your **RF-Dreamweaver** folder open the file "Harrisoncentercopy.htm". It contains some text that we're going to use in this exercise.

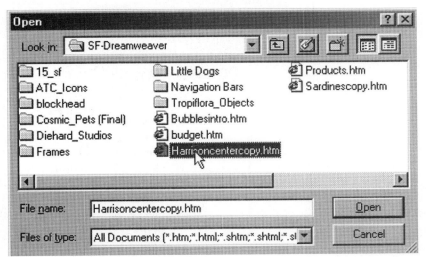

6. Click inside of the text and press Command/Control-A to select all the copy. Copy it to the clipboard using Command/Control-C. Close the file.

7. Go back to the Layers.htm page and click inside the layer. See where the bottom of the layer is now? It's at 400 pixels. Press Command/Control-V to paste the copied text into the layer. You may have to select the body text and increase its size so that your display matches ours.

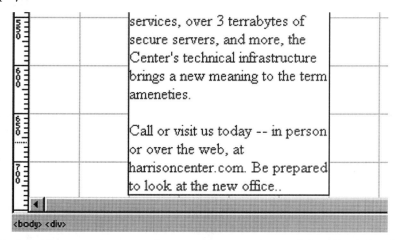

8. In the layer Property inspector is a pop-up menu (named Overflow) that lets you determine what happens in a case like this where the content is too big for the layer. Use it to select "scroll."

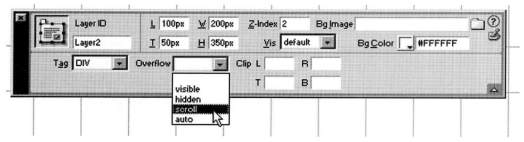

9. Paste the text back into the layer. What happened? The layer still grew to accommodate the overflowed text. Preview the page in the browser.

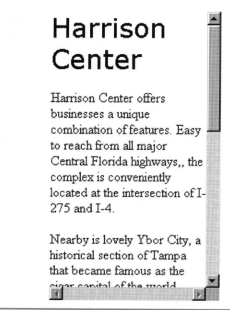

The keyboard command for activating the Layers panel is F2.

Remember to use F12 to preview in your primary browser. It's the single most important and often-used key command!

You need to be aware that the scroll bars won't show up in certain browsers. To be assured that they will work properly, you should preview them in Internet Explorer 5.0 (and above) or Netscape Navigator 6.0 and above.

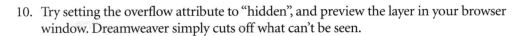

10. Try setting the overflow attribute to "hidden", and preview the layer in your browser window. Dreamweaver simply cuts off what can't be seen.

The Auto setting in the Overflow menu only puts scroll bars on the layer if the copy exceeds the size of its container. Otherwise it doesn't display them. This prevents having to unnecessarily set the horizontal width values.

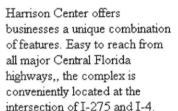

Harrison Center

Harrison Center offers businesses a unique combination of features. Easy to reach from all major Central Florida highways,, the complex is conveniently located at the intersection of I-275 and I-4.

Nearby is lovely Ybor City, a historical section of Tampa that became famous as the cigar capital of the world. Renowned for its rich Cuban heritage and

11. Save the page for now, but keep it open for the following exercises.

Every time you create a layer, it appears in the Layers panel. Dreamweaver numbers layers sequentially, but it's usually a good idea to give them names that make sense to you. That way, while you're working on your sites, you'll know exactly what's on each layer by looking at its name.

Adding and Managing Multiple Layers

1. Right now there's one layer in your document named Layer1. It was created when you drew the layer with the Draw Layer tool. Double-click its name in the Layers panel and rename it "Copy".

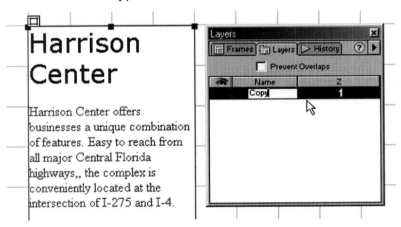

You can change the properties of several panels at once. Use Control-click to select more than one layer if you're on a Windows machine, and Shift-click if you're using a Macintosh.

2. You'll notice that there's a checkbox in the Layers panel that says "Prevent Overlaps." Checking this box will keep you from drawing layers on top of one another. Check it, and try drawing another layer over the top of the existing layer.

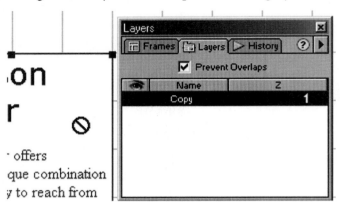

You can't draw overlapping layers when Prevent Overlaps is turned on.
The tool won't work from inside another layer, and if you draw
from outside, existing layer borders will stop the Draw Layer tool.

3. If you created a layer by experimenting in the last step, delete it. You can select it and press Backspace, or select its name in the Layers panel and delete it from there.

4. Select the Copy layer on the page and reposition it. It should reach horizontally from 250 pixels to 650 pixels (400 pixels wide), and down from 50 pixels to 450 pixels. Again, adjust the relative size of the body text if you need to.

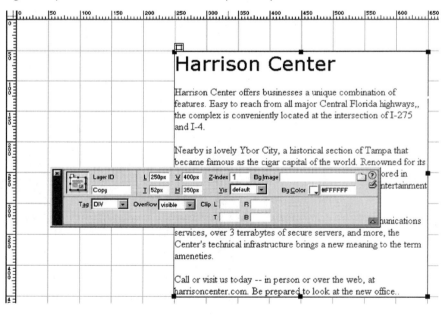

5. Make sure that Prevent Overlaps is turned off (unchecked) in the Layers panel. Draw a small layer in the upper left-hand corner of the page.

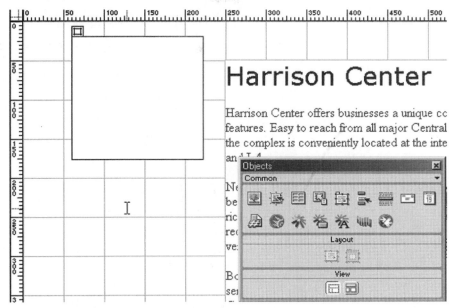

You can resize layers from the keyboard, which is a useful technique when you're visually sizing a layer. Just select the layer and press Opt/Control-right, left, or up and down arrow keys. Add the Shift key into the combination, and the layer will snap to the grid.

6. While it's still selected, enter "50" for the (L) position, "28" for the top (T) measurement, a width (W) of "750" and a height (H) of "514". Select #FFCC99 (a sandy-brown color on the lower-right side of the Color Swatch menu) as the Bg (Background) color for the layer.

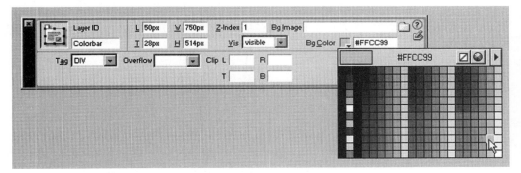

7. You've now created a layer that's going to represent the background for the layout; but it's covering the text — there's a problem with the stacking order. Save the file; we'll fix it in the next exercise.

Stacking Order — The Z-index

Whenever you create a new layer, Dreamweaver assigns it a value known as the *z-index*. The higher a layer's z-index, the higher it is in the stack. Therefore a layer with a z-index of 1 is going to be hidden by a layer with a z-index of 2, 5 or 15. As long as one layer's z-index is greater than another, it will hide the contents of the lower layer.

Controlling the Stacking Order of Layers

1. Look at the Layers panel. Rename the new layer "Background".

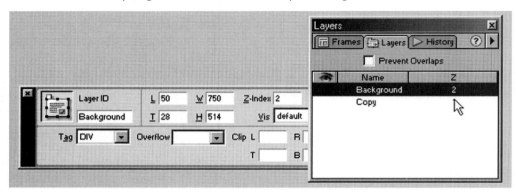

2. You'll notice that its z-index is 2, while the Copy layer's z-index is only 1. That's why the background is currently on top of the Copy layer. Change the Copy layer's z-index to 8 and it will always stay above the Background layer.

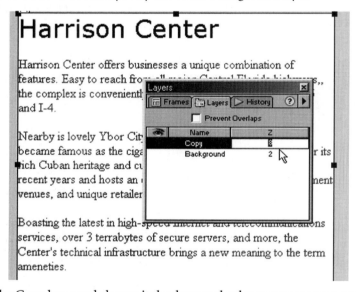

3. Select the Copy layer and change its background color to transparent, or none. Use the icon located in the upper right-hand corner of the color swatch. This will allow the color of the background to show through. If it's already transparent, then leave it as it is.

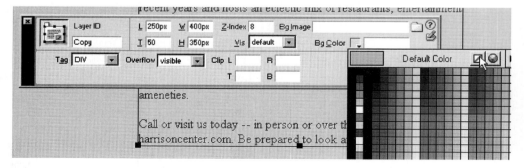

4. Draw a square layer in the lower-left corner of the page. The exact size doesn't matter; we're going to import a graphic into the layer and let it resize itself. In the Layers panel, rename the layer "imageleft".

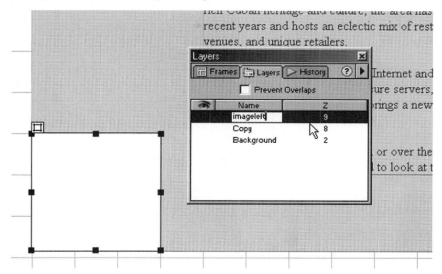

5. Click inside this new layer and, from the **RF-Dreamweaver** folder, insert the **tallprofile.jpg**. When it comes in, the layer will adjust to fit the size of the photo. The picture will be a little too big for the available space and overlaps the text. This problem can be fixed in several different ways.

6. Move the layer so that the picture fits perfectly into the lower-left corner of the page.

It seems that in their infinite wisdom, the engineers at Macromedia decided that using the same coordinate system on the Mac and Windows platform for the clipping attribute would be too logical. Instead they chose some incredibly weird method of sizing images on the Mac. Notice in this exercise that the values required to achieve the same effect are seemingly unrelated.

7. Activate the layer Property inspector (F2 or Window>Properties). In the bottom half of the panel is the Clip section with four fields that let you "clip" or trim the image on a layer. If you're on a Windows machine, enter "200" for the left side (L), "200" for the top (T), "50" for the right (R) clipping value, and "50" for the bottom (B) clipping value. If you're on a Macintosh, enter "40" for the left side (L), "0" for the top (T), "210" for the right (R) clipping value, and "400" for the bottom (B) clipping value. Press Return/Enter to apply, and observe what happens to the image.

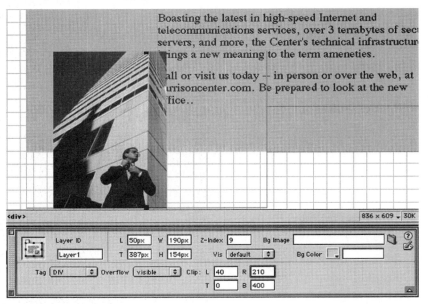

8. We need to adjust the clipping values so that the picture extends further to the left and doesn't obscure the copy on the right. If you're on a PC, Change the L value to "190" and the R value to "20". Reverse the numbers if you're on a Macintosh; the L value should be "20" and the R value "190".

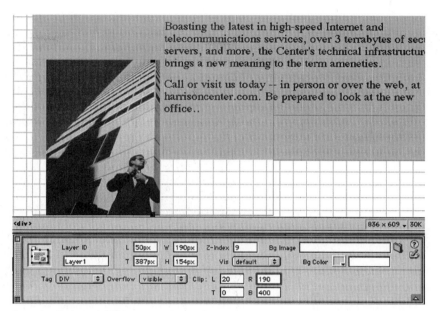

9. Select the "imageleft" layer in the Layers panel and select Edit>Copy. Deselect the layer on the page and use Edit>Paste. If you don't deselect the layer first, this will not work — it's very idiosyncratic. If you do it right, two layers with the same name will appear. Rename the new one "bottomimage". If you can't do it, simply select the handle of the layer itself and copy and paste it there — then rename it in the Layers panel.

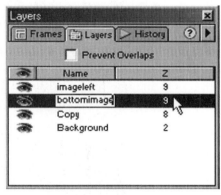

An open eye in the Layers panel means that the layer is visible; a closed eye means that it's hidden, and no eye means that the layer will inherit the attributes of the parent layer.

10. Click the eye icon in the upper row of the panel — directly to the left of the Name column. Open eyes will appear to the left of the four layers. Click the eye icon next to the imageleft layer to close the eye. The layer will be hidden.

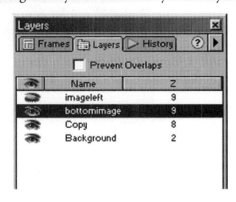

11. Now that the left image is hidden, select the bottomimage layer and adjust the clipping values so that only the lower-right side of the image shows. The values of L: 190, R: 400, T: 160 and B: 300 (Windows), or L: 190, R: 400, T: 155, and B: 400 (Macintosh) which should make the image fit. Be sure to work with the numbers until the image is properly positioned. We're trying to cut off the image at the bottom of the gray background layer. The left side of the bottomimage is transparent to accommodate the imageleft layer when it returns to view.

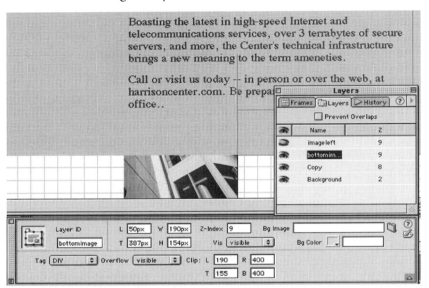

12. Make the imageleft layer visible again by clicking its eye icon in the Layers panel. Observe how, by using layers, the two cropped photos combine to appear as if one photo were being cropped to fit the text layout.

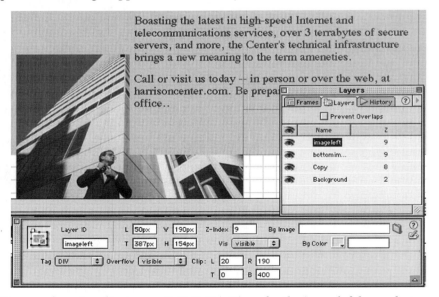

13. You may have to adjust some L, T, R, B settings for the imageleft layer photo so that it matches the bottomimage layer.

14. There are a few more images in the **RF-Dreamweaver** folder that you can use to continue experimenting with layers, clipping and stacking order. These images are named **tallwall.jpg**, **walkway.jpg** and **yborwatercolor.jpg**. Try experimenting with the placement of the images, stacking of the layers, and using background images in the Background layer.

15. When you're done, save the file and keep it open.

Converting Layers to Tables

In a perfect world, everyone would use the same browser, and the latest version would automatically download to their machines while they were sleeping, and install itself perfectly. When the person woke up they would be updated, and our lives would be much easier. Too bad for us.

Since many browsers don't support layers, in most cases it's best to convert your layer designs to tables before you publish the pages on a live site. Converting layers is simple in theory, but the conversion is not always reliable. You will, at times, have to experiment with different settings and options before you're happy with the results.

To convert a site designed with layers into a table-based site, simply select Modify>Convert> Layers to Table.

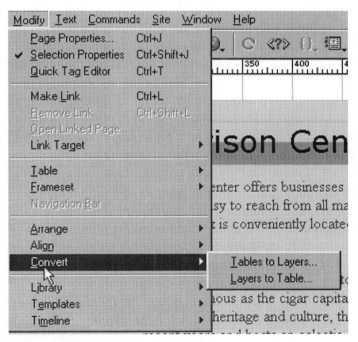

You can use this menu to convert tables to layers and, conversely, layers to tables.

There are a number of different settings available from the Convert Layers to Table dialog box.

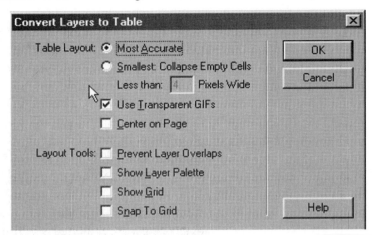

You can't convert layers to tables if any overlapping layers exist. This is a serious limitation, but understandable. Browsers that can handle layers, such as Microsoft Internet Explorer, have no problem displaying the pages without any conversion. Other browsers, such as any version of Netscape Navigator other then 4.0, can't handle the layers.

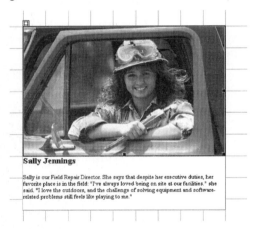

This personnel profile page, which was built using simple layers with no overlap, converted easily to a table site.

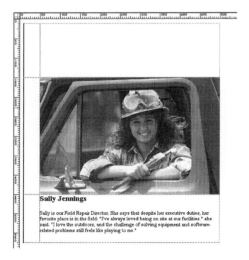

Using the Tables to Layers command, it converted back to layers with perfect results.

There are a few other conversion options available from the File menu. Try File>Convert>3.0 Browser Compatible. It offers conversion options that will — in most cases — make your pages work with older browsers.

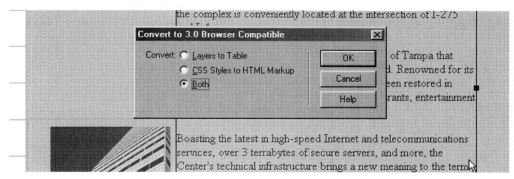

Again, you're limited to converting layer sites that don't have any overlapping layers. If there are layers intersecting on the page, Dreamweaver will return an error message, stating that the page couldn't be converted.

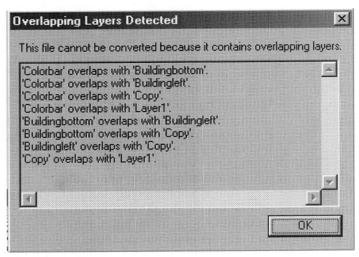

This same menu command lets you convert CSS styles to HTML. Remember to keep original versions of your files, though, so that if you make any changes to Cascading Style Sheets styles, you can re-create the file using the Conversion option.

Chapter Summary

In chapter 11 you learned about the use of layers in your documents. Although they're not supported by earlier browsers, they're a powerful design and creative tool, and they can be converted to the more commonly supported tables with a few mouse clicks. You learned how to add and delete, position, duplicate, hide and show, and add content to layers. You learned about the z-index, and how it determines the stacking order of layers. You also worked with the Layers panel and the layer Property inspector, and learned how to design a page using image clipping and layer positioning.

12 Creating Web Forms

Chapter Objective:

In chapter 12 we will learn how to incorporate forms into your site designs. To learn about the various components that comprise a form, and how to design forms that are simple to use and understand, in chapter 12 you will:

- Learn about the HTML </form> tag, and how Dreamweaver uses it to define forms within the body of your pages.

- Learn how to insert a form using the Insert Form object.

- Work with text fields and the text field Property inspector, which provides a range of important controls over how text fields function.

- Learn the difference between single-line, multi-line and password text fields.

- Learn how to create radio buttons, and how they function on a form.

- Create and position checkboxes, another important form object.

- Work with the Forms category of the Objects panel which provides a collection of common form objects.

- Experiment with file fields, which let the user download or upload documents to your Web sites.

- Create jump and list menus, which let you place multiple links in a pop-up menu that conserves space and reduces clutter.

Projects to be Completed:

- Cosmic Pets (A)

- **Tropiflora Order Form (B)**

- Diehard Digital (C)

- Mr. BlockHead's Challenge (D)

Creating Web Forms

The Web has become much more than just a way for people to research or post their stories and artwork for the world to see. With increasingly safer e-commerce, more and more people are starting to shop online. Forms are used to obtain information about these visitors, their buying habits and the services they may request from your site.

Forms are easy to assemble in Dreamweaver because each component of the form is its own object. By dragging the selected form objects onto your pages, you can create customized forms to suit your needs.

To get ready for this chapter, drag the **TOYBARN** folder from your **RF-Dreamweaver** folder into your **Work in Progress** folder. Go through the necessary steps to create a new site, with this (copied) folder as the root, and use the **index.html** file as the home page.

Remember that many people are still wary of the Web, and that they are uncomfortable providing personal information. Try to ask only about non-vital information such as electronics purchasing preferences or what albums they like to buy.

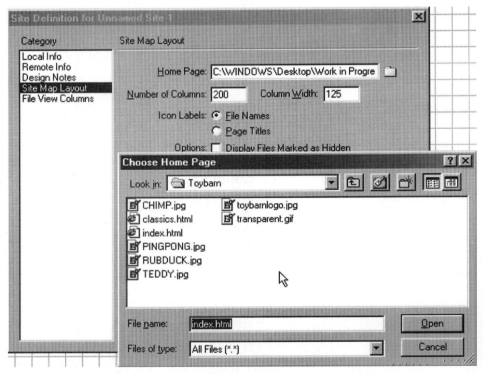

How Forms Work

To make a form function properly, you will need to know what CGI (Common Gateway Interface) your ISP is using on its server. The information that you want to collect must go through a specific protocol before its returned to you.

First, your guest fills out the information on your Web form. Then that information goes to a Web server for processing. Since it goes to a remote server (a computer other than your own), a server-side script takes the data in the form and places the information in a database located on the Web server of your ISP. The compiled information is then sent back to you, the client computer.

Sounds complicated? Well, it is, unless you are a programmer with knowledge of writing CGI scripts in either Java, VBScript, C or Perl.

Since forms rely on CGI to process data, it is important that if you don't know CGI, that you try to work with a programmer or contact your ISP. They may have a free CGI script that you can use to process your form.

Managing Form Objects

Forms consist of many individual parts that, when used in unison, can provide you with many ways to find out more about the people who frequent your site.

Form objects include:

Text fields: Your visitors will input their names, phone numbers, addresses and feedback messages in these containers.

Radio buttons: These are good for surveys and other questions you might ask your guests to choose an answer from. Normally, only one radio button — out of two or more buttons —in each question can be selected.

> Example:
> Your political party affiliation is (choose one):
> Democrat   Republican   Other

Checkboxes:
These boxes, which will display an "x" when selected, serve the same purpose as radio buttons. The main difference is that users can often place an "x" in as many answers to your questions as they'd like.

> Example: How many of these operating systems does your office use?
> Mac OX, Windows 95, Windows 98, Windows 2000, BE, OS.

Lists: Lists behave just like the drop-down lists in applications. When the users clicks the arrow, several options appear, and they can choose which option they'd like.

Submit and Reset Buttons: When your users have answered all the questions on the form, they can send their information to you by clicking the Submit button. In the event that your guests decide that they'd rather start from scratch, you should also provide a Reset button. This will clear all choices that they've made on the form and give them a fresh start.

Creating Your First Form

The best place to begin the creation of your new form is on paper. You should think of a logical order in which to ask and place your questions. Keep related categories together: shopping habits, favorite items, foods and so forth. Once you have a grasp of the information you will require of your visitors, you are on your way to creating a form that is efficient and, most importantly, one that visitors won't mind taking a few moments to fill out.

Creating a Form

1. Open a new document by choosing File>New.

2. Use the Draw Layer object to create a new layer on the page.

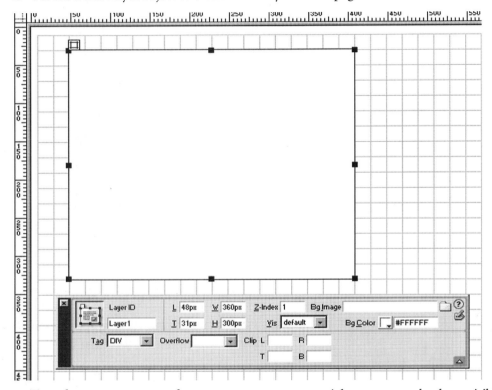

Forms automatically stretch to cover the entire width of your page. It's a good idea to place your forms in tables or layers. Doing so will ensure that the form doesn't resize and become jumbled.

3. To make sure you can see forms on your pages, you might want to make them visible using Edit>Preferences>Invisible Elements. Check the Form Delimiter and Hidden Forms Field boxes (if they're not already checked).

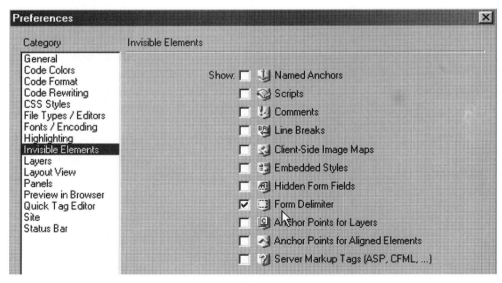

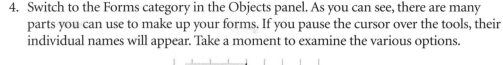

4. Switch to the Forms category in the Objects panel. As you can see, there are many parts you can use to make up your forms. If you pause the cursor over the tools, their individual names will appear. Take a moment to examine the various options.

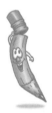

Once again, don't be confused if the grid is showing on our screen captures and not on your monitor. If you want to use grids (and we recommend that you do), turn them on using View>Grid>Show Grid. You can edit their size and color using View>Grid> Edit Grid.

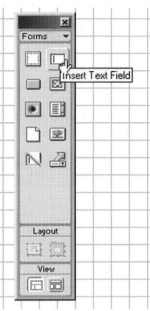

5. To use form objects, such as text fields, radio buttons, checkboxes, invisible fields, or a menu, you first have to insert a form tag. To do so, click inside the layer we just created, and then click the Insert Form icon or drag it onto the layer.

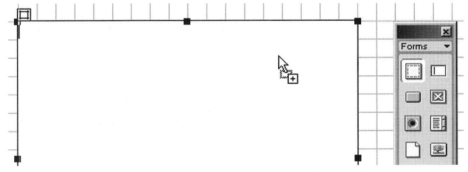

You can toggle your grids on and off using Control-Alt-G on the PC or Command-Option-G on the Macintosh platform.

6. If you've turned on the Form Delimiter attribute in the Invisible Elements preferences, you'll see a thin, dashed red line on the layer.

7. Switch to Show Code and Design Views. You'll see the </form> tag that Dreamweaver inserted into the code.

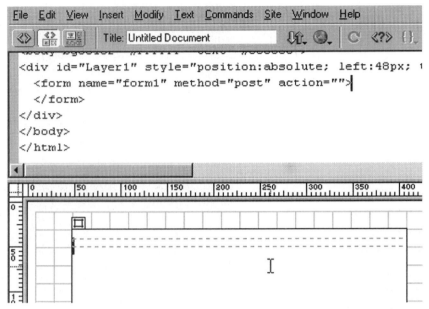

8. You can now go back to Show Design view. The reason we wanted to show you the code is because if you simply drag a form object onto a page, into a frame or onto a layer, without first inserting a form, Dreamweaver will assume you want to create a form, and present you with the following warning.

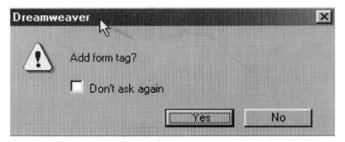

It's usually better to use the Insert Form object to create a form, and then add the form objects inside of the defined region.

9. Inside the form, type the words (make sure you put in the colon) "First Name:" Click the Insert Text Field icon on the Forms Objects panel.

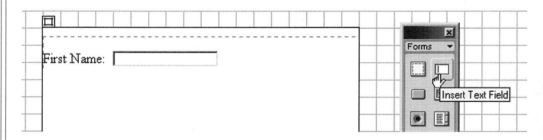

10. Click on the field and look in the Property inspector. On the left side of the panel, in the field for the name, type "firstname". Press the Tab key to apply the setting.

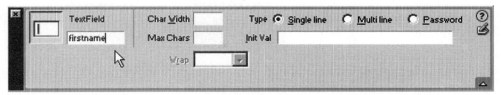

11. Preview the form in your browser by pressing F12. Although it's pretty useless at this point, you can see how Dreamweaver wrote the code to put the field on the page. If you want to, try typing into the field. Close the browser when you're done looking.

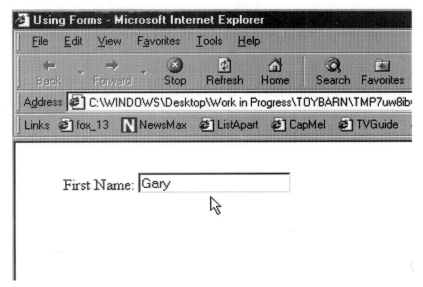

You may notice that we created a title for the page in Dreamweaver, naming the page "Using Forms". You can see the title at the top of the browser window.

12. Back in Dreamweaver, change the field's attribute to Multiline, using the radio button at the upper right of the inspector.

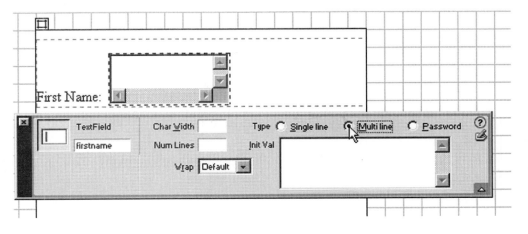

Dreamweaver will name your fields for you, using names like textfield1, textfield2, radiobutton1, checkbox9, etc. Using default names isn't a good idea. When you're using CGI (or other) scripts to process the information on your forms, logical field names will make your work go much easier.

13. Preview that field in your browser. It can now accommodate a really long name, including fond nicknames like "Bubba."

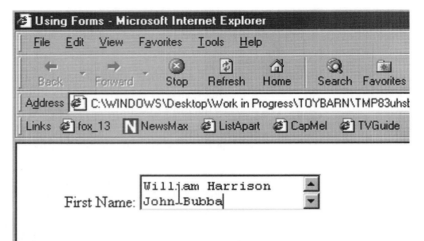

14. Continue experimenting with the Property inspector for the field, modifying its character width and other attributes.

15. Change the text on the page from "First Name:" to "Secret Code:" When you try the Password attribute, you'll see how those fields somehow hide what you're typing from prying eyes.

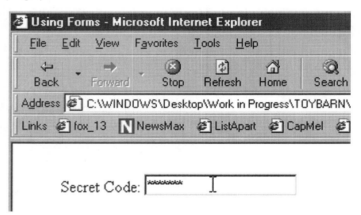

16. Put the cursor at the end of the line and press Return/Enter. First type "I am a spy for:". Press return and type the words on separate lines: "Russia", "China", "Chad", "Fiji" and "None of the Above".

17. Use the Insert Radio Button object to put a Radio button after each line of text.

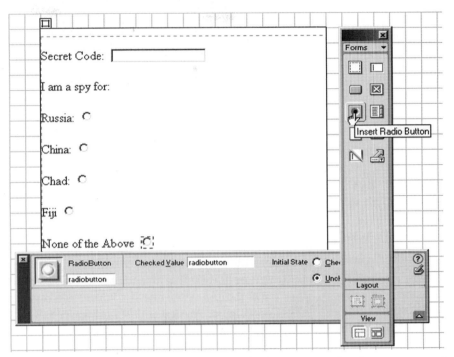

18. Try previewing the page, and playing with the buttons. Notice that you can only have one checked at a time.

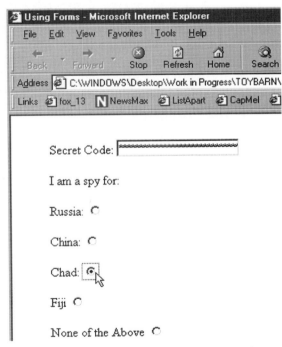

19. Continue experimenting with the various types of form objects available on the panel. Checkboxes, for example, work like radio buttons, except that you can check more then one of them at a time. When you're done trying out some of your options, save the page as "form.htm" and close it.

Default Fields and Other Form Object Attributes

There are a wide number of options available to you when building forms in Dreamweaver They all add strength to the argument that it's far easier to develop your Web sites using Dreamweaver than to writing the HTML code by hand.

You can automatically put a default value in any text field by entering the text into the Property inspector. The user can, of course, change the values, but the field starts out with a default response.

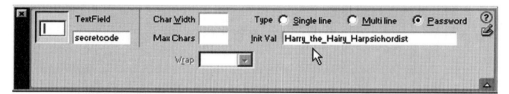

You can also limit the number of characters the field will accept, and control how type wraps in a field (using the Wrap attribute in the inspector). The manner in which the browser normally handles multiple lines of text in a field is the default selection. None means the user won't see the text that extends below the field. Virtual means that the text will wrap when it hits the end of the line, but will remain one long line of text with no breaks in the HTML code. Select Physical and Dreamweaver will automatically put hard breaks at the ends.

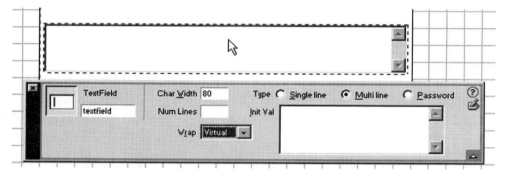

The File Field

The File Field is useful if you want to let users upload files to your site. Using the Insert File Field object, Dreamweaver inserts a field and a Browse button — allowing the viewer the option of navigating to find the file they want to upload.

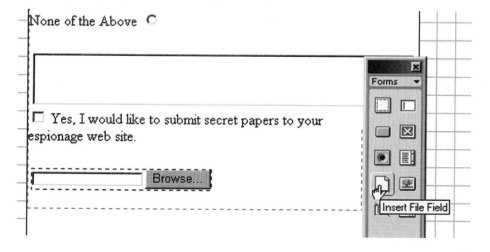

Jump Menus and Lists

Jump menus and Lists are pop-up navigation elements that conserve space and reduce clutter. They're particularly useful on busy complex sites.

Lists

Lists are fields that contain a number of predetermined responses to a field. An example might include a list of salary or age ranges. They're similar to a number of radio buttons that only occupy a single field. When the user clicks in the field, the list pops up, and they can scroll down to make their selection.

To add a list field to one of your forms, use the Insert List/Menu object on the Forms panel.

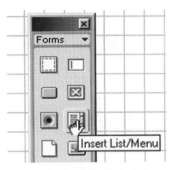

When you add a list menu, you can click the Edit Values button, and access a dialog box where you can enter the name of each item in the list, and a value to assign to that selection.

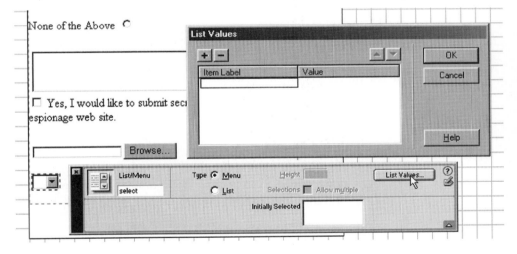

The value of a list entry is normally a number. Imagine that you wanted to know which alter ego our spy would like to assume while working undercover. In the following example, selecting "College Professor" would return a value of 1 when you received the information back from the form. If they selected "Harmless old man" instead, you would receive the corresponding value — in this case 3.

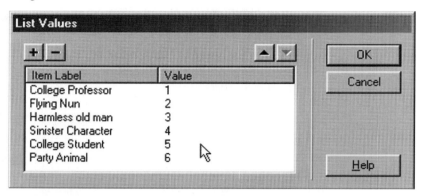

In the browser window, the list would pop up when users click on it, and they would be able to select their choice accordingly.

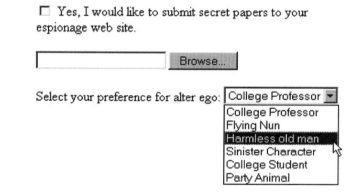

Jump Menus

If you're a regular surfer on the Web, chances are that you've come across sites that use drop-down menus as an alternate form of navigating the site. These menus are called *jump menus*, because they literally jump from one URL to another, using the items on the list.

Jump menus allow you to create a more compact selection area for your visitors because the list expands only when they click the drop-down arrow. Jump menus are a natural choice for the savvy Web designer who does not want his or her carefully planned page to be overwhelmed by buttons or links.

After all, surfing the Web should be a pleasant experience, offering timely information and popular features to visitors, but not at the expense of elegance and design.

Technological advances seem to be making options "smaller and smaller" for the user. The same is true in the way you can offer many options for your Web guests. Instead of having a long list of links on your page that can look rather ungainly and give you a headache, you can make a compact list that holds everything. With a jump menu you only see one thin button that is waiting to spring a list on you the minute you click it. It's compact, it looks great, and it's easy to make.

Creating a Jump Menu

1. Go to Site view. Select and open the **index.htm** file. It's (naturally) the home page for this small site.

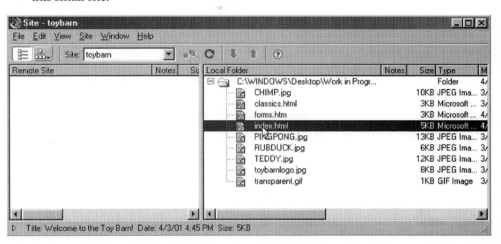

2. Look on the lower-right side of the page. There's a form already inserted into one of the table's cells. Click inside it.

3. Click the Insert Jump Menu icon in the Forms Objects panel.

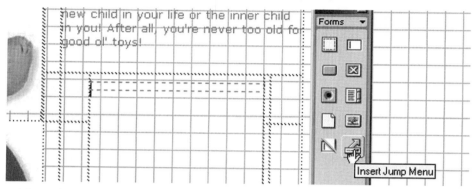

4. The Insert Jump Menu dialog box appears requesting the name of the items on the drop-down list and the URL the items will link to. Enter "New Toys" in the Text field under Menu Items. This will appear on the list a visitor will see when they click the drop-down arrow.

Jump menus are actually written in JavaScript, but, as usual, Dreamweaver does all the coding for you.

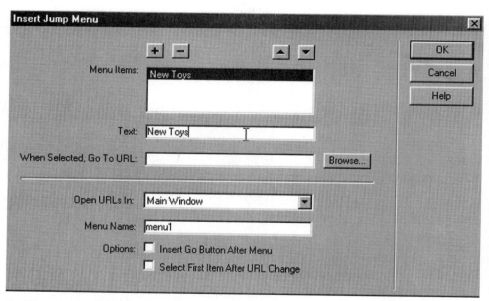

5. Now we need to tell the New Toys item which URL it should open when selected from the list. Click the Browse button and choose **classics.html**. You will notice that the name of the list button, as well as the link, appear together in the Menu Items field.

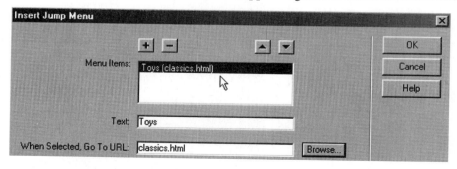

6. Place a check in the Insert Go Button After Menu checkbox. This option prevents your visitors from choosing the wrong item on the list, thus preventing them from being transported to the wrong page. The Jump list will only launch the intended page once the Go button is clicked.

fact, if we can't find the toy you're looking for, we'll build it ourselves! So, sit back and either buy a gift for the new child in your life or the inner child in you! After all, you're never too old for good ol' toys!

7. You can edit the list of items in your jump menu by clicking the Edit Initial List Values button (the button that says "List Values...") in the Property inspector. As was the case with list menus, you can add and edit the titles and values for each item.

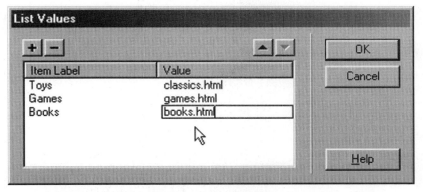

*Please note that the above example is for illustration purposes only.
The site doesn't contain these extra pages.*

8. Save and close the file.

Summary

In Chapter 12 you learned how to insert a form into a Dreamweaver page, and how the program handles the creation of the </form> tag in the HTML. You learned how to create text fields, and control how they work in a browser. You learned about multi-line and password fields. You learned how to include radio buttons, checkboxes, and file fields into your forms. You also explored the use of list fields and jump menus — two very common and effective techniques employed by professional Web site designers.

Complete Project B: Tropiflora Order Form

Notes:

13 Templates and Libraries

Chapter Objective:

In chapter 13 we will learn to work with templates and libraries — two features that Dreamweaver provides to ensure consistency between pages on the same site and the ability to re-use designs from site-to-site. To become familiar with using templates and libraries, in chapter 13 you will:

- Learn about the Library panel, which lets you add and manage components that you use repeatedly in one or more sites.

- Understand how to share assets among multiple pages or sites.

- Experiment with changing and modifying library items, which are automatically applied to any instance where you used the item in your designs.

- Learn to turn a design into a template, which can be used as the basis for other pages in your site. This ensures consistency and streamlines workflow.

- Work with creating "editable regions" — portions of your templates that can be changed to reflect different content while protecting the underlying design from changes.

- Learn to record your actions and create commands which can be used repeatedly when building templates, libraries or pages.

Projects to be Completed:

- Cosmic Pets.com (A)

- Tropiflora Order Form (B)

- Diehard Digital (C)

- Mr. BlockHead's Challenge (D)

Templates and Libraries

Sooner or later you'll may be faced with the task of creating and managing a large Web site comprised of dozens of pages. And, during the development of said site, your client or boss is going to make changes to the menu bar, the images, the buttons and possibly the entire site design. This is the life of a designer and it will never change. Without the use of libraries or templates, each significant or minor change requested would mean manually going through the entire site, editing and then updating countless revisions. Those days are over.

Understanding How Libraries Work

A *library* is a holding area for your most frequently used items such as menus and graphics. During the course of designing a Web site for a magazine, for example, you could simply drag an instance of the magazine logo directly into each page instead of having to continually browse for it on a disk.

As you might assume, this is an immense time-saver. But libraries offer more than that. A library also allows you to make changes to menus, graphics and text, and then automatically update all occurences of the library item used througout your entire site.

If you have completed Project A, you already have a site defined named Cosmic_Pets. If you don't, drag the **Cosmic_Pets (Final)** folder from the **RF-Dreamweaver** folder into your **Work in Progress** folder.

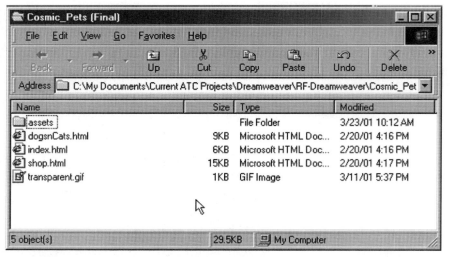

Use the Site>New Site command to make this the root folder of a new site named Cosmic Pets. Set the index.htm file as the home page. From that point on, everything should work as expected.

Creating a Library

We're going to create a library for our Cosmic Pets logo so that we can use it as many times as we need to in the future. Once you create a library, its items are available to you in any site you build in Dreamweaver.

1. Open the **index.html** page of **Cosmic_Pets.com**. Select Window>Library to display the Library category of the Assets panel.

2. Select the **Cosmic Pets** logo. Choose one of these options:

    (a) Drag the Cosmic Pets logo into the Library category.

    (b) Select Modify>Library>Add Object to Library.

    (c) Click the New Library Item icon on the bottom of the Library category.

3. Enter "Cosmic Pets logo" for the new item where it reads untitled.

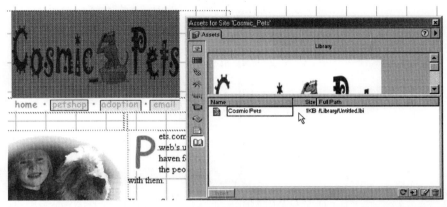

The keyboard command for adding an object to a Dreamweaver library is Command/Control-Shift-B.

Once you've added an item to a library, it can be used by any site regardless of its location or root folder. Dreamweaver will let you automatically add library items to a site's asset list.

Once you take the time to create a library for your site, the speed in which you build and maintain your Web documents will greatly increase. Think about the interface, the buttons, the icons and everything else that will be a part of the whole site, then make a checklist of the items that will serve you best as library items.

Using Library Items

1. Create a new document.

2. Choose the **Cosmic Pets** logo from the Library category and select one of these options:

    (a) Drag the logo from the Library category onto the page.

    (b) Click the Insert button on the Library category.

As your sites grow, you will want to make cosmetic changes to the logos, the navigation systems, and so forth. This means that you will have to edit some of the items in your library. That's the bad news. The good news is that once you've finished your housekeeping, Dreamweaver will automatically update every page that contains the Library item.

Editing Library Items

1. Select Window>Library to open the Library category of the Assets panel if it is not already open.

2. Double-click the item to open it in its own window.

3. Draw a hotspot linking the word Cosmic to index.html so it will link back to the home page.

4. Save your changes and elect to update any pages associated with the library item. Even something as simple as changing the color of one word will prompt you to update all the pages in the site.

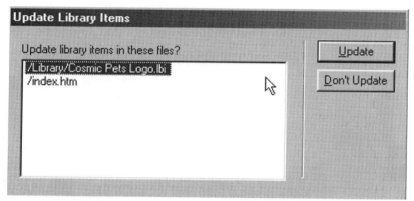

5. You have the option of updating all the links at once.

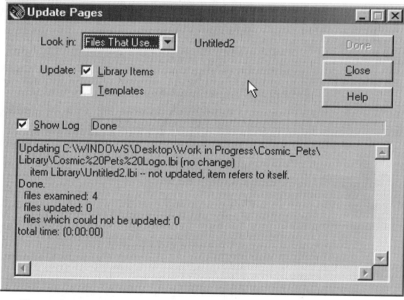

If you want a library item to automatically update any changes you've made, edit the item within its own window inside the Library category. Editing an instance of the item will detach it from the library and make it a stand-alone object.

Using Templates

A *template* is similar in function and convenience to a library because it saves you development time. Once you have created a page that you know will contain repeating elements troughout your site, you can convert it into a template. You can even base a template on a page you've already designed.

Templates contain editable and non-editable regions that you define, allowing you to make designing and maintaining a Web site a simple and enjoyable task.

Unlike libraries, a template is a static document and does not offer the flexible drag-and-drop that a library does. Still, templates are a powerful tool that can streamline your workflow and give uniformity to your entire site.

Like creating a library, taking the time to plan out a great looking page that will be used as the backbone of the entire site is worth the effort. What you will save in time in the future more than makes up for this critical stage of pre-planning your site and all of its shared components in a sketchpad.

Creating a New Template

1. Open **index.html** of **Cosmic Pets.com** from your **RF-Dreamweaver** folder.

2. Select File>Save as Template. Name the file "MainPage".

3. Locate the site in which the template will reside.

4. Click Save. Dreamweaver will place the extention ".dwt" at the end of the name of the new template.

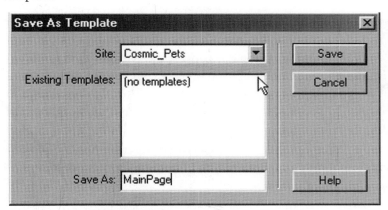

5. Once you've saved a template you'll see that it appears in the site's Asset panel under the Templates category.

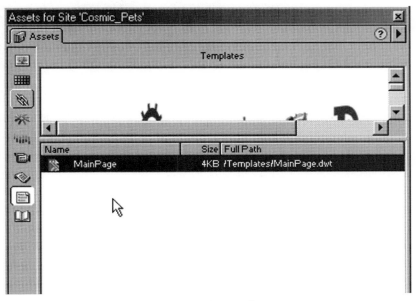

6. Save the file once you've created a template within your site.

By default, all areas of your template are locked and cannot be edited when you first save your document as a template. You'll notice this when you open a new document based on the template and are given a warning that the entire document is locked and uneditable.

We need to select the areas of the template that will be editable so that you can update the items you need and keep the other items locked.

An example of this is a coporate site where you need to place new company news into a page each week while leaving the logo and menu alone. The layer that contains the text is marked as editable and the rest of the document as locked.

Templates are more rigid than libraries because you're dealing with one large preformatted document instead of smaller items that can be placed on a page at your whim. That doesn't mean you can't edit the elements within. One of the main attractions to many Web sites is how often the content is updated to provide new services or entertainment value. The minute visitors see that nothing has changed, they will move on to the next site. Keep them excited by editing your templates regularly.

Making a Template Editable

1. Select the the text welcoming visitors to the Cosmic Pets site. We're going to identify it as "editable" so that it can be changed as we update the site.

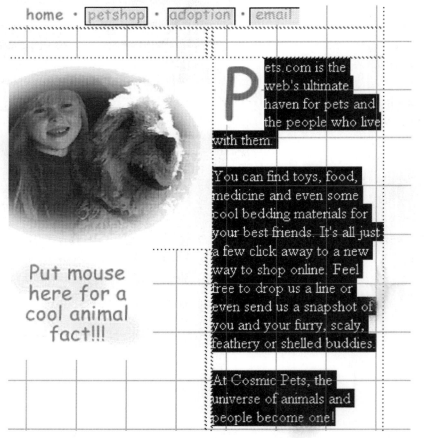

2. Select Modify>Templates>New Editable Region.

3. Once you make the menu selection, Dreamweaver will ask you to name the region. Use "Welcome Copy" as the name.

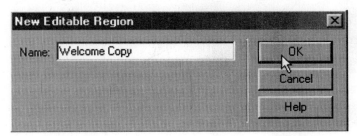

4. Save the file and keep it open.

Like a magazine cover, the main page of your site should have a color or graphic that changes each time you update it. It will take only a second for your visitors to notice that there is something new and fresh to be seen at your site. Make sure that you leave an editable region on your templates that can quickly be changed.

Using Templates in Site Construction

Before we use a template in the construction of a site, it is a good idea to color editable regions to allow you and your fellow designers to easily spot them. There's no reason to have to click every part of a template to guess what is and isn't editable when colors do the job.

When you open a new document from a template, the locked regions are highlighted in the color you select. While editing or creating your template, the editable regions are highlighted.

Dreamweaver is a fantastic tool for solo or team designers. Selecting colors to indicate editable and locked regions can speed up workflow and lessen the time it would take to guess which areas can or cannot be updated.

Coloring Editable and Locked Regions

1. Open the new **Cosmic Pets** template. We're going to make changes.

2. Select Edit>Preferences and choose Highlighting.

3. Choose the colors you wish to mark editable and locked regions using the color chips.

4. Place checkmarks in the Show column. These might already be checked; it depends on what the settings were when you started the chapter.

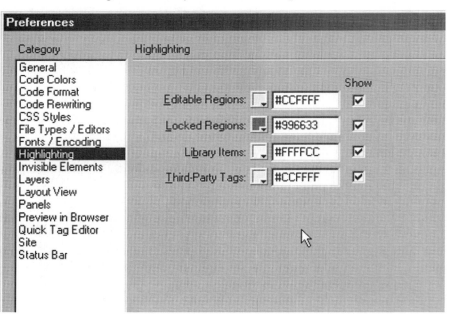

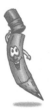

An idea that may prove useful is to think of a traffic signal when assigning your colors. Red can mean locked areas. Green can be used to mark editable areas.

5. Click OK when done.

6. To view editable and locked regions, make sure you choose View>Visual Aids>Invisible Elements.

When you create a new document from the template (File>New from Template), the only area that you can edit is the editable region named "Welcome Copy."

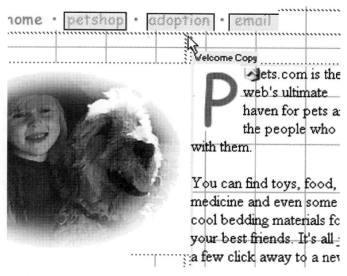

Automation Techniques

Web design embodies a wide range of different jobs — from graphics to text content — and you will surely find that you are constantly repeating some of the same tasks.

The History panel is an amazing tool for the Web designer. It allows you to go back in time to fix a mistake or to copy a set of motions, allowing you to apply the steps to a new part of your document.

Using the History Panel

Several applications have implemented a way to travel back in time to help designers fix mistakes that *undos* take too long to reach. Imagine that you have been working on a document for two hours and have made twenty different changes to it and need to go back to the second edit you made. Normally, you'd have to click the Undo arrow 18 times. Do that long enough and you'll go insane. Thank goodness there is a solution to this in the form of the History panel.

1. Select Window>History to display the History panel.

2. If there's not one already open, created a new untitled document. Enter a few lines of text, separated by returns.

3. Select a word or two and change the color and make the text bold. Center the text with the alignment tools in the Property inspector.

I am sitting by the pool

I am drinking a Seabreeze

I am playing hooky from work

I AM HIDING FROM THE FBI!!

I am going to ride my bike to the store

4. Observe your steps displayed in the History panel.

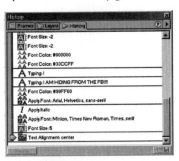

5. Click the slidebar on the left of the History panel and scroll up several steps. Notice that your document reverts to that state.

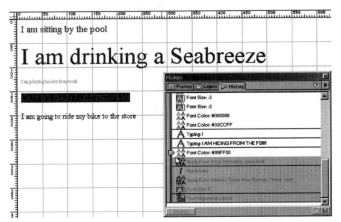

Sliding the bar goes backward to previous steps.

Copying and Pasting Code

Fixing mistakes is just one of many uses of the History panel. With the History panel, you can even record the steps you have made, and then apply them to a similar area in your document.

1. Create a new document in Dreamweaver.

2. Enter text and format it by changing the alignment, colors and size. Insert a horizontal rule.

3. Select the steps in the History panel.

4. Click the Options arrow to the right of the History palette and choose Copy Steps.

5. Press Return a few times to move your cursor down the Document window.

6. Select Edit>Paste.

Even though Dreamweaver is packed with automation features, you can create your own custom commands using steps made in the History panel.

You can bypass steps in the History panel and choose only those you want to copy by holding down the Command/Control key.

Creating Commands

You're going to create your own customized commands to be used as often as you'd like. These commands can even be used in all of your future sites created in Dreamweaver.

1. Select one or more of the steps you have made using the History panel.

2. Save the selected steps as a command button on the History panel.

3. Enter a name for your new command and click OK.

To use the command, all you have to do is go to the Commands menu and select the command — the ones you define will be displayed at the bottom of the menu.

Chapter Summary

In Chapter 13 you learned how to use the Library function in Dreamweaver, which lets you use the same common objects on multiple pages or within separate sites. You learned how to make changes to a library item and how to apply those changes to every instance of a library object. You learned to create Templates — predesigned pages which are used to gain consistency from page-to-page. You learned to create editable regions — areas that can be edited from page-to-page (such as text) while protecting the remaining regions of the design. Lastly, you learned how to record your actions, how to rewind your actions to a specific point and how to save recorded actions as a command.

Notes:

14 *Animation*

Chapter Objective:

In chapter 14 we will learn to use Dreamweaver's animation features. To learn about animating layers and objects within those layers, in chapter 14 you will:

- View and work with the timeline, which gives you control over objects in real time.

- Learn about frames per second, or fps — the basic measurement of time in the development of an animation, and a determining factor in playback quality.

- Understand the definition of frames and keyframes — the two components of a timeline that control animation and timing.

- Add a layer to the timeline as an object.

- Work with tweening — a technique that lets you move objects across the page and over time.

- Learn to control when your animations start or stop.

Projects to be Completed:

- Cosmic Pets (A)

- Tropiflora Order Form (B)

- **Diehard Digital (C)**

- Mr. BlockHead's Challenge (D)

Animation

Everyone loves animation, especially on the Web. More and more sites are offering animation as a way to keep surfers coming back. Nothing works as well as movement to grab the eye when going from site to site. While it doesn't offer the horsepower of its sister program, Flash, Dreamweaver's animation capabilities can still add motion to an otherwise static page.

As with most applications, it is not necessarily the tool set, but the creativity of the user that makes all the difference. You should begin by storyboarding a sequence for your animations. Have a good idea on paper, then begin to build the pieces for each frame. There's a good reason it takes Disney three years to finish an animated feature film — and planning is a huge part of the equation. Though smaller in scope by far, you should still know exactly what your goals are before constructing your masterpiece in Dreamweaver. Dreamweaver creates animation through the use of layers and the timeline.

The Timeline

The *timeline* allows you to animate layers and/or the images that you place within them. From an airplane flying across the screen to an image that change from time to time, you can use the timeline to do almost anything, as long as you can think past it's limited abilities. You already know that Dreamweaver animates layers and their content, but how you animate the content is what will set your animations apart from other animations on the Web.

The timeline relies on JavaScript to perform its wonders, and all of the code is written as you animate. You have all the fun while Dreamweaver toils in the background. Let's go over some of the elements that you should become intimate with as you delve into the timeline.

Creating Movement

If you're going to be a professional animator, it's likely that the tools available in Dreamweaver won't prove powerful enough to meet all your needs. Creating the sense of movement on your Web pages, however, by using a combination of layers and the timeline, is quite simple.

Anatomy of the Timelines Panel

1. Open Dreamweaver so that you have an untitled document in which to work.

2. Choose Window>Timelines to open the Timelines panel. Familiarize yourself with the buttons and other parts of the timeline.

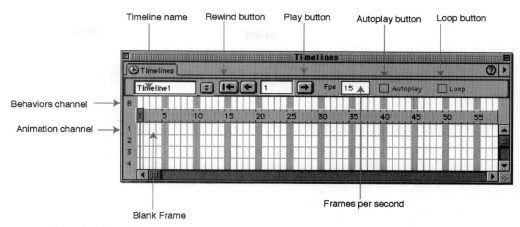

Timeline name   Rewind button   Play button   Autoplay button   Loop button

Behaviors channel →

Animation channel →

Blank Frame

Frames per second

3. Close the file without saving.

Some of the major features of the timeline are:

- **Animation channels.** This is where the actual animation takes place. Each channel is filled with boxes called frames, and each frame represents movement in the timeline.

- **Frames per Second, or fps.** The number you put here represents one second of actual time. Dreamweaver defaults to 15 frames per second. You should note that at 12 fps the human eye can detect individual frames.

- **Keyframes.** A keyframe indicates a change in an animation state. For example, a pitcher winding up to throw a ball would be the first keyframe. When the pitcher has fully stretched into the end of the throw would be the last keyframe. In simpler terms, if you had a ball moving across the page from left to right, the first keyframe would show the ball in its leftmost position, in-between frames would be used to contain images of the ball at various positions in its path, and the last keyframe would be where the ball stopped.

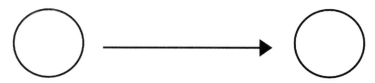

- **Behaviors channel.** You can apply behaviors to frames to perform specific instructions that are triggered by an external event. For example, you can open selected URLs when an animation is finished playing, or make an image appear on cue. We'll cover behaviors in chapter 15.

- **Play and Rewind.** You can click and hold down the Play button to preview your animation from within Dreamweaver's Document window. Rewind takes you back to the first frame of an animation. You can also step backward using the left arrow to reverse your progress.

- **Loop.** The Loop button causes animations to repeat. You control the number of times you would like an animation to loop.

- **Autoplay.** The Autoplay button tells the browser to begin playing the animation when the page loads.

In traditional film, television, movies and 3D animation, somewhere between 24-30 frames are played per second. Since we're dealing with the Web and keeping slower machines at the top of our priorities list, 15 is the lowest common denominator that ensures that the most people will be able to view your animations without taxing their machines or seeing choppy animations.

Moving Objects

We've just learned a few terms that relate to what makes the timeline tick. Let's discuss how to actually apply these concepts and make something move across the page. Remember that 15 frames equals one second of animation.

Timelines give you the power to manually control what happens on the stage when you want it to. You can also have Dreamweaver automatically add the keyframes of an animation. Let's work on a manual animation first.

We know you can't wait to make something move across the page, but we have to first become familiar with all the steps involved in building an animated sequence. The first thing we need to learn is how to add an object to a timeline.

Adding a Layer to the Timeline

1. Inside your **RF-Dreamweaver** folder is another folder named **Jumbo_747**. Open the folder and take a look at the pieces we're going to use for this page. As you see, you don't need a lot of artwork to give the illusion of movement to a page.

2. Open the **jetworld.htm** file in Dreamweaver.

3. We're going to use the timeline to create the animation of a jet flying across the page. Choose Window>Timelines to open the Timelines panel. Take a moment to examine the panel again. Locate the frames, the Play button, Rewind, and the Behaviors channel. Rename the timeline "Jumbo Jet".

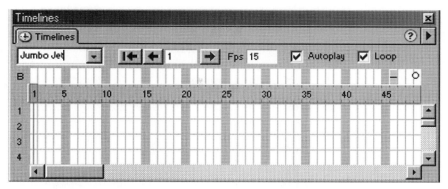

4. We need to add a layer to the timeline, and then put an airplane on the layer. Use the Draw Layer button to draw a small layer underneath the main logo at the top of the page. There's enough space there to do it. If you can't access the Draw Layer tool, just click the Standard View icon (at the bottom left of the Objects panel). The Draw Layer tool is disabled if you're in Layout view.

Dreamweaver can only animate layers, so if you use animations that you create in the program, the viewer must have a recent browser that supports layers (IE version 5.x and higher, and the beta version of Navigator 6). Alternately, you can use Flash to create animations, and if the user has the Flash plugin, they'll be able to see the animation. More browser versions support Flash than do layers.

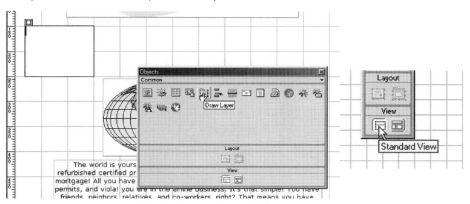

5. Use the Insert Image button to insert the **747.gif** file into the layer from the same **Jumbo_747** folder. Once it appears, resize the layer to fit the image.

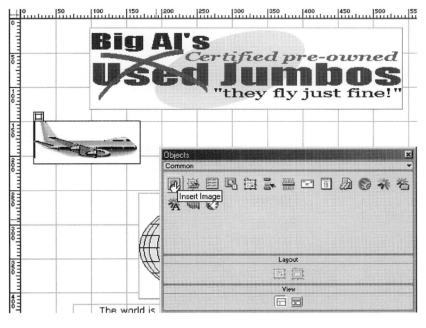

6. Click the selection handle of the Jumbo Jet layer and then click the pop-out menu arrow in the upper-right of the Timelines panel. Select Add Object from the list.

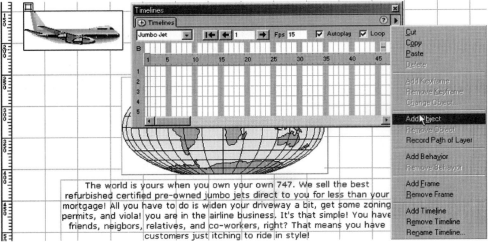

7. Name the layer "Jet" in the Layer Property inspector.

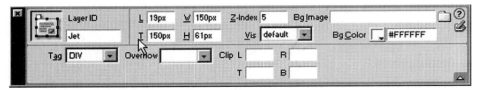

8. Notice that the animation has been given a default of 15 frames. Your first keyframe is in frame 1, with the second, and last keyframe, on frame 15.

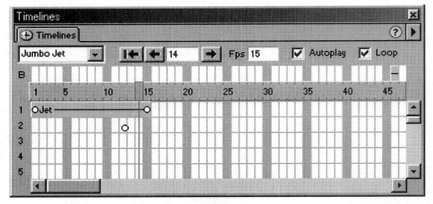

9. Our jet is ready for lift-off in the timeline. Now let's check with the control tower because it's time to fly the friendly skies. Save the file and keep it open.

Tweening

Tweening is the term for creating the illusion of motion in Dreamweaver, Flash and Macromedia's other superstar application, Director. Tweening is short for "in-betweening," or the frames that go in between the two keyframes. All you need to do as an animator is to set the start and end positions of a layer, and Dreamweaver will interpolate the in-between movement for you. And to top it all off, tween is just a fun word to say.

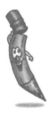

You might get a warning when you select the Add Object command that says that Netscape Navigator can't handle layers and animation. As of the date of this book, Netscape had just released Version 6 in a relatively stable condition, and it seemed to handle the JavaScript for Dreamweaver layers just fine.

Animating a Layer

1. Make sure you deselect the frames in the Animation channel so that none of them are dark blue. Click and drag the selection handles of the Jet layer to the left edge of the Document window.

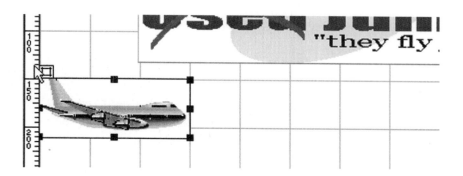

2. Now, while the layer is still selected, click the last keyframe, which is on frame 15. The selected frame will turn dark blue.

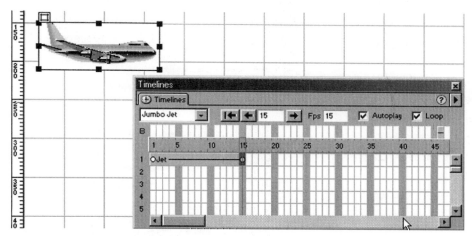

3. Drag your Airplane layer to the right of the Document window.

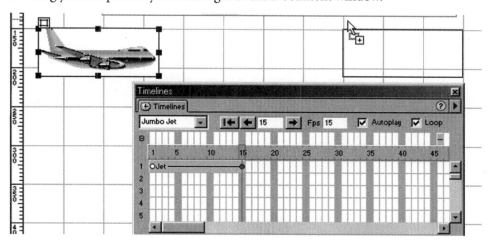

4. If everything worked OK, you'll see a line indicating the motion path for the plane. We moved the plane down a little in addition to moving it to the other side of the Document window.

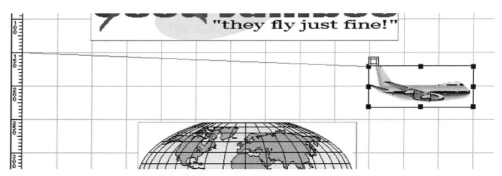

5. At the top of the timeline, directly over the frames, is a small red rectangle. It's called the Playhead. Grab it and move it back-and-forth, left-to-right. You'll see the airplane flying.

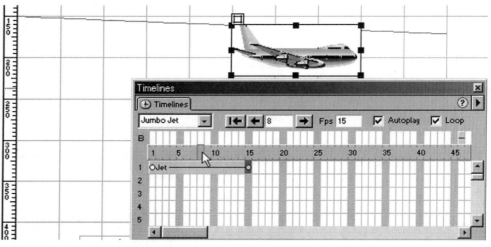

6. Press the Rewind button to move the animation to frame one. Now press and hold down the Play button to preview your jet in flight within Dreamweaver.

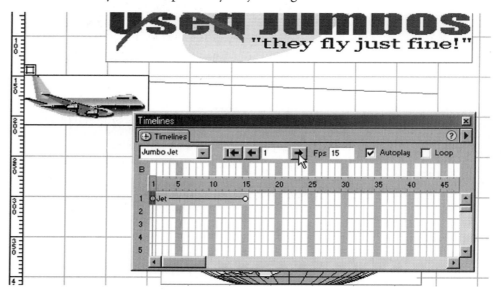

7. Rewind the Playhead and preview the page in your browser. Try turning on the Loop function using the checkbox on the right side of the timeline and preview it again.

8. Save the file.

Controlling Speed and Timing

You can use the timeline to control the speed and timing of your animations. For example, if you wanted to slow the plane down, you could extend the last keyframe by clicking it and dragging it to a new location. In this example, we dragged the last keyframe out to frame 45. This means that at 15 frames per second, it will now take the plane 3 seconds to move from left to right; before, it made the same trip in 1 second.

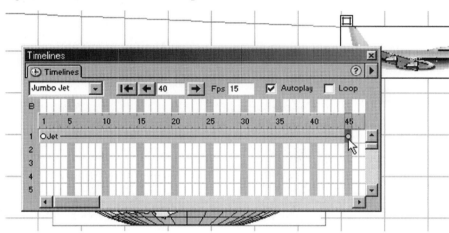

Conversely, if we dragged the last keyframe all the way back to frame 5, we would make the plane fly across the page in about 1/3 of a second.

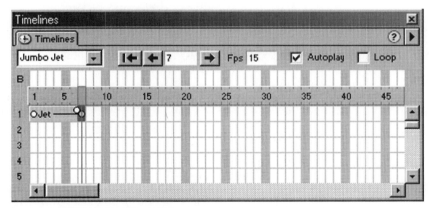

Recording the Movement of Objects

Dreamweaver can help you animate in the way in which a video camera records your every move. All you need to do is move a layer anywhere in the document and Dreamweaver will record the path for you.

Make sure that if you drag the last keyframe out to extend an animation that you either move the loop behavior or take it out. Otherwise the loop will still happen at the same place, and your intended extension of the timeline won't take effect.

Be careful using loops on your sites — they can get annoying.

Automatic Animation

1. Open the file **flighttest.htm** from the **RF-Dreamweaver>Jumbo_747** folder. Save the page in your **Work in Progress** folder.

2. The page contains one layer named Jet, and a timeline named Flight Test. The Jet image has been imported into the layer and positioned at the left side of the page.

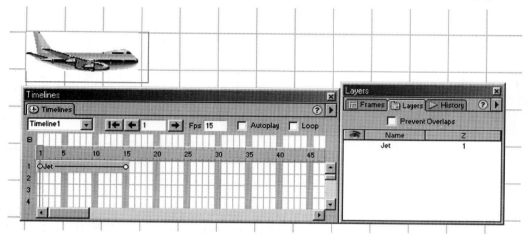

3. Click the selection handle of the Jet layer to let Dreamweaver know which element we want it to record for the next step.

4. Choose Modify>Timeline>Record Path of Layer from the Menu bar.

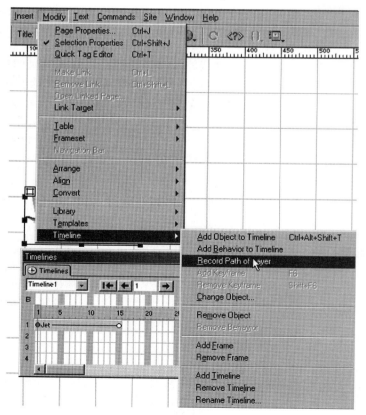

5. Drag the Jet layer in two circles and then across the page in a crooked line.

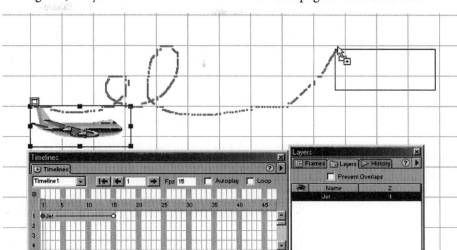

6. Notice how many keyframes Dreamweaver calculated to match your mouse movements. Click and hold down the Play button to see it work.

7. Check the Autoplay option and click OK to the Alert dialog box that appears. We'll learn about behaviors — the subject of the Alert dialog box — in a subsequent chapter. For now accept the message.

8. Make sure you reset the Playhead back to the beginning of the movie. Preview the animation in your browser. Save the file and close it.

In chapter 15 we're going to explore the use of behaviors. Behaviors can be used to affect how layers react. For example, when you turn on the Loop function in the timeline, Dreamweaver is actually creating a simple behavior that is activated when the Playhead reaches the last frame of an animation. The instruction simply repositions the Playhead back at frame 1, and the process starts over again.

Animation is a vehicle you should use to ensure that your site is dynamic and fun to visit. As with all the many offerings available to you in Dreamweaver, use animations wisely. Don't use them just to add movement to a page where it isn't appropriate. Just because you are a doctor, it doesn't mean you need an animation of a pumping heart on each page.

With careful planning you will be able to create animations that help make your page stand out among the millions of pages on the Web. Just think Disney, but on a much smaller scale.

Chapter Summary

In chapter 14 you explored some of Dreamweaver's animation features. You examined the timeline, and reviewed its major functions. You learned how to add a layer to the timeline as an object, and how to name timelines. You learned about keyframes, and how objects can be moved on the page using tweening, or the creation of in-between frames. You also learned how to speed up and slow down animations, controlling their playback time when viewed on the Web.

Complete Project C: Diehard Digital

Notes:

15 Using Behaviors

Chapter Objective:

In chapter 15 you're going to learn about behaviors — Dreamweaver's definition of JavaScript instructions that add control over how your pages interact with the viewer. To learn about using behaviors on your pages, in chapter 15 you will:

- Work with the Behaviors panel, where you can add, delete and modify built-in behaviors, and where you can add new behaviors.

- Learn about onLoad, the simplest behavior, which tells Dreamweaver to perform a specific function (such as starting an animation) when the page is loaded into the user's browser.

- Use a behavior that sends a user to another URL.

- Add behaviors that send a message to the viewer either in the browser window or in a pop-up alert box.

- Learn about extensions, and how JavaScript can be used to identify browsers, download extensions and more.

- Understand how to validate user input in forms and other interactive environments.

- Learn the relationship between the timeline and behaviors.

- Learn to modify the parameters by which behaviors determine their effect on the page.

Projects to be Completed:

- Cosmic Pets (A)

- Tropiflora Order Form (B)

- Diehard Digital (C)

- **Mr. BlockHead's Challenge (D)**

Using Behaviors

It's important in Web design to understand something of what is happening behind the scenes. ASPs, JavaScript and PHP are a few of the scripting languages that communicate with the Internet. What we see on the Web is a visual representation of the code that has been decoded — or interpreted — by a Web browser. To understand what behaviors are, you must first understand that concept.

Dreamweaver lets you use behaviors to control objects and layers without actually using any scripting languages. This makes Dreamweaver extremely expandable. There are many elements, plugins and objects that can be purchased or downloaded for free to enhance Dreamweaver's capabilities. Although we will discuss this more in the chapter 16, it is through the use of behaviors that extensibility is achieved.

Defining a Behavior

A *behavior* is pre-written script (JavaScript) that holds all the coding (event and action) needed to produce a specific result. However, in order for them to be flexible, they also hold a series of questions that allow you to customize them with additional scripts and images.

JavaScript

JavaScript was developed by Netscape as a cross-platform scripting language for the World Wide Web. It should not be confused with "Java," which is a trademark that represents a programming language that focuses more on building applications for the Web. They are related but not the same. JavaScript is a more simplistic scripting language that allows you to enhance a Web site, not necessarily create an application (unless you are really good at scripting). JavaScript works alongside HTML; for example, JavaScript is placed inside HTML tags; it acts like a little program inside the opening and closing HTML tags.

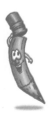

Web-compliant programming languages such as HTML, Java, JavaScript and XML are decoded, or interpreted by the browser used to view the pages.

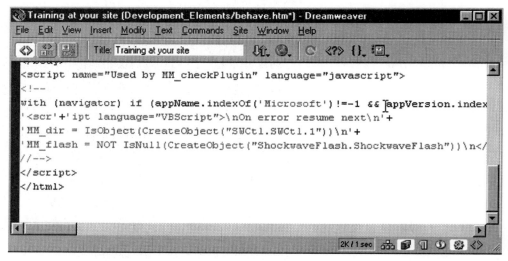

Working with Behaviors

Using behaviors on your Web sites is very easy in Dreamweaver. Behaviors are available in the Behaviors panel.

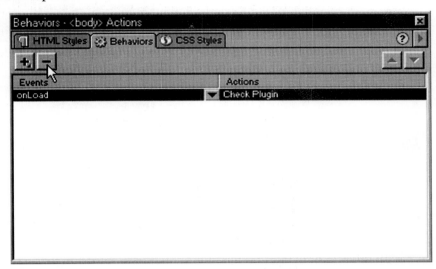

The default keyboard equivalent for activating Behaviors panel is Shift-F3.

Adding Behaviors

Some behaviors apply to objects, such as images or text for rollovers, while others refer to event handlers — such as how the Web page is loaded in the browser.

Adding a Behavior

1. Open Dreamweaver so that you have an new untitled document. Save it in your **Work in Progress** folder and name it "behaviors.htm".

2. Make sure your Behaviors panel is open. To open it, use Window>Behaviors.

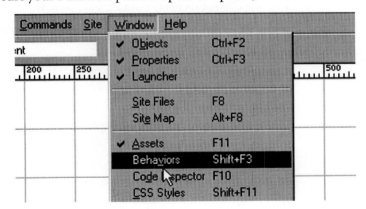

3. Click on the Plus (+) sign in the Behaviors panel. You'll see a list of predefined options. Select "Go To URL."

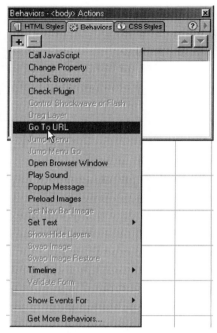

Using the "Go To URL" Behavior is useful if you move a site from one ISP to another; simply create a page on the original site that says "we've moved." Let the page display for 30 seconds, and then execute the Jump.

4. The Go to URL dialog box will appear. Type in your favorite Web address next to URL and click OK. You can probably tell from this screen capture what our favorite Web site happens to be.

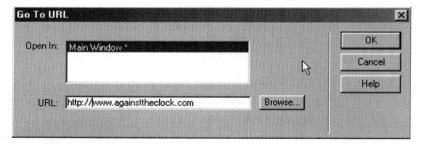

5. Examine the Behaviors panel. You will see the new behavior that you just added to the page.

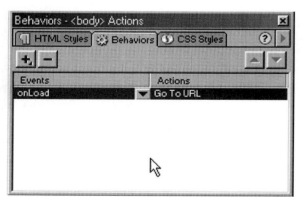

6. Under the word "Events" you'll notice the word "onLoad". This code refers to a browser event. When the browser finishes loading the page it will read this behavior and respond by performing the action. This particular action will immediately send the viewer to the Web address you typed in the URL box inside of the dialog box.

7. View the HTML code of your document. Even though your document does not have any text or graphics, it contains the JavaScript generated by the behavior.

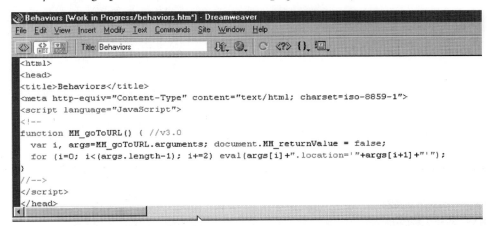

You'll probably notice that the colors of the script tags and the word "location" are different than the rest of the HTML code. To observe why Dreamweaver colors certain code differently, check out Edit> Preferences>Code Colors.

You can see the code that the behavior generated. It starts with <script language = "JavaScript> and ends with the end script tag </script>.

8. Preview the page in a browser window by pressing Command/Control-F12. If you have an Internet connection, the browser will open and take you to the URL that you typed into the dialog box; this is what makes behaviors so powerful. They have the ability to perform with or without visual attachments (like an image).

9. Save the file and keep it open.

Objects

Almost any element in Dreamweaver can be an object. The Objects panel is full of objects such as images, characters and invisible items; and they're all considered objects.

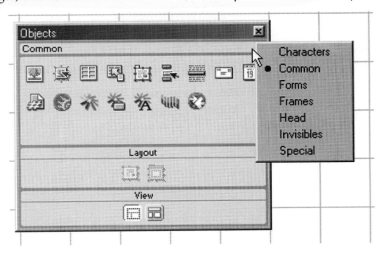

Lets examine the practical concept of an object. For example, a rollover button may consist of several images — each representing a different "state" that the button might be in. Another way of looking at it would be to think of actions on the part of the viewer (like moving the mouse over the top of the button, or clicking it) that change the condition, or state, of the button.

Each state of the button shows a different image, and each image is an object. In short, it could take three or four objects to create one rollover. To create a rollover in Dreamweaver we need the assistance of a behavior to tell each object how and when to change. We do this by using an event handler and an action.

Event Handlers

Event handlers are the part of the script of a behavior that defines when an action should take place. In the exercise where we added a behavior, the event handler was "onLoad."

"Loading" is the event, and the word "on" states when the event will take place. Many event handlers begin with the word "on,"; for instance, "onMouseup," "onMousedown," "onMouseover" or "onLoad."

There are hundreds of different events defined in the HTML and JavaScript communities, and you can download hundreds, perhaps even thousands, more. Naturally, we couldn't cover all of them in this book unless we dedicated the entire work to events. We will, however, cover a few of the more important ones in this chapter.

Actions

Actions are the flip-side of an event handler. Once the event has taken place, the action is the result. For example:

Event: onLoad (when the Web page is loading in the browser).

Action: GoTo URL http://www.myfavoritesite.com (sends browser to the Web page "myfavoritesite" when the browser loads the original page).

Actions are the key to dynamic Web sites. Dreamweaver has provided a plethora of information in the Help file and on the Macromedia Web site.

Working with Actions

1. Open the **behavior.htm** file from your **Work in Progress** folder. Activate the Behaviors panel (Window>Behaviors or Shift-F3).

2. Delete the gotoURL action by selecting it in the Behaviors panel and clicking the Minus (-) button.

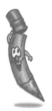

We discussed in chapter 8 how a button could have an "over" state (the mouse hovers over the button), a "down" state (the user clicks on the button) and an "up" state (the image is displayed when no one has touched the button); these are Behaviors.

3. Click on the Plus (+) button in the Behaviors panel and select Set Text>Set Text of Status Bar from the submenu.

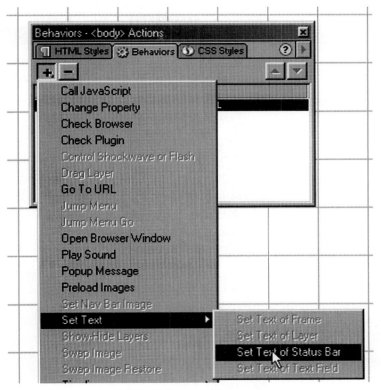

4. In the Message window type your name and click OK.

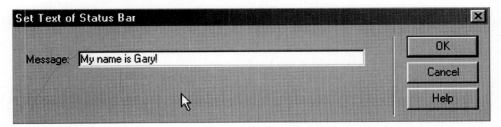

5. Preview the page in a browser window. Since this is an onLoad event, when the page loads you should see the message in the lower left of the window.

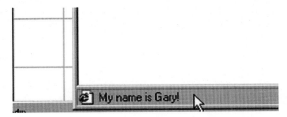

6. Add another behavior by clicking the Plus (+) button in the Behaviors panel. Select Popup Message from the list of available behaviors. Enter the following text in the Message text field: "Hope you come back and visit us again!".

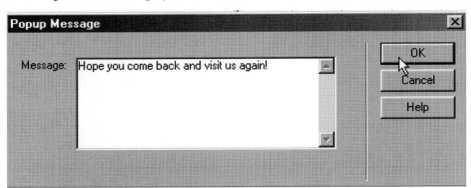

7. In the Behaviors panel click on the black triangle to access the available behaviors and select "onUnload". This changes the event handler to trigger the action when the viewer is leaving the Web page.

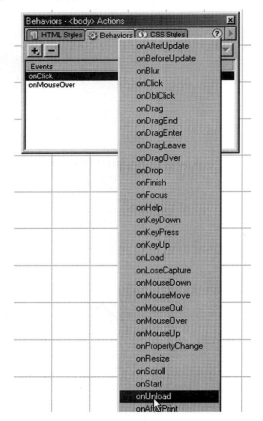

8. Type the word "Link" on the page.

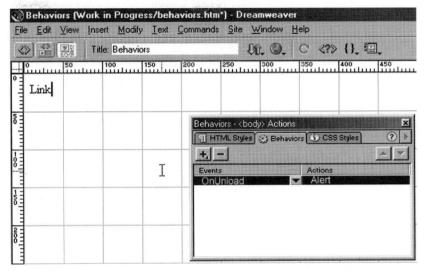

9. Select File>New to create another page. Type the words "I am a new page". Set the text size to +5. Save this page in the **Work in Progress** folder and name it "new.htm".

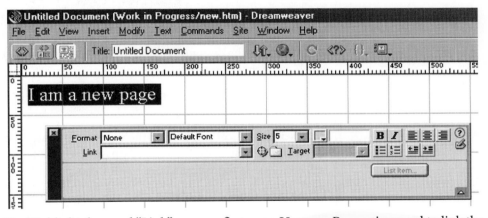

10. Highlight the word "Link" on your first page. Use your Properties panel to link the two pages together. To the right of the Link field in the Properties window, click on the folder to browse and find **new.htm**. Select the page and click OK.

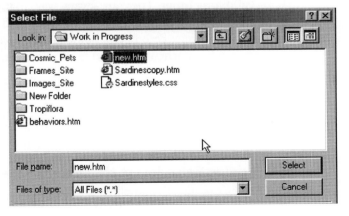

11. Make sure the Link page is selected and previewed in your browser. If everything worked OK, you should see your name in the Status bar. Click on the link, and an alert box should appear stating "Hope you come back and visit us again!". Click OK and you should see your "I am a new page" page.

12. Save the page when you're done.

Here's an overview of some of the more commonly used behaviors. For more on behaviors and extensions, visit the Dreamweaver site at http://www.macromedia.com/dreamweaver.

Status Bar Messages

Status bar messages provide the designer with the ability to place a custom message in the Status bar. The Status bar is located at the bottom of your browser window. This feature is not compatible with all browser versions.

Go To. Allows the designer to send the viewer to a specified Web site or timeline created inside of Dreamweaver.

Popup Menu. Allows the user to create an alert box with a custom message that is displayed when a certain event (onLoad or onUnload) takes place.

Browser Identification. Checks the viewer's browser version and can send them to a specified Web site to download and upgrade; or if it is within the parameters you have set, it will continue to the Web address of your choice.

Extensions. One of the advantages to Dreamweaver is its ability to expand. Extensions help create this versatility. Extensions allow you to add features and capabilities to Dreamweaver, such as quickly formatting a table or connecting a database. You can download many extensions for free from the Macromedia Exchange Web site.

Validating Input. There are several ways to input information into Dreamweaver. The Validating Input behavior works directly with a text field that is an object. The text field can be set to receive certain types of data such as an email address. The Validating Input behavior can be attached to the text field; if users enter text or numbers that are not an email address, they will get an alert box.

Behaviors and the Timeline

In chapter 14 we worked with animating layers — making objects on layers move across the page. We also discussed how a timeline can contain behaviors as well as pages.

Adding Behaviors to the Dreamweaver Timeline

If you examine the timeline, you'll see that one of the horizontal rows is labeled with the letter "B." This is where you insert behaviors.

In the following screen image, we've created a layer called "imagelayer," and added it as an object to the timeline. We stretched the length of the animation to frame 45.

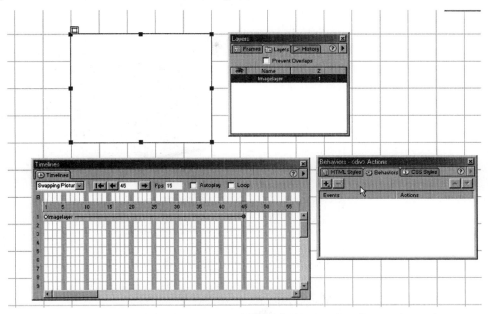

The next thing we did was to import an image into the layer. The effect we're trying to achieve is similar to a pre-planned rollover — an image that changes every second or so.

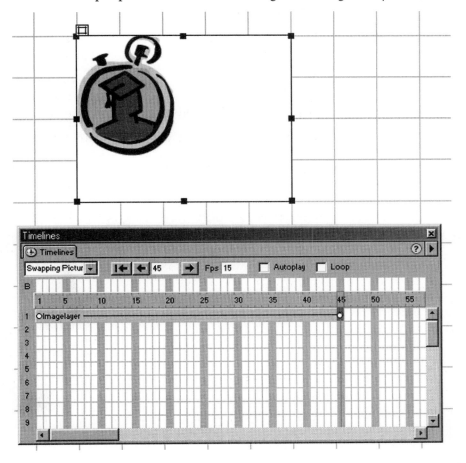

You can place as many behaviors as you want on the timeline: simply make certain that the Behaviors panel is open, click in the Behavior row in the frame where you want the behavior to occur, and click the Plus (+) button on the Behaviors panel to add the appropriate behavior. In this image, we've selected Swap Image from the pop-up Behaviors menu.

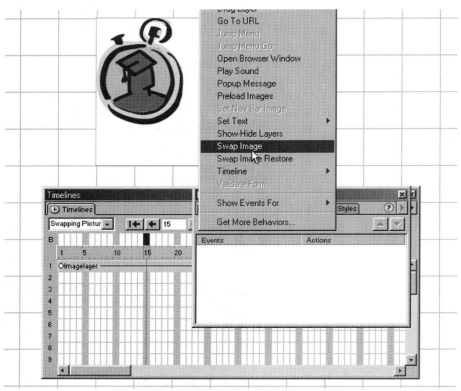

In frame 30, we added another Swap Image behavior. Every time you do, you're presented with a dialog box that lets you browse for the file that you want to use as the swap image.

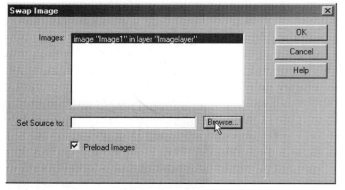

The Preload Images checkbox makes the browser download the three images along with the page; this makes the swap appear instantaneous. Not preloading the images will cause a delay when the swap first occurs, which is not such a good idea.

The last action we took was to check Autoplay and Loop. Doing so actually adds behaviors to the timeline — an onLoad action that starts the timeline running when the page loads, and a Goto Frame action in frame 46 — one that sends the animation back to the first frame and begins it running again. The results of this behavior-enhanced timeline is a page that loads three images, and swaps them out with each other every second.

When you check these options to turn them on, you'll see that the behaviors have been added to the timeline. Dreamweaver will display a dialog box that tells you what it's doing when you turn on the features.

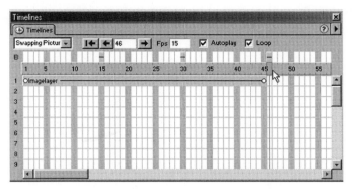

Dreamweaver automatically adds behaviors to achieve the Autoplay and Loop options available as checkboxes on the Timelines dialog box.

One final note about behaviors. Make sure that you preview them in more than one browser: they may, at times, behave poorly. We checked this small animation in both Internet Explorer and the latest version of Netscape Navigator; it worked fine in both programs.

Chapter Summary

In chapter 15 you explored the use of behaviors. You used the Behaviors panel to add and delete behaviors, starting with a behavior that instantly sends the viewer to another URL when the first page is loaded (onLoad). You used the Behaviors panel to send messages to the viewer, and to create a pop-up message when they left a page. You learned some more about JavaScript, and explored the use of browser identification actions. You learned about extensions, and how to validate user input. Lastly, you examined adding behaviors to the Timelines panel.

Complete Project D: Mr. BlockHead's Challenge

Notes:

16 Plugin Technologies

Chapter Objective:

In chapter 16, you will work with plugins — programs that enhance the functionality of your Dreamweaver pages. To learn how to include plugins on your pages, in chapter 16 you will:

- Learn the definition of "rich media" — external objects that can play animations, movies and sounds.

- Understand how to import Director movies in Shockwave format.

- Import QuickTime Movies.

- Work with Flash objects — animations created in Macromedia's popular Flash animation program.

- Understand how to use behaviors to determine whether or not a visitor has the required plugins; and how to direct them to a site where they can download the file.

- Insert a variety of rich media formats and learn to play them both from within Dreamweaver as well as within your browsers.

Projects to be Completed:

- Cosmic Pets (A)

- Tropiflora Order Form (B)

- Diehard Digital (C)

- Mr. BlockHead's Challenge (D)

Plugin Technologies

The concept of *plugins* for Web browsers was created by Netscape to act as a decoder for the browser so that it understands how to show certain types of external media. (Adobe Photoshop was among the first applications to feature plugin technology.) This concept allowed the viewer, for the first time, to see movies or animations inside of their browser window as opposed to having to download them and play them from a player on his or her computer's hard drive. Most browsers come with the most common plugins already installed and automatically play external media. As the plugin changes you can download a new plugin for (usually, but not always) free to keep your plugins up-to-date. The most popular formats of external media at the time of this writing are Flash, Shockwave, QuickTime and Real movies.

It is critically important to make sure that any rich media content — QuickTime movies, Flash animations, Shockwave objects created in Director, Real content, and others— are at the root level of your site. If you put them into nested (child) folders, many servers will not be able to link the content to the page. Keep them at the same level as the home page and you won't have any problems.

Developing dynamic Web sites with external media presents some challenging issues. First, adding external media requires more processing power, meaning the viewer's computer and connection speeds come into play. You only have 3-5 seconds or less to capture your viewer's attention. Many think that dynamic media is the answer to capturing someone's attention as connection speeds increase. Remember that although connection speeds are increasing, your viewer's patience is not. Therefore, even if you choose to use dynamic media, try to provide an alternative site for those who are not yet on a high-speed connection. Second, not every Web site requires external media. Just because it is available does not mean it is the best option. Web sites are built to serve a certain purpose, or to attract a certain audience.

Inserting external media in Dreamweaver is simple. You can insert media into your file from the Objects panel.

We've resized the Common category of the Objects panel for this image, which shows the icons for inserting interactive content along the bottom row, beginning with the second icon on the left. The first object inserts Fireworks HTML objects, the second Flash movies, the third Flash Buttons, then Flash Text, Shockwave and finally Generator — a Flash object that lets you create dynamic pages.

The Special category of the Objects panel, shown below, lets you put in Java Applets, plugins and ActiveX programs.

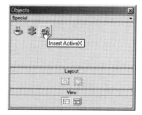

Some of the more advanced objects, such as Java Applets and ActiveX controls are far beyond the scope of this book. For more information about using Java and ActiveX, visit the macromedia. com Web site. There are several links from that site pointing you in the right direction for becoming a Java programmer.

Inserting Flash Content

Flash is Macromedia's animation and vector-art drawing program for the Web. It's estimated that over 500,000 people use Flash to either develop or view rich-media Web sites.

One of the major advantages of using Flash content is its extremely small file sizes. The reason Flash movies and objects are so small because the file format is based on vectors — or mathematical equations — to describe images. A Flash file doesn't remember that each pixel comprises an image, but rather the mathematical equations necessary to recreate it.

Before Flash, all images on the Web were raster or bitmap images such as JPG or GIF. Macromedia was at the forefront of creating vector graphics that can be distributed on the Web, which in turn created the possibility of creating Web graphics that are resolution-independent. Flash not only lets you use vectors, but also allows you to animate them.

Adding Flash content is as simple as any other image. Flash content requires the user's browser be equipped with a plugin to display properly. Therefore it may be necessary to create a splash page that doesn't contain any Flash objects, so that you can check the viewer's browser for the plugin.

The following exercise will lead you through the steps of inserting a Flash movie. You will also set up a screen to have the viewer check to see if they have the correct Flash plugin. Be careful when working through the exercise; there are many variables, and it is sometimes difficult to get a specific reaction when working with plugins.

There are many ways to check the browser to determine whether or not the Flash plugin is available. Visit http://www.flashkit. com and examine its download areas — it offers a few different options.

Adding Flash Content

1. Open Dreamweaver.

2. Create a new page if one is not already open. Save it in your **Work in Progress** folder as "flashcheck. htm".

3. Insert a table with 3 rows and 3 columns. Center the table on your page using your Property inspector and change the border to 0.

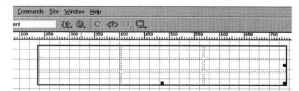

4. In the top-center cell, type "Can you see this movie?". Center the text.

5. In the bottom-left cell type "Yes". In the bottom-right cell type "No". Center those text elements as well.

6. Click in the center cell and then click on the Insert Flash icon in your Objects panel and insert the file **flshtest. swf**, which can be found in your **RF-Dreamweaver** folder. Click on Open or Choose (you may get a dialog box. Click OK and then No in the next dialog box that appears). You will see a gray box with a Flash icon in the center.

7. Make certain that the Flash movie is selected. In your Property inspector, click onPlay to view the Flash movie. This will show you what the Flash movie looks like without having to switch to a browser.

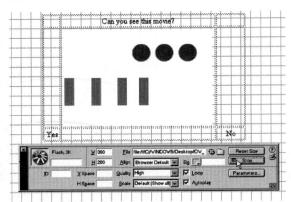

8. We still need to make a link. For the purposes of this exercise we will only link the No option. The Yes option would traditionally take the viewer to the opening page. The No option will take them to a Web site that allows them to download the correct browser. Highlight the word No on your page. In the Property inspector, type http://www. flash.com in the box next to the link.

9. Select File>Preview in Browser. If you see the movie playing, you have the latest version of the Flash plugin; if not, click on No, and download it from the Flash site for free.

This exercise showed one way to help your viewers check to see if they have the correct plugin. By placing a small test movie (such as the one you just used), you can warn the viewers that they may not see the site correctly without the appropriate plugin.

Director and Shockwave

Macromedia has been a leader in the interactivity market for many years. *Director* is a Macromedia product that allows you to create stand-alone interactive presentations that can be delivered on CD ROM. Director actually creates a small application, or program, that contains its own programming language; it has a long learning curve, but is incredibly powerful, and is often used to create games and training software.

Shockwave is a file format created by Macromedia that is the link between Director and the Web. *Shockwave* is a compression system that creates small files from Director content that can be effectively distributed over the Internet.

Placing a Shockwave movie is identical to placing a Flash movie, except you will use the Insert Shockwave option instead of Insert Flash. You'll discover that it is almost easier to use the HTML page Director has created, and then format it to fit within your specifications, rather then trying to insert it and then reformat. The following exercise will use an HTML document with a Shockwave movie already placed in it (placed by Director) and then reformat it. Then we will test the viewer's browser for a plugin, by using a behavior instead of a test movie.

Using Shockwave Content

1. Use File>Open to open **shock.html** from the **RF-Dreamweaver** folder.

2. You should see a gray box with a Shockwave icon on a blue background.

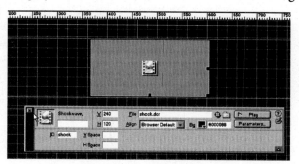

3. Select the Shockwave movie and, in your Property inspector, click on Play to preview the movie. The happy face should move away from the mouse when you try to click on it. Click Stop.

4. Deselect your Shockwave movie, and click on the Add Behavior button in your Behaviors panel (Plus (+) sign). Select Check Plugin from the submenu (if that option is grayed out, make sure your Shockwave movie is not selected).

5. In the pull-down menu, select Shockwave. This dialog box lets you set a Web page to go to if the viewer has the plugin, and one to go to if the viewer does not have the plugin. In the Otherwise field, type in "http://www.shockwave.com". This will take the viewer to the Shockwave site, where the correct plugin can be downloaded.

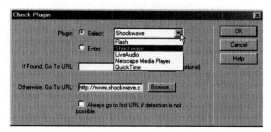

6. Choose File>Preview in Browser.

7. If you have the Shockwave plugin you should see the movie without a problem. If you do not have the Shockwave plugin you should have been taken to the shockwave.com site.

8. Close the file without saving.

It is always difficult to predict what might happen with plugins. Sometimes the viewer has the plugin, just the wrong version. If you use the behavior that you just attached in the exercise, the viewer will automatically be taken to a site (which you specify) to download a plugin; however, a novice user may not understand why they are there or what they need to do. That is why many people use the test movie instead of a behavior. It is good to know how to use both options.

Remember that Shockwave can generate its own HTML that places the Shockwave movie in the document, which makes it easy for you to reformat. You can then make changes to the HTML document and add a behavior to test the viewer's browser for the Shockwave plugin.

QuickTime

Apple Computer developed the *QuickTime* format. QuickTime is a movie format that allows streaming (as soon as part of the movie downloads it begins to play while the rest of the movie finishes downloading), some interactivity and panoramic viewing. QuickTime is a cross-platform format but requires a QuickTime plugin for the viewer to see it. Within the QuickTime format there are several different kinds of compression systems. For instance, "Sorenson" is a type of compression that can be applied to a QuickTime movie. This is the most important part of using movie files in a Web page. Size is always an issue.

Dreamweaver does not have a specific insert option for QuickTime like it does for Flash or Shockwave. However, it is does have a generic plugin option under the special section in your Objects panel that allows you to insert a QuickTime movie. The following exercise will walk you through inserting a QuickTime movie.

Inserting A QuickTime Movie

1. Open Dreamweaver if it is not already open and create a new document.

2. In the Objects panel, select Special from the pop-up menu at the top.

3. Click on the Insert Plugin icon (it looks like a puzzle piece).

4. Locate the **qtime.mov** file in the **RF-Dreamweaver** folder and click Open. Click OK and No in the dialog boxes that appear.

5. Select the Plugin icon in your document and change the width and the height to 265 × 205 by using your Property inspector. If you do not change the size of the Plugin icon to match that of the movie, it will only show the part of the movie that will fit inside the icon. You can click the Play button to watch the movie inside Dreamweaver.

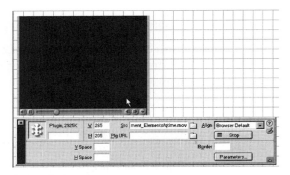

6. Choose File>Preview in Browser.

7. The QuickTime movie should play in your browser, unless, of course, you do not have the QuickTime plugin.

8. Close without saving when you're done watching the movie.

Notice that we didn't set up a way for the viewer to be warned about a potential plugin problem. If you are not able to see the movie, then you have just had a firsthand experience of what is like to be the viewer. You can download the plugin from the Apple site, http://www.quicktime.com.

The Insert Plugin option in Dreamweaver allows you to insert more generic types of media, or media that Dreamweaver cannot accommodate with its standard Insert command. QuickTime is one of those formats with many possibilities, but it does not have a direct insert option in Dreamweaver.

Sounds

Sound files are another type of external media that can help create dynamic Web sites. Before using sound, though, you must consider your audience. Just as other external media takes time to download, so does audio. It is important to keep audio file size as small as possible.

Sound Formats

.aiff/.aif	Audio Interchange Format, a Macintosh sound format from Apple.
.au	Sun Audio Format.
.midi/.mid	Musical Instrument Digital Interface.
.mp3/.mpg	MPEG-1 Audio Layer 3. Offers great compression and great quality.
.ra/.ram	Real Audio, offers streaming capabilities for the Internet.
.rmf	Rich Music Format is used in the Beatnick plugin.
.swa	Shockwave Audio, developed by Macromedia for Director and Flash.
.wav	Wave Audio Format was developed by IBM and Microsoft and plays on either a Windows operating system or Macintosh system.

Importing

Dreamweaver has provided simple ways to incorporate audio files of various formats into your Web site. In the following exercise, you will insert a sound file using a plugin and a behavior.

Importing Sound

1. Open Dreamweaver, if it is not already open, and create a new document. Click on Insert Plugin under the Special category of your Objects inspector.

2. Find the **music. aiff** file inside the **RF-Dreamweaver** folder and click Open or Choose. If you get a dialog box, click OK and then No.

3. Choose File >Preview in Browser. Notice the small player controls in the top corner of your browser.

4. Another way to use audio is via a behavior.

5. Create a new page (File>New) in Dreamweaver.

6. In the Behaviors panel click on the Add Behavior button (+) and drag down to the submenu Play Sound. Browse to find the sound file **music. aif** and click OK.

7. Choose File>Preview in Browser. If you get a dialog box, click Cancel. This time you should see a control bar that allows you to play the streaming audio.

In this exercise you learned two ways to place audio in your site. Both of these methods allow the music to play immediately, and will loop the music back to the beginning when finished.

Size Consideration

The biggest issue in Web design, especially when it comes to dynamic Web pages, is size consideration. Adding sound adds size; there is no way around it. File format can be considered, though, when examining size. Shockwave Flash files will provide a small file and are easy to use. They are cross-platform, and allow for flexibility. Macromedia suggests that you always use Shockwave Flash Audio, since the newest browsers are already set up to read this audio format without any problems. Other audio formats may sound different in different browsers.

Summary

In chapter 16 you learned how to build pages containing "media rich": animations, movies, sounds and Flash objects. You worked with Director movies and Shockwave content, which are both created in other Macromedia applications. You imported and worked with QuickTime movies, which are a popular movie and sound format originally developed by Apple Computer and are used by developers and media professionals everywhere. Lastly, you began to learn how to determine if the viewer has the required plugins to properly view rich content that you build into your pages.

The term "weight" is often used to describe relative file sizes. A 2k image is said to weigh five times less than a 10k image.

17 Managing Your Site

Chapter Objective:

In chapter 17 we will learn the ins-and-outs of managing a remote site using Dreamweaver's site-management features. To learn to manage the sites you create from your desktop, in chapter 17 you will:

- Learn the definition of site-management, and explore the tools that Dreamweaver provides to facilitate this critical, ongoing task.

- Learn how to use File Transfer Protocol (FTP) to access and manage your sites.

- Learn to upload and download sites from a remote server

- Learn to synchronize a remote site with a copy kept on your development system, and how to ensure that the process worked properly.

- Learn to use the site map to view both remote and local sites side-by-side.

- Work with Dreamweaver's reporting functions — specialized tools that let you generate a wide variety of printed reports from which to analyze the current state of your sites.

Projects to be Completed:

- Cosmic Pets (A)

- Tropiflora Order Form (B)

- Diehard Digital (C)

- Mr. BlockHead's Challenge (D)

Managing Your Site

Site-management is one of the most important aspects of Web development. Many people may feel it is easy to skip this section and start creating fun Web sites right away. We assure you that you will be back to read this more carefully, or will be desperately looking for a book on site-management. It is difficult to convince those new to Web design that this is important; but it is the nuts and bolts that hold all your assets together.

The first important concept to grasp is the difference between a Web site and a Web page. A Web page refers to a single page in a site. Many sites will let you customize their home Web page with your preferences. For instance, your personal stocks and regional weather can be set to show when the page opens in the browser. A site can consist of hundreds of pages, thousands of graphics and be connected to a database, or ten pages with a few graphics. It does not take long to rack up the pages and graphics. Built into Dreamweaver's workflow are site-management tools that can help you organize, update or even work in a group.

Remote Sites

Two types of sites exist. The first is a local site; your Web site resides on your computer. The second type is a remote site; your Web site resides on, and is delivered from, your Web server.

Connecting to Your Site

To gain access to a remote Web site, you have to communicate with the server. To communicate with the server you need to know specific information. Dreamweaver allows you to define this information with your server through the Site window, which is located under the Window menu.

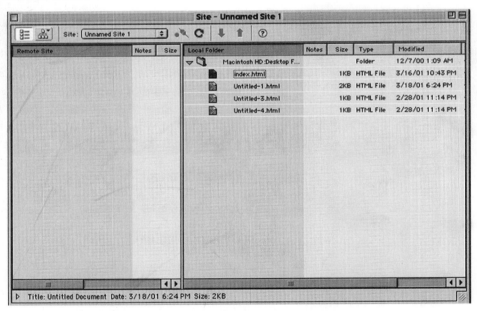

The Site window allows you to see your main site folder and all of your files hierarchically. It is also through this window that you can transfer data to a server.

Once a local site is created you can use that site to create a remote site. Whenever possible, you should start with a local site and then set up the remote version at a remote site. In the Site window, the left-hand column labeled Remote Site would show what your actual site looks like on the server. On the right, the Local folder should look similar, mirroring the same files as the remote site.

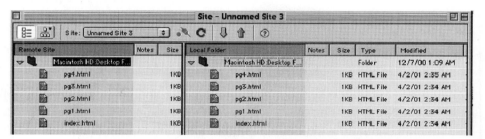

FTP

FTP stands for File Transfer Protocol, which is a method of transferring files to your server. Dreamweaver has a built-in utility that allows you to use FTP from inside of Dreamweaver.

The Site window contains most of the information you will use to manage your site. The FTP function is in the Site window under the Remote Info category of the Site Definition window. To get to this window, select Site>Define Sites; choose Edit, and then the Remote Info option. If you have multiple sites, this has to be done for each one of them.

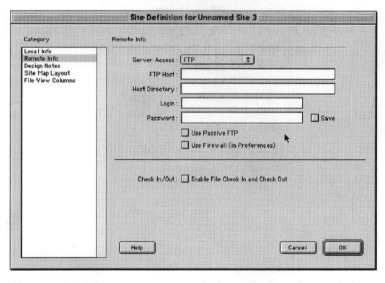

Transferring files via FTP contains its own vocabulary. The list of terms below will help you understand what you are looking at in the above screen shot.

FTP Host: This is your server. Host is a common term referring to the people that hold your account and are providing you with a Web server. The information that is entered in this section will look something like ftp.servername.com.

Host Directory: This is the folder on the server where you place your site to make it available to the world. Commonly, the directory folder is called "public," referring to the ability of the general public to see the files using their browser when they type in your Web address and connect to you server or host. Please note that the appropriate folder is not always called public, and you will need to ask your server administrator to double-check.

Login & Password: This is specifically for security reasons, although this is not the only caution you should take. Your login name and password will allow you to control who has access to uploading and changing files that exist on your site or server.

Use Passive FTP: Checking this option will allow your local computer to setup the FTP connection rather than requesting that the remote server set it up.

Use Firewall: This is the option you should use if you are trying to connect from behind a firewall. If you are not sure, you need to ask your system administrator.

Downloading and Uploading

Transferring files to and from your remote server is the only way to update the information on the remote server. Downloading is a common term used on the Web referring to copying something from the Web to your computer or disk (like an image on a Web page or an email attachment). Downloading means basically the same thing in this case, except that you are referring to your site (pages and assets) controlled by the down (Get) arrow. Uploading is the process of transferring data to your remote server controlled by the up or "put" arrow.

Synchronizing Your Site

Web sites are being updated constantly. You rarely can put a site out there and expect it to still be timely and current in six months. Dreamweaver makes it easy to update your site. If you build and change everything in your local site, Dreamweaver will let you synchronize an updated local site with your remote site. It will look for changes and update links and make your remote site match your local site. The Synchronize option is located under the Window menu and will copy the files from your local folder onto your remote site while checking for changes in links and pages.

Site Navigation

A site map is like a flowchart that shows you how everything is connected. Dreamweaver builds a site map automatically for you as you build your local site. You can view the site map at any time from the Site window. You can also export a site map and place it on your site so that your viewer can see how all the pages are connected.

To view your site in "map" mode you can select the Site Map icon in the Site window.

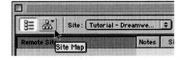

You will then see a flowchart of your entire site. If you click on the Plus (+) button it will show you all of the links connected to that page.

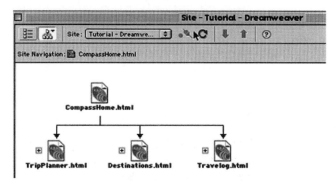

To export this map as an image, select Site>Site Map View>Save Site Map, and state the file format. This is nice if you have a large site that needs some direction. Remember that it will only show the main levels, unless you click on the Plus (+) button and expand the views before exporting.

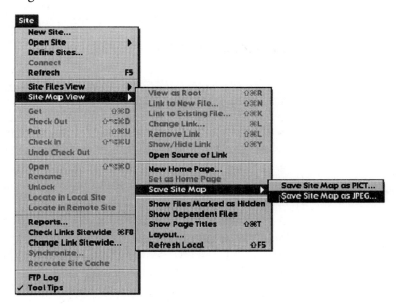

Direct Access to Individual Files

Within the Site window you have access to any individual files you may need to work with. Double-clicking on the page you want to access will automatically take you to that page in Dreamweaver. This is a wonderful tool when sites become large and you need to change a few elements on specific pages. Once the changes have been made, do not forget to synchronize with your remote site to keep everything updated.

Checking your Changes

Dreamweaver allows you to run several reports to help you know what is going on. By doing this, Dreamweaver keeps track of various types of data, so it can help you change information or find something. You can run a report that checks on group activity or changes, and will update the links, as well as many others.

The Reports window gives several options to run reports for both workflow and HTML, allowing you to catch potential mistakes or extra information that you do not need. You can access the Reports window from the Site window.

Besides the basic reports, Dreamweaver has provided a way to check your links over an entire site and then change them. Once they are changed, you need to make certain that you synchronize your local site with the remote site.

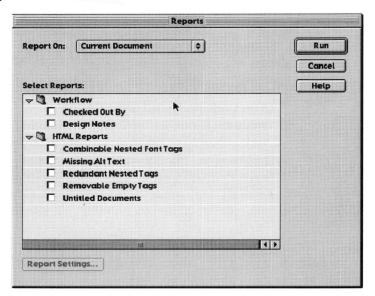

Once your site is synchronized, it is important that you take it for a test drive. Check it in Netscape Navigator, MS Internet Explorer, AOL and any other browsers that you can obtain. Test it in several different versions of those browsers. You will be surprised at how different your site can look. It is also a good idea to let someone else check it as well, since you may not be able to find those little details after so much examination.

Summary

In chapter 17 you learned that site-management is one of the most important aspects of Web development. Dreamweaver has many built-in tools to help you stay organized and update your remote site quickly and easily. You learned to synchronize and update a remote site via FTP, which resides in your Site window along with your site map and report options. Now that you know the basics, you can start creating Web sites with Dreamweaver, one of the best programs available for Web site development and management.

Notes:

Free-Form Project #2

Assignment

Next year is your grandparent's 50th wedding anniversary. You've decided to give them a Web site as a gift. You have a large family — there are five kids besides your mom, and more then 20 grandchildren. Not to count the 14 great grandchildren.

Your assignment is simple: design a workgroup site that grants permission for people to upload pictures, stories, sounds and video about the family. Design a series of templates with editable regions that your extended family can use to post their own data. You have to think about contacting everybody to determine who is going to get involved, and to what level.

Applying Your Skills

As you develop your family site, you'll need to apply several techniques and methods that you've worked with throughout this book. While you shouldn't be afraid of trying new things, at the very least you should:

- Create the site with blank (or just titled) pages. Create whatever folders you're going to require. Remember that rich media (like QuickTime movies, Real movies, Shockwave and Flash content) must reside in the same folder as the page on which they're used.

- Draw a flow chart and a navigation system.

- Design at least three different formats to fulfill the requirements of the assignment.

- Secure a domain name — or at least do the necessary research to see what is available.

- Use layers in the design. Add a simple animation to at least one page.

- Experiment with various text styles until you're satisfied with the headings, body text, lists and paragraph formats. Define HTML or CSS styles for the primary elements.

- Gather the graphics. Use an external image-editor to ensure consistency and optimization. Create any graphic text treatments that you might need.

- Create templates for all the pages. Use editable regions to allow for varying content while protecting the basic design.

- Add behaviors to make sure that anyone viewing the site has plugins for Flash, Shockwave, Real, QuickTime or other rich media. Add rollovers and swap images to the site as well.

- Use Define Sites>Edit to access the remote access privileges. Select FTP as the access method, and enter access privileges for your family members.

- Write the copy for your site along with instructions for all participants.

Specifications

If you have family images, then by all means use them. If you don't have a family, or if the pictures they've provided you with are more appropriate for a wanted poster than for this project, then check out the images in the RF-Dreamweaver>family_album folder. All of these images are from http://www.pdimages.com. Visit them if you get a chance.

Make at least the home page 640 pixels × 480 pixels — or even a little less. This will eliminate the need for the user to scroll to see the contents.

Use layers to construct the site, but make sure that you check the results in a variety of browsers. Although IE and the newest version of Navigator can properly display HTML layers, many older versions cannot. If you have problems, use the Convert Layers to Tables command to turn the designs into more compliant tables.

Publisher's Comments

You would be amazed at how many pictures, stories and even home movies are lying around in someone's attic. They're just waiting to be brought into the digital age.

Something to consider is the addition of a link page for genealogy sites. Do a search on Yahoo or one of the other major search engines and you'll find dozens — even hundreds — of sites where you can do research on your family's past.

Review #2

Chapters 10 through 17

In the second half of the book you worked with many of Dreamweaver's powerful features. After completing the discussions, exercises, and projects, you should:

- Understand how to build frame-based pages, and know how to target specific HTML content into a framed page. You should know about framesets, and how to save them along with your pages. You should understand the limitations of frame sites.

- Be comfortable with building pages with the Layers function. You should be fully aware of the compatibility problems associated with layers, and which browsers and versions are unable to properly display layered pages. You should also know how to convert pages from layers to frames and back, and how to use the Layers panel to control the positioning and attributes of layers. You should know how to create layers and populate them with images or text, and how to hide, view and lock layers to facilitate effective design.

- Be able to build forms, using a wide variety of objects available in the Forms Objects panel. You should know how to insert text fields, and the difference between single and multi-line text fields. You should be able to populate your forms with images, and use radio buttons, checkboxes and pop-up menus. You should be able to create jump and list menus that save space while providing navigation tools. You should know how to insert buttons and provide upload and download capabilities with the File field.

- Know how to use the Library to hold commonly-used items. You should be able to use the Template function to ensure consistency from page-to-page, and be able to create templates that provide specific regions where you can change content.

- Be comfortable with the timeline feature to animate layers and their contents. You should know the definition of fps, and how the frame rate controls the speed at which objects move. You should know how to add layers to the timeline, define frames and keyframes and understand their relationship to tweening — or the creation of movement between keyframes.

- Know how to work with behaviors and the JavaScript scripting language. You should be able to describe the relationship between the timeline and behaviors.

- Have worked with adding rich media objects in your pages. You should be able to play movies, animations and sounds on your pages.

- Know how to upload a site to a remote server and how to access it through FTP. You should be able to synchronize a local site to a remote site to maintain and update from your local machine. You should also be able to repair broken links, and generate reports to aid in the management process.

Project A: Cosmic Pets

This project will introduce you to the process of developing an integrated multi-page Web site. The client, Cosmic Pets, is a "brick and mortar" pet supplies and adoption agency that wishes to feature its services online. They want a clean, clutter-free design with a touch of humor. You will use a combination of Dreamweaver's features, such as rollovers, image maps, tables, horizontal rules and email links.

Before you build this site, it's a good idea to examine the finished product. Once you've had a chance to do so, we'll proceed to build it ourselves.

Pre-planning

Every project requires pre-planning. In this case, we already have the finished site to work from — but even on new projects you should take time before you start, to plan your actions, the order in which you're going to perform certain tasks and what your goals are for the finished project.

Looking at the finished site

1. Inside your **RF-Dreamweaver** folder is another folder named **Cosmic_Pets(Final)**. Open the folder and take a look inside.

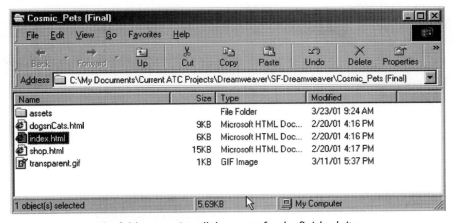

The folder contains all the assets for the finished site.

2. The **index.html** file is the home page. Double-click this file and the site will open in your Browser window. Click around until you're comfortable with the way it works.

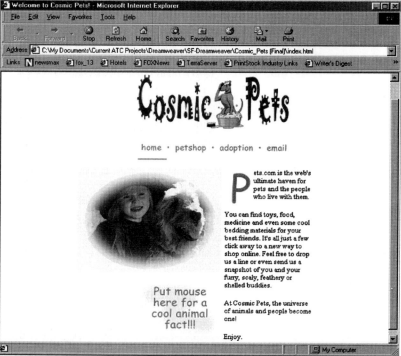

3. As you move through the pages, take a look at each one to see if you can determine what techniques were used to achieve the various effects. For example, you'll see data tables on the Petshop page.

Item	Weight	Price
ProFood	40 lbs.	12.98
FishFlakes	18 oz.	2.98
CatProChow	28 lbs.	11.89
TurtleMeal	20 lbs.	12.69
GoatBoat	13 lbs.	14.98
LeezardChow	17 lbs.	19.89
HamsterStuff	12 lbs.	10.89

4. Rollovers were also used. Moving your mouse over the pet images will display a graphic treatment that lets you know what's on their minds.

(to find out what our furry friends are thinking, move your mouse over their picutres)

"Man, what I wouldn't do for a steak, with a side order of fries right about now..."

Name: StarGazer
Age: 1 year, 5 months
Breed: Alaskan Husky

Stargazer is an amazing pedigree Husky right from America's frozen tundra! He's a good companion and loves to eat hot dogs and mustard and a good potato chip every once in a while. To adopt, send an e-mail to us with a paragraph telling us why you think you'd be great parents to Stargazer. Good luck!

5. Keep the Browser window open.

6. Every site you create should start with a piece of paper and a concept. Sketch out the basic form of the site and you'll save lots of time when you actually start building pages. Look at the home page in your browser and sketch out the structure of the page. Remember our lessons using tables? That's how we're going to build this site.

Preparing the Site Structure

Once you've determined what you're doing to do, what the basic pages will look like, what graphics you need, what techniques you're going to use to accomplish your goals and what copy you're going to use to deliver your message, it's time to prepare the site. This includes creating a root folder, moving the site assets into place and using Dreamweaver's Define Site tools to build the basic structure of the site.

Preparing the Root Folder and Home Page

1. Create a new folder inside your **Work in Progress** folder. Name it "Cosmic_Pets". Drag the Assets folder from your **RF-Dreamweaver>Cosmic_Pets (Final)** folder into the folder you just created. This is going to be the root folder for your new site.

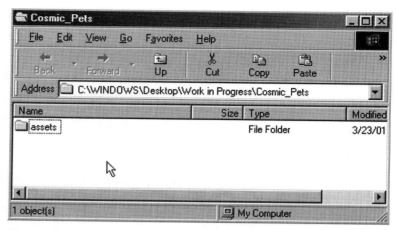

Storyboarding, or drawing loose sketches of the entire site before using Dreamweaver, can speed up your production time. Have the client sign off approval on the sketches, and then proceed to build the site in Dreamweaver.

2. Start Dreamweaver. Save the untitled document into the **Cosmic_Pets** folder as "index.htm".

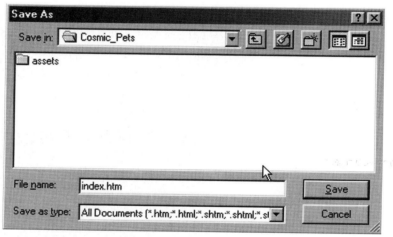

3. Now that we have a root folder, an assets folder and a home page, it's time to define the site. Select Site>New Site. In the dialog box, under the Local Info category, type in the Site Name and select the **Cosmic_Pets** folder as the Local Root Folder.

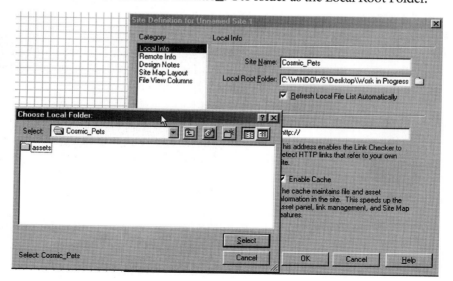

4. Select the Site Map Layout category, click the Browse icon (the small folder to the right of the field) and locate the **index.htm** file. Click the Open button to establish it as the home page for this site. Click OK to finish.

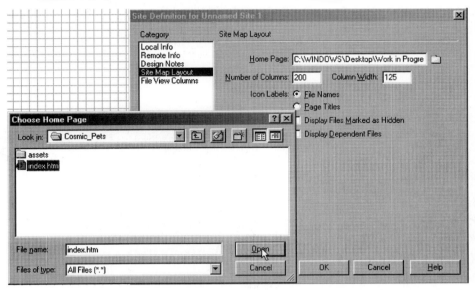

5. Dreamweaver will respond by displaying a dialog box stating that the program will now build the Cache file for the site. Click OK.

6. Select Window>Assets or press F11 to activate the Assets panel.

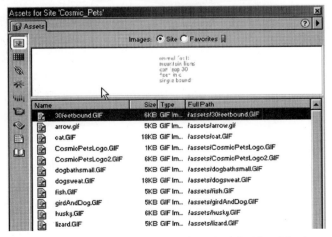

Notice that the Image icon is selected on the left side of the Assets panel. If you don't see the list of images, that's probably what's occurring

Several of Dreamweaver's dialog boxes — most notably the Cache message and Help page that appears when you select Layout view from the Objects panel — can be permanently turned off by selecting the "Don't show me this message again" checkbox. We suggest that you don't do this until you're very familiar with the program.

7. Dreamweaver automatically recognizes any folder named "Assets," and brings its contents into the Assets window. From there, you can preview them, and later you'll be able to drag them into position on your page. Take a minute to examine the assets in the panel.

The default keyboard equivalent for showing the Assets window is F11.

8. Save the file but keep it open.

Building the Page Format

Most sites display a great deal of consistency from one page to another. While certain pages may have a different layout, good design theory states that the less the layout change from one page to another, the easier it will be for the viewers to find what they're looking for. That's certainly true in the Cosmic Pets site — each page uses the same layout, but with different pictures, text and content.

Designing the Pages

WINDOW > OBJECTS

1. At the bottom of the Objects panel is the Layout View icon. Click it.

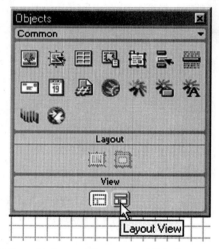

2. The Layout View Help window will appear. This is one of those dialog boxes we spoke about before; you can turn it off forever, but it's a good idea to let it show until your fully comfortable using the feature. Read the copy and click OK.

You might notice that our Objects panel looks different than the one on your monitor. That's simply because we keep ours re-sized so that it's square instead of tall — this provides screen shots that are shaped better. Re-sizing the panel has no effect on its function.

Although many designers choose to "freeform" their sites, there's no question that using grids and rulers make it much easier to position elements visually, align page elements and create a solid, structured look to your pages. Even pages that seem very fluid and not structured often were built on a grid.

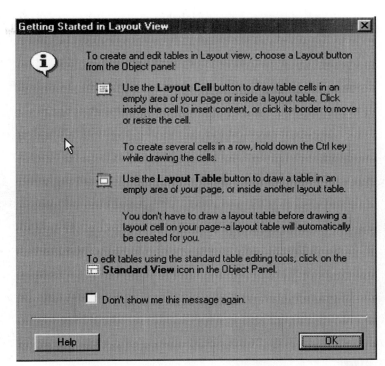

3. Select View>Grid>Edit Grid. Set the Spacing to 50 Pixels and click OK.   *FROM MENU BAR*

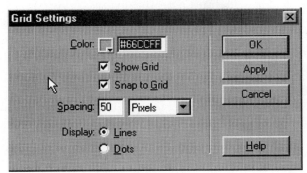

We usually use a light blue for the grid color. In the old print world, "non-repro" blue pencils were used to mark films. When duplicated, the special color disappeared.

4. Make sure to use View>Grid>Show Grid to make sure the grid is visible. Display your rulers by selecting View>Rulers>Show Rulers. If they don't align perfectly to the grid, click in the intersection of the two rulers (in the upper-left corner of the screen) and drag them to the corner of the grid. You might have to set them to Pixels as well. Use View>Rulers>Edit Rulers to change the setting.

VIEW>RULERS>PIXELS

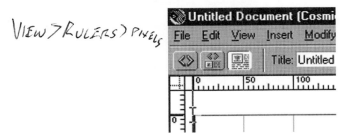

5. Select the Draw Layout Table tool. Draw a rectangle 450 pixels wide × 500 pixels high.

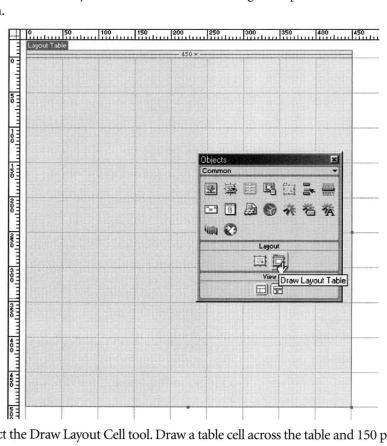

You can move the intersection of the rulers (sometimes called the Zero point in other applications) to any position on the page by dragging it out. It's a good measurement tool. To reset it, double-click the intersection of the rulers.

6. Select the Draw Layout Cell tool. Draw a table cell across the table and 150 pixels high.

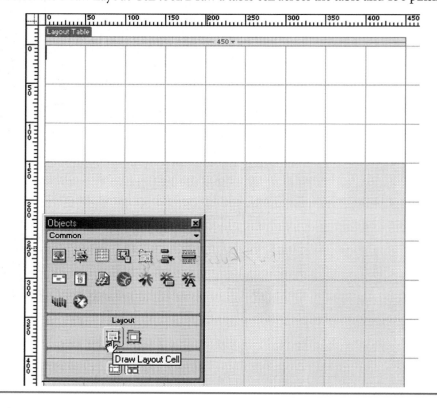

7. Underneath the first table cell, draw another thinner one — make it 25 pixels high. If you can't draw it perfectly the first time, simply type the height into the Property panel in the H field.

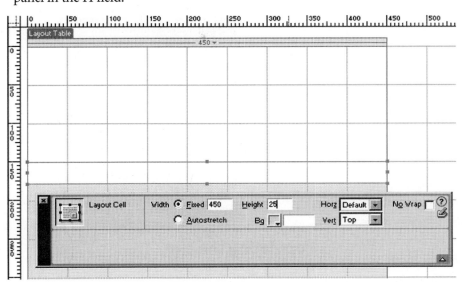

8. If the Assets panel isn't visible, activate it by selecting Window>Assets or pressing F11. Drag the asset named **Petsmenu.gif** from the panel into the thin cell you just made. Drop it there.

VIEW >
TABLE VIEW >
STANDARD VIEW

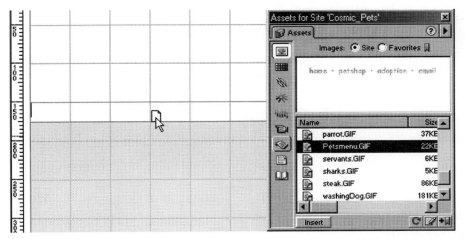

9. Use the Center Align icon in the Property inspector to center the image in the cell.

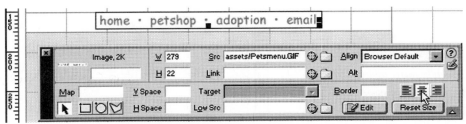

10. Save the page. Use File>Save As to create two more pages for the site. Name one "petshop.htm", and the other "adoption.htm". Make sure you save them into the correct folder — the Cosmic_Pets root folder we created in the beginning of the project.

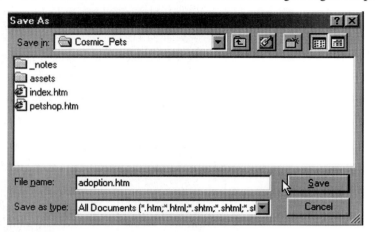

By building a table to contain the page elements, we can ensure that each page will have consistent visual structure — elements won't jump around every time the user changes to another page.

Populating the Site

Now that we've built the basic structure for the Cosmic Pets site, it's time to populate the pages with the content that the client wants to deliver to their visitors. It might be a good time to surf the final site again, so that you can see how the various pages are built, and what they contain.

Inserting Content

1. Make sure you have the **index.htm** file active (check the Window menu). Click the Show Code and Design Views icon. Scroll to the top of the Code window and change the title of the document to "Welcome to Cosmic Pets!".

You could also use the Title field at the top of the Design View window to change the page title. We just wanted to remind you that HTML code was being written while you're laying out these pages. Another way to change the page title is to use Modify>Page Properties, which can be accessed with the shortcut Command/Control-J.

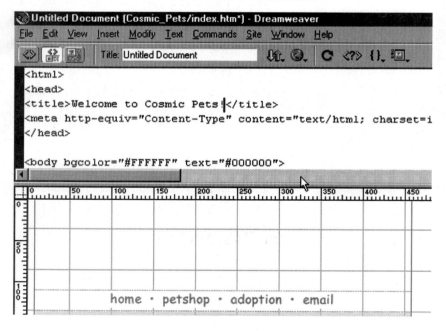

2. Close the Code window by selecting the Show Design View icon when you're done. Click on the page and the Title bar will display the new page title.

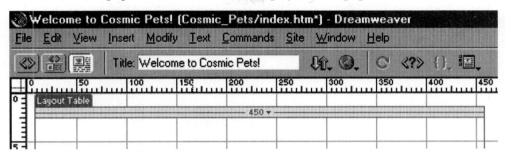

3. From the Assets panel, drag the **CosmicPetsLogo.gif** into the cell at the top of the index.htm (home) page. Once it's there, center it using the Center Align icon on the Property inspector.

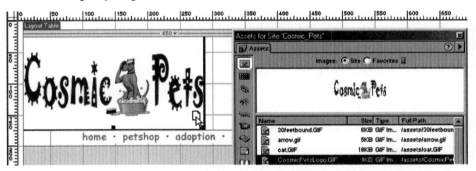

4. Create table (layout) cells for the picture of the girl and her dog, the rollover image (it looks like type in the browser but it's actually a graphic) and the type column on the right-hand side of the page.

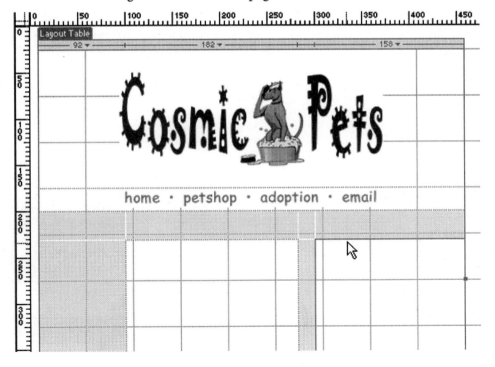

5. Drag the **girlanddog.gif** file into the cell on the upper-left side. If necessary, readjust the size and position of the cells to properly balance the page.

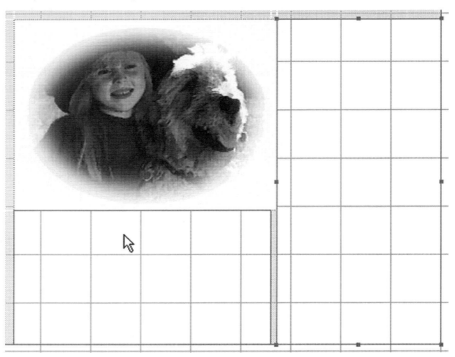

6. There are many ways to import text into a Dreamweaver page, but the easiest way that we know of is to copy it from somewhere else (such as a word processor or page layout program) and paste it into place. Open the original **index.htm** file from inside of Dreamweaver. Select the copy in the right-hand column and press Command/Control-C (or select Edit>Copy from the Menu bar).

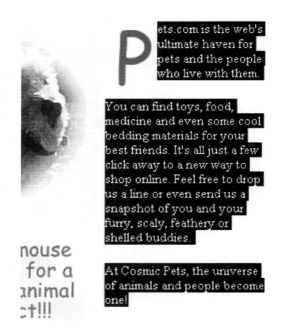

7. Click in the right-hand column cell on your home page. Paste down the copy using Command/Control V. There it is. Notice that the first sentence is missing the letter "P". It's a graphic that we'll import in a moment.

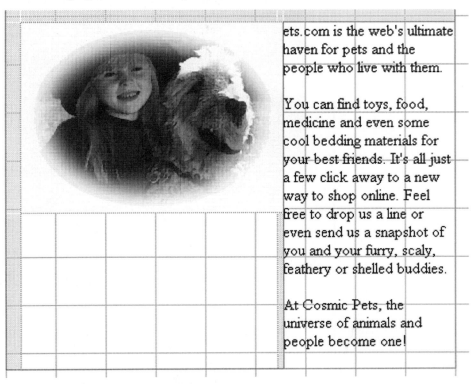

8. Drag **p.gif** from the Assets panel in front of the copy in the right-hand column.

9. Click the graphic and select Left from the Properties panel pop-up Align menu.

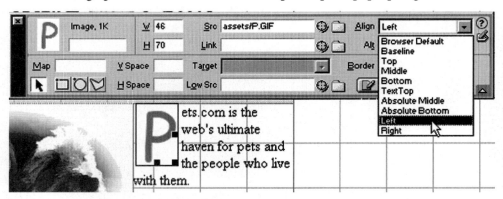

10. Time to create the rollover. Click inside the lower-left cell and select Insert>Interactive Images>Rollover Image.

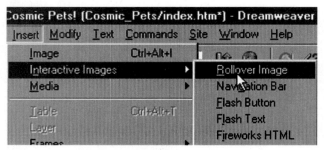

11. The Insert Rollover dialog box appears. For the original image, click the Browse button, and from inside the Assets folder, select **mousehere.gif**. For the Rollover Image, do the same thing and select the **sharks.gif** image. You can leave the URL blank, because this isn't going to a link — but it could be if you wanted it to be.

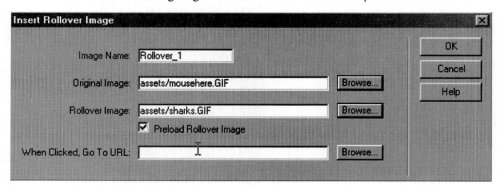

It's always best to bring images into Dreamweaver at actual size. Otherwise the browser is forced to recalculate the image upon loading, slowing it down considerably. Even if the image is used small on your pages, Dreamweaver still has to download the full sized version for it to properly display.

12. Click OK. Select the image and center it using the Property inspector.

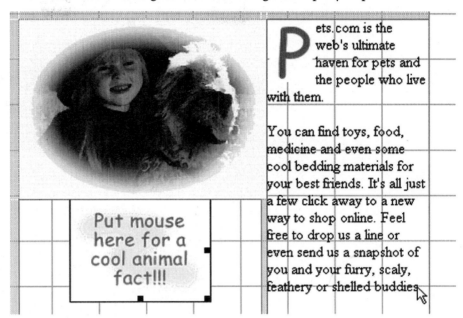

13. Preview the page in the Browser window by pressing F12.

14. Close the Browser window and save the index.htm file.

15. Begin to build the other pages, using the Final file as a visual guide for placement of your page elements. Use it as a visual guide only — there are no shortcuts in the real world. If you need to copy text from the other site, that's fine — just as long as you don't borrow anything else. Browse through the Assets panel to see what images go on what pages, and what images are used for rollovers.

Rollovers are a great way to add impact to your site without excessively slowing down the browser. Use them for text effects and to give the viewers a hint that certain items are clickable.

16. On the Petshop page, build the price list, with a nested table built of rows and columns. Use the Insert Table command.

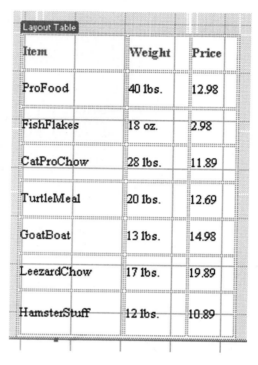

For best results, make sure both images for your rollover are the same pixel size. If not, one of the images may stretch to fit the cell boundary.

17. Save the files.

Wiring the Site

Once you've built all the pages that make up your site, it's time to put in the links — what we refer to as "wiring the site." This site doesn't use any buttons or sophisticated navigation techniques — just a simple site map.

Creating the Links

1. On the **index.htm** page, select the Menu bar. From the Property inspector, select the Rectangle Image Map tool.

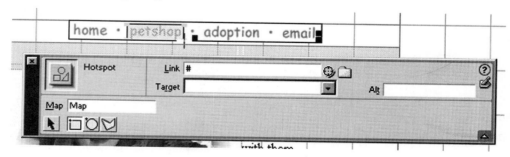

2. Link the hotspot to the **petshop.htm** file.

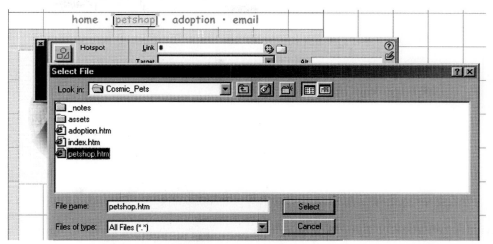

3. Do the same thing with the Adoption menu item. Create a hotspot with the Image Map tool, and link it to the appropriate page — **adoption.htm**.

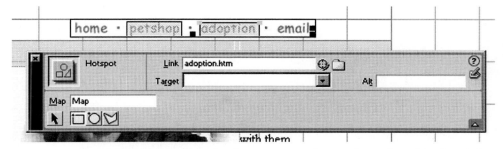

4. Create an email link. Draw another hotspot over the word email, and in the Link field of the Property panel, type "mailto:courseware@againsttheclock.com".

5. Go through the entire site, linking all the pages and checking your work often using the Preview in Browser (F12) command.

Although quite simple in design and complexity, this site still delivers what the client wants — a clean, fun and effective way to get their name in front of the Internet user. While small local and regional sites might not be as glamorous as MSNBC, CNN or the Whitehouse, they still play an important role in the marketing and contact strategies for smaller companies.

However, building a site like this might be simple for you to do with Dreamweaver; it's the content that actually comprises a site. Solid images, tasteful use of type and an easy-to-understand interface are all components of the design and creative process. Without good content, the most flashy and dynamic site is just another flash-in-the-pan.

A few, well-designed images should be your goal in your site-development. Try to design for the lowest common denominator modem speed, which is generally 33bps to 56bps. Not everyone has a cable modem or a high-speed T1 or DSL line.

It's tricky designing a site that looks the same in all browsers. Try to preview your pages in Netscape Navigator, Internet Explorer and America Online. Tweak the pages until you are satisfied with all three.

Notes:

Project B: Tropiflora Order Form

Tropiflora offers many services on their site; we need to make it easy for customers to order products. The client wants you to create an easy-to-use form that will be intuitive and require no instructions. In this project you will learn how to make a form that includes text fields, checkboxes and drop-down lists. We'll also use a table to construct our form, to make it easier to align the various fields and form objects.

Before you Get Started

It is important that you design your forms to be as easy to understand as possible. A confusing form could cause a potential customer to move on to another site to place their order.

Before we start the project, there are a few details to discuss. First, there's a folder inside the **RF-Dreamweaver** folder named **Orderform**. The files for this exercise are inside that folder, along with an Assets folder. Drag the Orderform folder and all its contents into your **Work in Progress** folder before you start going through the steps. Staying inside that folder will keep pathnames and links from becoming an issue.

Second, we should discuss a bit about form handling. Form handling refers to doing something with the information you collect from the completed form (when the user clicks the Submit button). There are a lot of free programs out there that will collect the information for you and send it back as an email or an email attachment. We strongly suggest that you talk to your ISP — they probably have programs you can use for free as well, and they must provide you with information about how their servers want to collect information and give it back to you.

Third, inside the Orderform folder, there's a file named **completedform.htm**. Open the file and take a look at it. We're going to reconstruct this form from the ground up.

Please note that you might have to spend some time formatting font sizes and styles if you want the form to look exactly like it does in the screen images used throughout the project. Feel free to use any font combinations you like. However, it won't have any effect on the results.

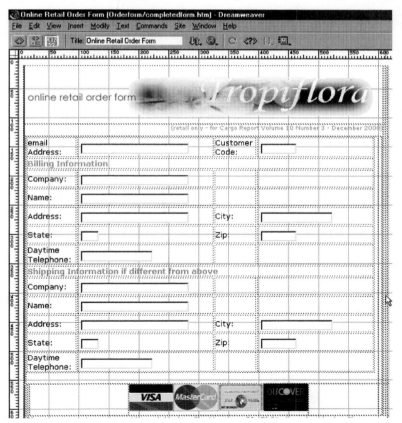

Creating the Form

1. Start a new document in Dreamweaver by choosing File>New from the Menu bar. Save it into the Orderform folder as "newform.htm".

2. Select View>Grid>Edit Grid. Change the Grid Spacing to 20 Pixels.

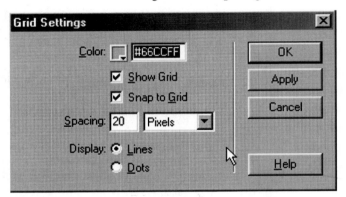

3. Activate the Layers panel (Window>Layers), and check the Prevent Overlaps option.

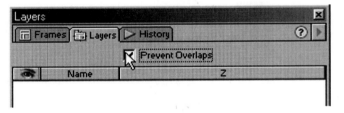

4. Create a new layer by clicking on the Draw Layer icon in the Objects panel. Be sure you are in Standard view or the tool won't work. It doesn't have to be very large; the image we're going to insert onto the layer will automatically size it correctly.

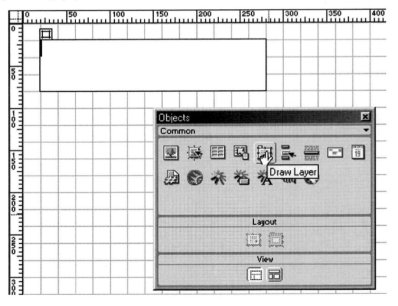

5. Click inside the layer, and click the Insert Image object in the Common category of the Objects panel. Select the **masthead3.jpg** image from the Assets folder (which is inside the orderform folder) and click Choose/OK.

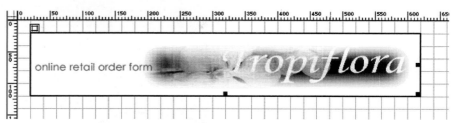

6. Underneath this layer, draw another layer as wide as the first one and extending down to 600 pixels.

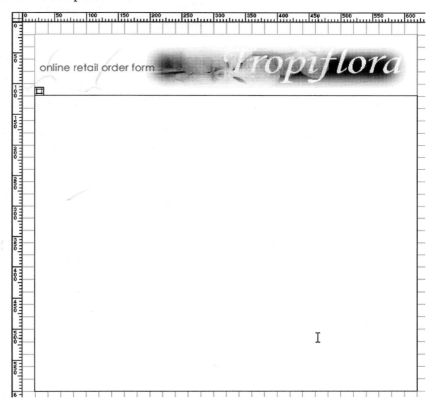

7. Change the Current Tools panel on the Objects inspector from Common to Forms.

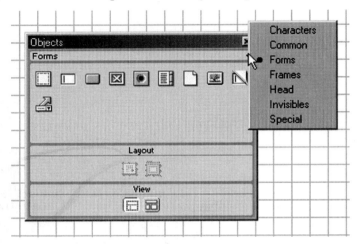

8. Select the menu option View>Visual Aids>Invisible Elements. You won't be able to see the form's outline correctly if Invisible Elements is not selected.

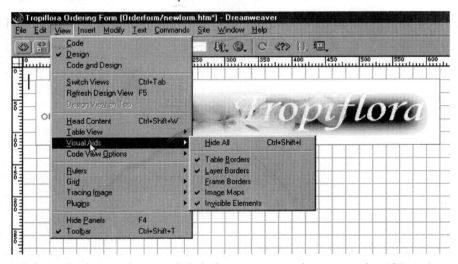

9. Click inside the new layer and click the Insert Form button on the Objects inspector.

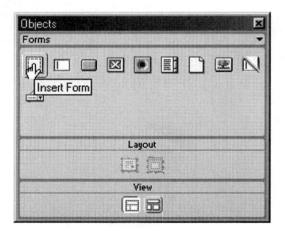

Inserting a Table for Alignment

1. Click the Insert Table button from the Common category on the Objects inspector.

2. When the dialog box appears, enter 13 for Rows and 4 for Columns. Set the Width to 100% and set Border, Padding and Spacing to 0.

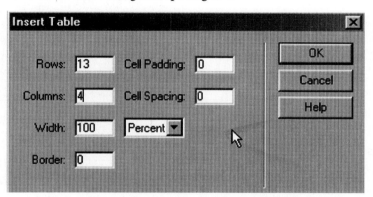

3. Select the entire second row by dragging across it, and from the Modify>Table menu, choose Merge Cells.

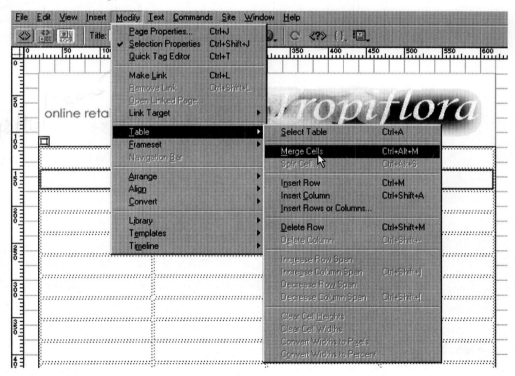

This ability to grab colors from images that are on the page is an excellent technique. It adds color consistency and can help give a page a finished, detailed look.

4. Type "Billing Information" in the second row. Select all the text, and press the Text Color chip in the Property inspector. Drag the Eyedropper to an orange color in the Tropiflora masthead. This gives the page a more uniform look, while minimizing the number of colors on the page.

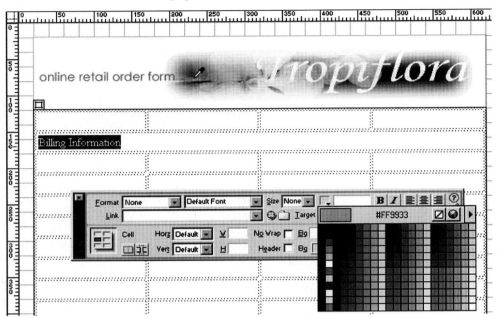

5. Repeat steps 3 and 4 for the eighth row. Type "Shipping Information if different from above".

One of the most common problems designers face when working with forms is alignment. To overcome this, insert a table within the form and place your elements in separate cells.

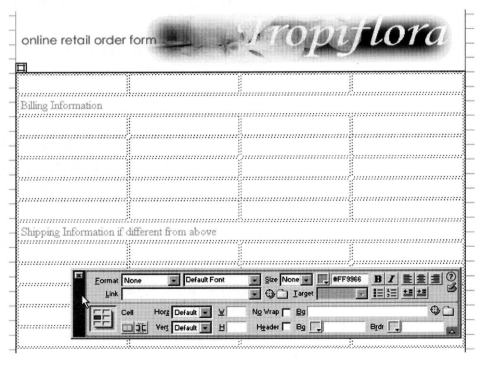

Inserting Text Fields

1. A flashing I-Beam in a cell indicates that you can enter text or a field. Click once in the first empty cell in row one, column one, and type "email Addressee:".

2. Press the Tab key to move into the cell to the right and click the Insert Text Field button on the Forms Objects panel.

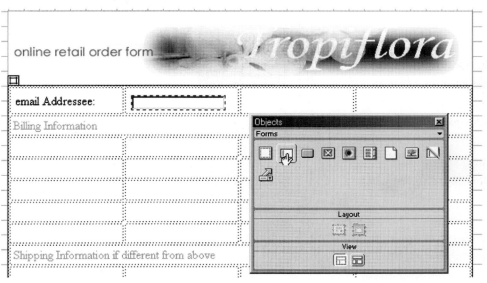

3. Click once on the newly created text field. Look at the Property inspector. It has changed to reflect the currently selected text field. Enter "32" for Char Width. This will create a text field that is 32 letter spaces wide. You can always increase or decrease this number by clicking the text field later.

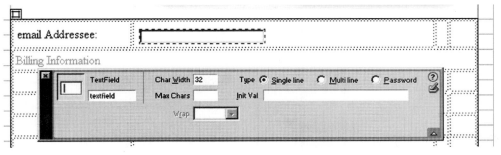

4. Choose the Single line radio button. This will keep the entered text on a single line in the form. If you'd like to give the customer more space to enter their information, you could select the Multi line radio button.

5. Press Tab again to move to the next available cell.

6. Type "Customer Code:" and then insert another text field in the next cell after the words. You can adjust the width of cells by dragging the borders to the desired position.

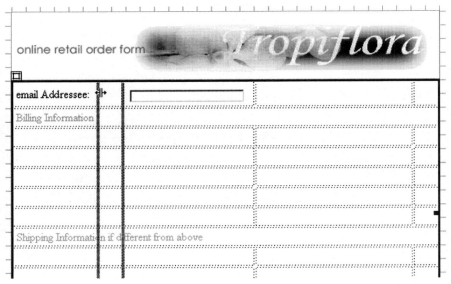

As you develop the form and need to add rows, simply tab to the last cell in the lower right-hand corner of the table, and press the Tab key. Dreamweaver will automatically insert another row.

7. Following the sample page, create the rest of the text fields. Remember, Tab moves you from left to right and the arrow keys move up and down. Shift-tab moves you backward from right to left.

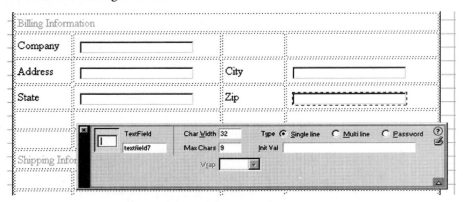

8. When you've finished the fields and field descriptions for the shipping information, select the next three rows — one at a time — and use Modify>Table>Merge Cells to make three cells that have only one column each.

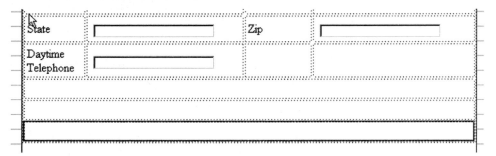

9. Skip one row and insert the four credit card images in the next row down. Insert them all in the same row, one after another. Their names are **visa.gif**, **mastercr.gif**, **amex.gif** and **discover.gif**.

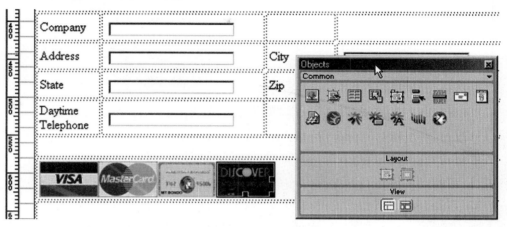

10. Control/Shift-click the four images and use the Align Center icon in the Property inspector to center them on the form.

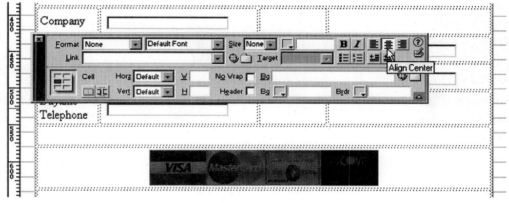

11. Copy the credit card copy from the finished sample and paste it into place on your new form — in the row directly below the credit card images.

12. Save the file but keep it open.

Using images on your forms makes them friendlier and easier to understand. Don't go overboard and use images without any relevance, but whenever it's appropriate to use a picture or graphic to help the visitor better understand or navigate around a form, by all means do so.

Many forms require that the user select from a list of items — as is the case when selecting which credit card to use. Let's look at how to insert pop-up lists as form objects.

Inserting Lists

1. Place your cursor after the credit card copy we just pasted in and press the Tab key a few times to add some more rows.

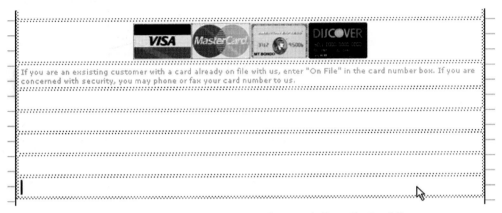

2. In the next row after the credit text, enter the words "Credit Card:".

3. After the text, press the Space bar and choose the Insert List/Menu button from the Forms category of the Objects inspector.

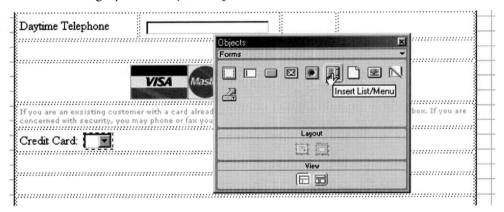

4. Click the List Values button at the top right of the Property inspector.

5. Enter "Visa" in the first field and give it a value of 80. Press the Plus (+) button to add a new value and type "MasterCard" with a value of 81. Finish by entering "American Express" with a value of 82 and "Discover" with a value of 83. Click OK.

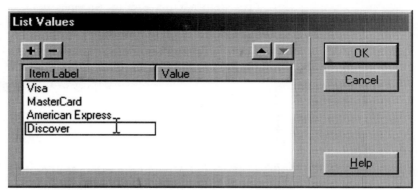

6. Click on the List/Menu you have just inserted and examine the Property inspector. Choose Visa by clicking once where it's highlighted under Initially Selected. This makes Visa the default selection in the browser. Customers will click on the button to reveal alternate forms of payment.

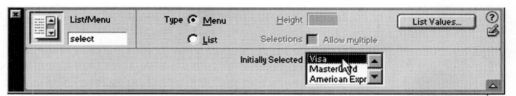

7. Continue building the form until you have reached the two Choice fields. You can insert all the copy and fields in one row, since the objects don't really require any special positioning to look good.

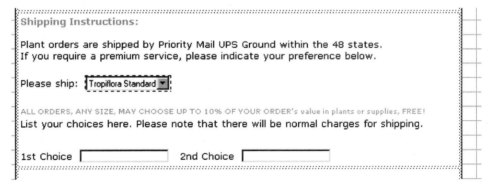

8. Save the file and keep it open.

Checkboxes are another common form element . In the last part of the project, we need to allow customers to make other choices regarding their order. This time, we'll offer additional options by way of checkboxes. Customers will be able to choose as many of the checkboxes as necessary.

Checkboxes and the Submit button

1. Press Return/Enter after the second Choice field and click the Insert Checkbox button. You can continue to work in the same row.

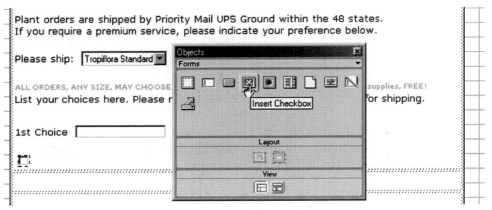

2. Click the checkbox once that you have just inserted and select the Unchecked option where it says Initial State on the Property inspector. Selecting this for each checkbox you insert ensures that all of the boxes will be unchecked on the broswer. Fill in the remainder of the checkboxes on your own. At the end of each line, use Shift>Enter to create a line break — this will keep the lines close together.

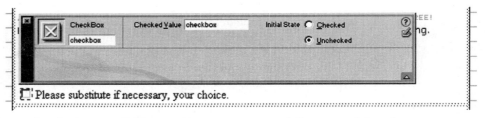

3. After the last text field, press Return to create a full paragraph break.

4. Enter the text "Please only click Submit ONCE" and choose the Align Center button on the Property inspector.

5. Choose the Insert Button button on the Forms category of the Objects inspector to insert a button directly after the warning message.

Make sure to name all of your fields and form objects so the information you receive back makes sense. Do so in the Property Inspector.

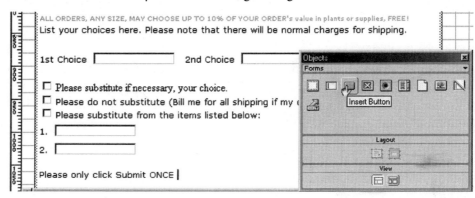

6. Submit is the default label for this button, but you can easily rename this button anything you'd like. You can even make this a Reset form button, which will clear all the choices made by the customer on the form. All these choices can be made by clicking the Submit button once, and making appropriate alterations on the Property inspector.

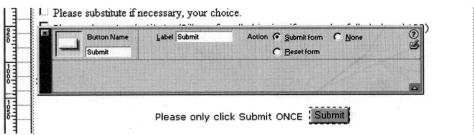

7. Save the file. Preview the form in your browser.

The form that you built was actually a real-world update to an older, existing form that used to be on this company's site. The new form is much cleaner, easier to navigate and provides several important pieces of information that weren't available on the older form. The client and their site visitors are both very pleased with this updated, visually-pleasing form.

Notes:

Project C: Diehard Digital

Diehard Studio specializes in graphic design and animation and is known for its popular published and televised characters. The owner wants to convey this in the design of the home page. You will achieve this by using layers for precise control over the page's design. You will also add animation by using the power of Dreamweaver's DHTML timelines.

This project involves the use of sliced images. A sliced image is one large graphic that's literally cut into several smaller (hopefully) seamless tiles. The widely-used technique lets you use images that would normally be too big and take too long to download. By optimizing one large image and slicing it into smaller pieces, they'll load faster and still look perfect.

We'll be using files that can be found inside the **RF-Dreamweaver>Diehard_Studios** folder. Before we begin, make a copy of the entire **Diehard_Studios** folder inside your **Work in Progress** folder for use during the remainder of this project.

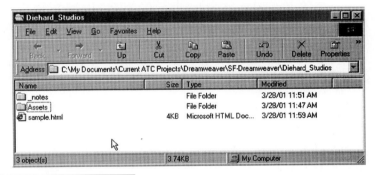

It is important that you design your sites to complement the clients' needs and the services they offer. You would not design a toy store site to look like a financial corporation nor would you put toys all over a Wall Street site's pages.

Looking at the Finished Result

1. Start Dreamweaver and open the file **sample.html** from the **Diehard_Studios** folder. Take a look at it.

2. You'll probably notice that there are two layers used in the construction of the page. The top one — the one containing Dwayne's face — makes use of a technique called "slicing." Click somewhere inside that layer and you'll see one of the slices that make up the image.

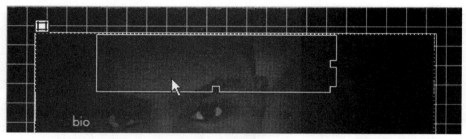

3. Once you're done looking at the sample file, you can close it. Keep an untitled document open, though; we're going to recreate this page, and add an animation to make it interesting.

Although Dwayne is a contemporary designer whose cartoons and illustrations are considered cutting-edge, he does subscribe to an old-fashioned technique every time he designs a site, a printed piece or an animation: he draws them on paper. Here's the original sketch he used before he started building his own site:

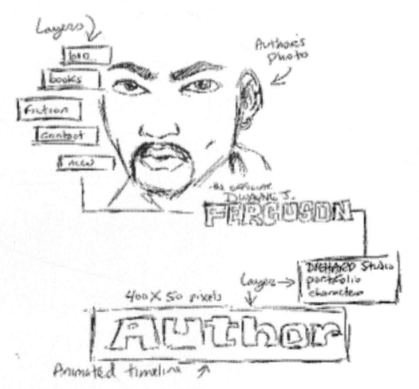

Sketching your ideas on paper is a technique used by many top professionals in the design field. It provides a solid foundation from which to start the actual work of putting the design together. Another benefit to the process is that it keeps your work from looking like it was designed on a computer.

Good design doesn't jump out of the box that your Macintosh came in and stick on your clothes. Nor is it a feature of the latest version of Microsoft Windows operating system.

Advanced Layout with Layers

1. You should have an untitled document on your monitor. If not, start a new page. Save it into your **Diehard_Studio** folder and name it "index.htm". Use Site>New Site to create a site using this folder as the root, and the index.htm file as the home page.

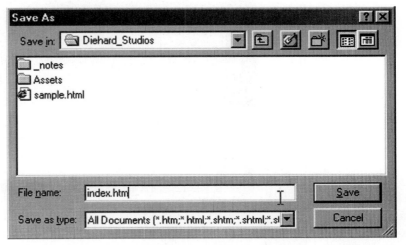

The sample file that you see in the folder was created on a Macintosh — hence the .html suffix.

2. Select Modify>Page Properties and change the background color to black. You can either pick the color from the color swatches or enter its hex number — #0000000. Change the Title to "Diehard Studios — Home of the Hunter".

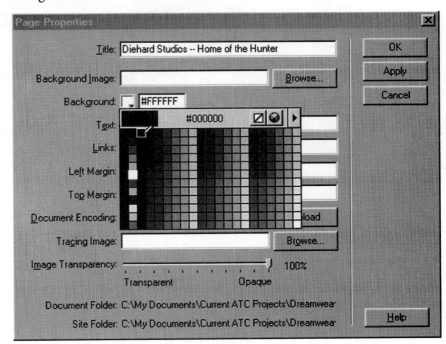

You could use the Page Properties dialog box to actually put one of your sketches on the page as a tracing image. Dreamweaver tones down the image and locks it on the page. When you're done, simply turn the feature off in the same dialog box.

3. Using the Draw Layer object, draw a layer starting at 100 pixels from the top and left of the page. Make it 400 pixels wide × 280 pixels high. You can draw the layer exactly the right size, or draw it small and enter the values in the layer Property inspector.

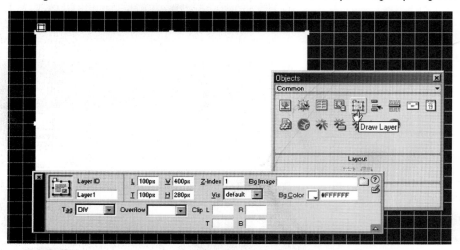

The default keyboard command for activating the Assets window is F11.

4. Set the fill of the layer to None so that the black page background can show through.

5. Activate the Assets panel. You can do this from the Window menu or from the Launcher panel.

6. Insert a table onto the layer. Make it 4 rows by 3 columns, with no padding or spacing between the cells. Use a Border setting of 0.

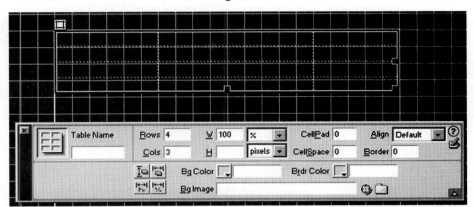

We try to use the name "Assets" for folders containing a site's images and other items. Just remember that if you're using Flash, Shockwave or QuickTime media, it has to be kept in the root folder — many browsers won't link to these types of media if they're not available at the same folder level as the page that uses them.

7. Drag the **DHSmenu_1.gif** file from the Assets panel into the first cell on the top left of the table. Don't worry, it's just black — there's nothing wrong.

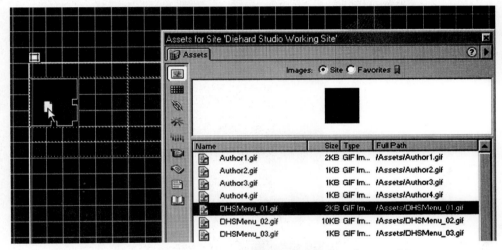

8. Drag the first cell border to the left until it's tight against the graphic.

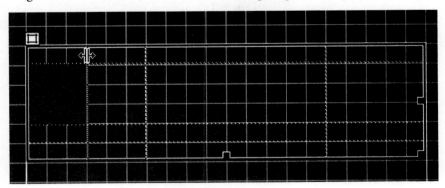

9. Drag the **DHSMenu_02.gif** image into the second cell of the first row and the **DHSMenu_03.gif** image into the third cell on the top row.

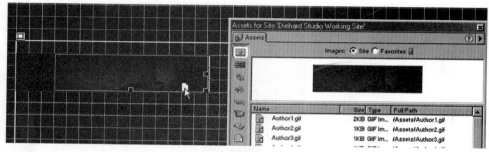

10. Build the second row using images 6, 7 and 8.

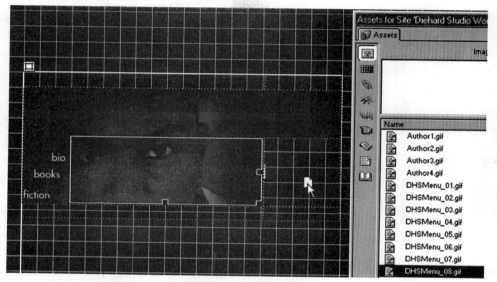

11. Build the third row with images 10, 11 and 12.

12. The last row is built with images 14, 15 and 16.

13. Preview the page in your browserr window. It should be seamless.

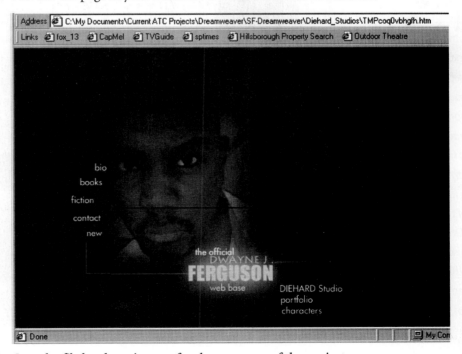

14. Save the file but keep it open for the next part of the project.

The days of Web pages that don't have any motion are becoming extinct. Because software is able to compress graphics more efficiently, more designers are using animation to liven up their pages. The key to using this new power is not to abuse it by putting in animation just for the sake of it. Make certain that if you are going to distract a viewer from reading the information you have posted, that the animation enhances, not detracts from your message.

The timeline is similar to traditional animation: it uses keyframes for animation. On an animated feature film, a Master Animator supplies the starting and ending frames of an action, called keyframes to his team. This team, called "In-Betweeners", draws in the missing illustrations to fill in the blanks between the two keyframes. The Master Animator draws just two or three keyframes, and the In-Betweeners draw the missing frames. There are normally 24 frames per second, which can add up to hundreds or more drawings for even a short clip.

Animating Images with the Timeline

Unlike animation packages such as Flash, or more sophisticated programs, Dreamweaver can only animate motion — it can't change shapes or build character animations like programs with more horsepower. Think of a racetrack with a single car going from the first keyframe (the starting line) to the last keyframe at the end of the track (the finish line). Dreamweaver can fill in the motion of the car from the first to last keyframes. The timeline cannot fill in the complex frames of someone doing a spinning roundhouse martial arts kick.

1. Choose Window>Timelines to display the Timelines panel.

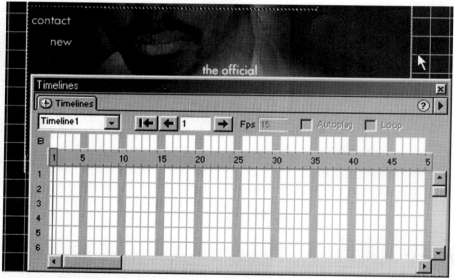

2. Draw a new layer underneath the one containing the sliced graphic. Click the layer's selection handle so we can change its dimensions in the Property inspector. Resize the layer so that it is 400 pixels wide × 50 pixels high.

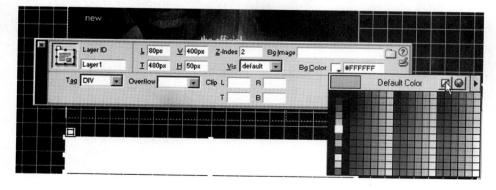

3. Rename the sliced image layer "main", and the new layer "animation". To do so, activate the Layers panel if it's not already visible (Window>Layers).

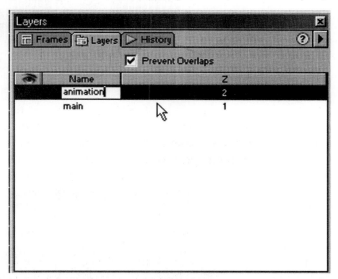

4. Select the animation layer by clicking on its handle. Add it to the timeline using the Add Object selection from the pop-up menu. *(RT Click on Timeline)*

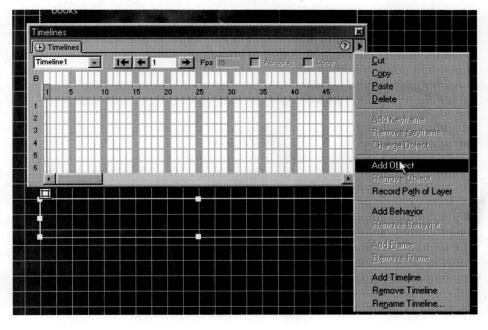

5. Rename the timeline to "Change images". Make sure that the Animation layer is now showing as an object on the timeline.

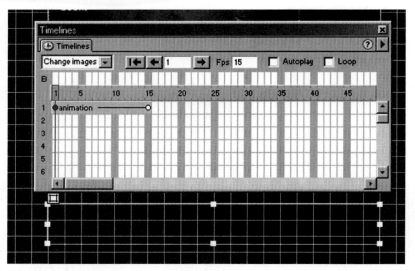

6. Drag **Author1.gif** into the new layer from the Assets panel. You'll notice that the image was saved to fit the layer precisely at 400 × 50 pixels in an image-editing program like Fireworks or Photoshop.

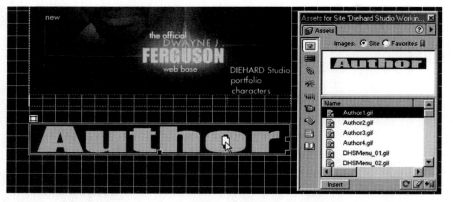

7. Click the second keyframe of the image in the Timelines panel and drag it to frame 110. This extends the total duration of Author1.gif from 1 to 110. We are going to insert our remaining images by substituting them at specific keyframes.

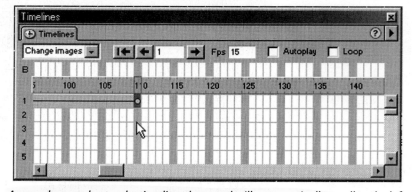

As you drag and extend a timeline, the panel will automatically scroll to the left. Sometimes it's tricky to drag precisely to the frame you want.

8. Add a keyframe at frame 10. You can do this by Command/Control-clicking in the frame. A small circle will appear indicating that the frame is a keyframe.

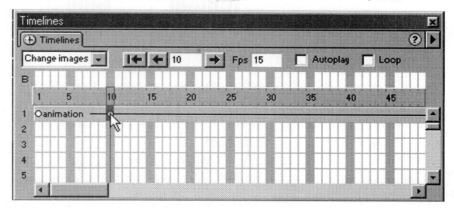

9. Insert a new keyframe on every tenth frame from 20, 30, 40 and so on until you reach frame 110. We don't need to add one to 110 since it is the endpoint of our animation and therefore, by default, already a keyframe.

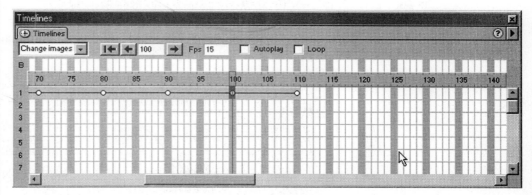

10. Select the keyframe at frame 10 by clicking on it once. If you look at the name of the image in the Property inspector, it says Author1.gif. This instance of the image is only one of four variations created in an image-editing program. To create the illusion of animation, four separate versions of each word have been created. We are going to place each new iteration of the words on each successive keyframe.

11. If you look above the first object in the Timelines panel, you'll see a blank row that's labeled with a capital "B" on the left of the panel. Activate the Behaviors panel (Window>Behaviors).

12. Click in the "B" row above the keyframe at 10. Immediately click the Plus (+) button on the Behaviors panel and select Swap Image from the pop-up menu. Make sure you have the Author1.gif file selected before you do this or you might animate some other image.

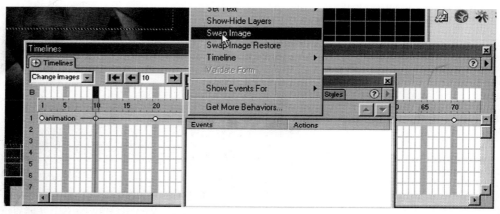

13. Use the Browse button on the Select Source dialog box that appears to find the **Author2.gif** image in the Assets folder. Select the file.

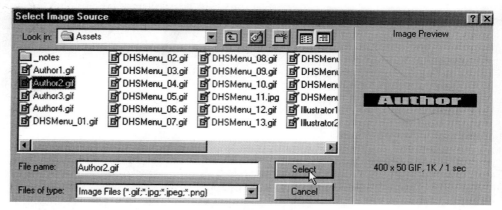

14. You'll see a small horizontal line appear in the Behaviors row, and the behavior itself will appear in the Behaviors panel — "onFrame10, Swap Image." This is JavaScript code that tells the browser to swap the picture at that frame.

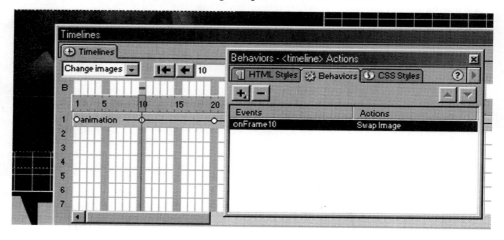

15. Complete the animation by placing Swap image behaviors at frames 20, 30, 40 and so on until you hit the last frame. The animation starts with the three *author* images, then moves on and uses the *illustrator* images, and lastly the *needs coffee* images.

16. Before you're done, check the Autoplay and Loop boxes on the Timeline. You'll get a message that Dreamweaver is going to add behaviors to accomplish these two commands. Click OK when you see the dialog box.

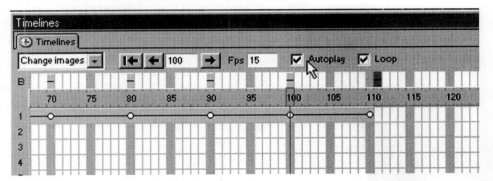

17. Save the file and preview it in your browser.

The project that you just completed is a rather challenging page whose construction was made simple through the use of Dreamweaver's powerful animation and JavaScript tools. To code this page by hand would have been horrendous — or at least far less fun than it was doing it this way. The animation not only adds motion to the page but a little humor as well; Dwayne runs on coffee and adrenaline.

Notes:

Project D: Mr. BlockHead's Challenge

One of the features many Web sites provide for their visitors is entertainment. Whether it's a movie trailer, a cartoon or music downloads, many enjoyable pastimes are available online. We are going to create an electronic version of a jigsaw puzzle game using Dreamweaver's pre-written scripts called "behaviors".

The game is fairly simple to build, and was designed primarily to show you some of the capabilities of Dreamweaver as an interactive development tool. The most intense games and interactive cartoons are being done in Flash. For examples of what can be done in that medium, visit jaydonaldson.com or joecartoon.com. Be forewarned, however, that some of the humor and interactive games on those sites are considered "edgy," and may not be amusing to some viewers.

Before you Get Started

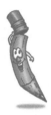

When designing a game with many pieces like a jigsaw puzzle, remember the total size of the assembled image. You should strive to keep the total size of images on a page below 60k. As always, think about the lowest common denominator connection speed.

Load the **BlockHeadPuzzle.html** game file in your browser and take a quick look at the finished project. The files for this project are in the **RF-Dreamweaver>blockhead** folder. This project will not work if the browser doesn't support layers.

Although the final game is built on a black background, we thought it was easier to keep the background white while you're constructing the project. At the end, we'll change the background to black.

Assembling the Pieces

The files for this project are in the "blockhead" folder, which is located inside of your **RF-Dreamweaver** folder. Move this folder into your **Work in Progress** folder and work from there for the remainder of the project.

1. Start a new document in Dreamweaver by choosing File>New from the Menu bar. Save the file as "puzzle.htm". If you want, you can go ahead and set up a new site just for this project. If you decide to do this, do it now.

2. Create nine layers, roughly 150 pixels wide × 120 pixels tall. We will resize the layers to snap to the contents after we've imported all our images. The easiest way to do this is to create one layer, and in the Layers panel, copy and paste eight more copies. They'll all sit on top of each other in exactly the same location as the original. To copy and paste in the Layers panel, you have to make sure that no layers are selected.

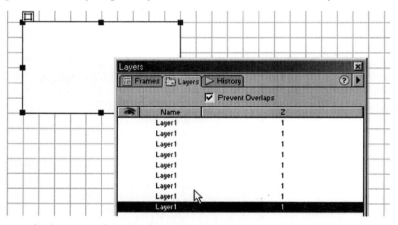

To name a layer, click its selection handle. To name the image inside a layer, click once on the image. You can rename both layers and images in the Property inspector.

3. Arrange the layers so that they're in three columns and three rows — not in a table, mind you — just arranged next to each other. Be sure to check the Prevent Overlaps box on the Layers panel, and then drag the layers off the pile of copies in the upper-left corner.

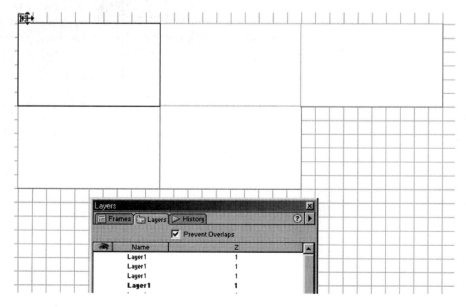

4. Choose the layer at the top-left corner by clicking its selection handle and rename it "L1". Moving down the column, name the next two layers "L2", and "L3".

5. Move to the next column of layers and continue naming them as such: "M1", "M2", "M3"; move to the next column and continue: "R1", "R2", "R3". We are doing this because we will need to know which layers we're working with when we start to apply behaviors.

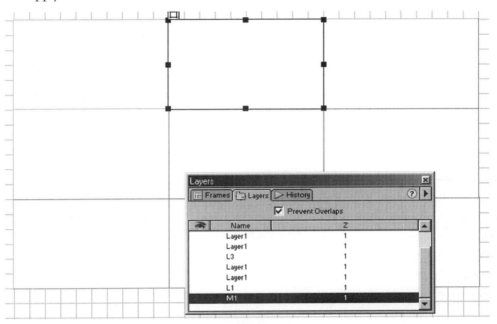

6. Insert the **BlockHeadPuzzle_01.gif** image into the first layer in the upper-left corner. It's inside of the images folder where the original file was found.

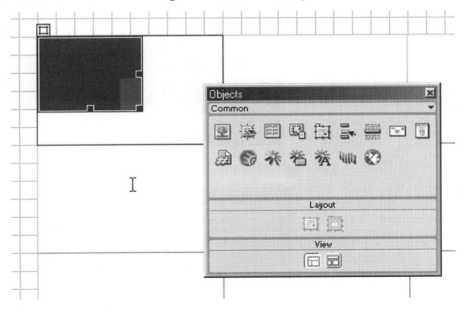

7. As you import images into each layer, drag its handles until they are flush with the images within the layer boundaries. Each piece of our puzzle needs to fit together as tightly as possible, so having extraneous layer space will work against us here.

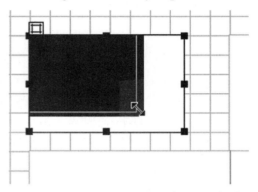

8. Complete the first row, importing images 2 and 3 into the layers and resizing them as you go.

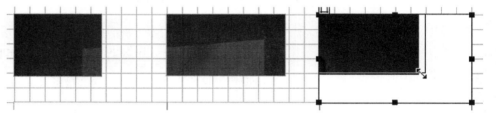

9. The second row contains images 7, 8 and 6 — in that order.

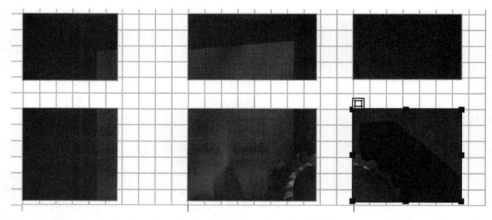

10. The last row contains images 9, 11 and 13. Resize the layers to fit the images.

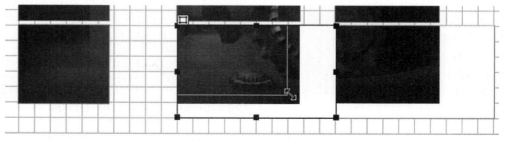

11. Save the changes to the file, but keep it open for the next part of the project — we're going to build a game.

As you become more familiar with Dreamweaver, make it a habit to name every element from images to layers for the sake of organization and clarity. The Web changes on a daily basis, so you must be well organized to minimize time wasted on guessing which layer or image you need to manipulate.

Behaviors give you the opportunity to add actions to layers and their contents. Fortunately, Dreamweaver writes all the JavaScript for you, so all you have to do is focus on creating exciting content. We are going to add actions to each layer, to make the pieces of the jigsaw puzzle draggable by the Web surfers who will play this game online. It may seem labor-intensive, but the results are well worth the effort.

The behaviors process relies on events and actions. An *event* is something that the end user does to trigger an action to take place. An example of this is when you click a link (the event), which then opens a new URL on your browser (the action that the event has triggered). The pre-written JavaScript in Dreamweaver will write the onLoad events for us. This means that our puzzle will be ready for action when the page loads into a browser.

Assigning Behaviors to Layers

1. Choose Window>Behaviors to display the Behaviors panel. This panel gives you access to several built-in Behaviors that you can apply to layers. You can also specify in which browsers you'd like your behavior event(s) to execute. Browsers that are version 4 or higher should be your choice; but this still does not guarantee that the actions will function as planned, since browser incompatibility remains a Web designer's greatest trouble spot.

Behaviors and their effects on the browser will change depending on the browser and its version number that you select in the Behaviors panel drop-down list. The more current 5.0 and greater browsers offer the greatest flexibility and choices. Experiment to see what does and does not work across the widest range of browsers.

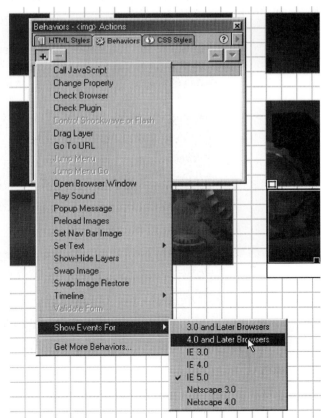

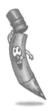

2. Put the puzzle pieces together so that the puzzle is complete.

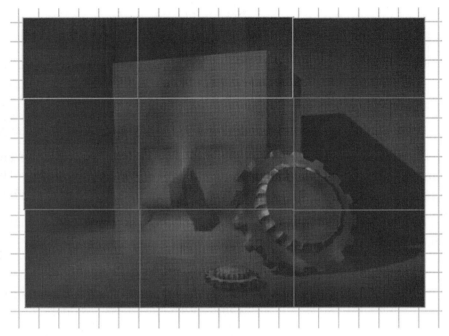

3. Deselect all layers. This next step will not work if any layers are selected.

4. Click the Plus (+) button on the Behaviors panel to open the Actions submenu. Select Drag Layer from the available actions.

5. The Drag Layer dialog box appears. Choose layer "L1" from the Layer drop-down list.

6. You now have the option to constrain the movements of the layer or to allow the player to drag the layer around the monitor. We will leave the layer Unconstrained.

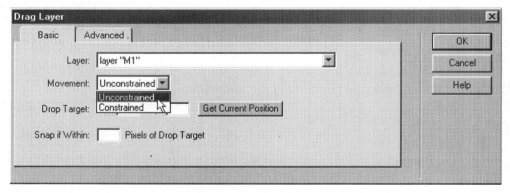

7. In order to know where each piece must be placed before it locks into the jigsaw, we have to define its current position. This is called a *Drop Target*, or the spot where the piece must be before the action to lock it in place occurs. To set the drop target for layer "L1," click the Get Current Position button. As you can see, Dreamweaver automatically fills in the exact coordinates of the layer based on its left and top pixel location on the page.

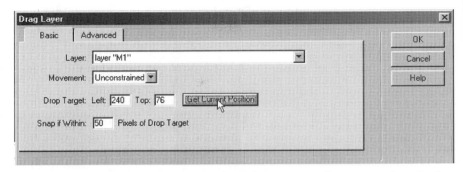

8. We also have to decide how close to the Drop Target a player must drag the layer before it snaps into its position on the puzzle. The default is 50 Pixels. Its best to leave this number at 50 or slightly higher so the player won't have to work so hard to complete the game.

9. Save the file but keep it open.

To make the game more interesting, we're going to add in two additional pieces that can be tossed into a trash can on the game screen. By setting The z-index or the order in which layers are stacked in the Layers panel, we can easily create this illusion.

The Z-Index

1. Click on the L3 layer selection handle and choose Copy and then Paste to duplicate both the layer and its contents. Do the same for layer R3. Be sure to check the Property inspector and rename the layers by placing the letter "B" after their names. For example, your copy of Layer L3 should be called L3B.

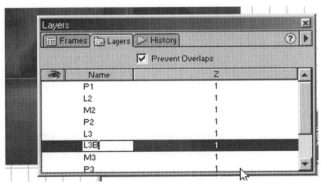

2. Draw another layer and insert the **trashcan.gif** image. Rename the layer "trashcan". Look at the sample page for the position of the Trashcan layer, but place it near the left side of the page for now.

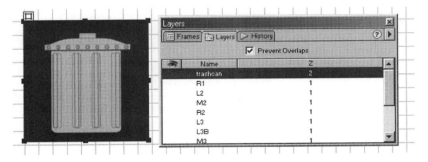

3. Use the eye icon on the Layers panel to hide all but Layers L3B and R3B. This will make the next step easier.

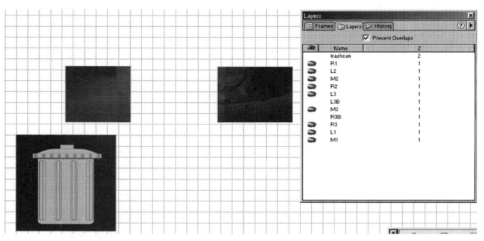

4. Place the L3B layer where the trashcan will eventually rest on the page. Deselect Layer L3B and choose Drag Layer from the Behaviors panel. Pick the L3B layer from the pop-up menu, and click Get Current Position. This tells Dreamweaver where this piece should be for it to stay in the trashcan once it is dragged here.

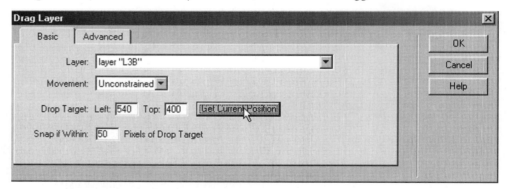

5. Click the Advanced tab on the Drag Layer dialog box. Make sure a there's a checkmark in the Bring Layer to Front box and choose Restore z-index from the drop-down list. This tells each duplicate piece that the Trashcan layer is to remain in front so that when we drag these pieces on top of the trashcan, they look like they have gone into it.

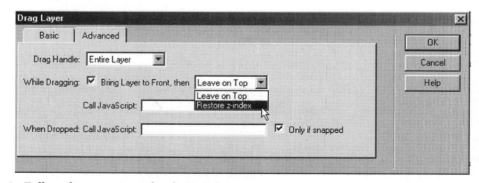

6. Follow the same steps for the R3B layer.

7. Turn off Prevent Overlaps in the Layers window. Place the Trashcan layer in its spot near the bottom right of the page as it is in the sample page.

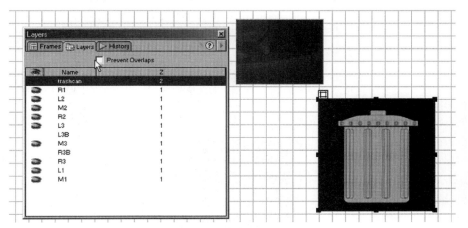

8. Drag the Trashcan layer to the top of the other layers.

9. Save the page as "Blockhead.htm", and preview it in a 4.0 or later browser.

We're going to use two different methods to incorporate a sound into our page. The first method will open the sound in its own browser window. The second will play the sound within the same document on the Web.

Adding Sound

1. To insert a sound, click the Plus (+) button on the Behaviors panel and choose Play Sound from the drop-down list.

Some browsers may display an alert to locate an extension or plugin required to play audio.

For best results, use 8-bit sounds. Stereo takes up twice the space and mono is more than adequate for a Web game.

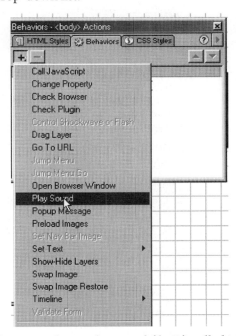

2. Click the Browse button to locate the sound file. It's called **Music.aiff** and it's in the Blockhead folder.

3. To increase the options for when the sound will play, change to a 5.0 or later browser in the drop-down list in the Behaviors panel.

4. Save the page and preview in a browser.

Now let's incorporate the second method, which is probably the one you will prefer to use. In our earlier example, Dreamweaver opens a new browser window by default because it uses an onLoad behavior. This time we will embed the sound file within the page.

1. Draw a new layer, approximately 50 × 50 pixels and place it near the bottom of the document.

2. Click once inside the layer. Choose Insert>Media>Plugin from the Menu bar. This places a plugin directly within the page itself. Now when the window opens in a browser, the sound will play on the same page.

3. Save your document and preview in a browser.

Completing the Puzzle

1. Add the other components to the puzzle — the first graphic at the top is called **Challenge.gif**, the second is called **instructions.gif**, and the third is a layer into which you should enter yellow text to match the type above it.

2. Position all the pieces around the outside edge of the Puzzle field, making sure to add the Drag Layer behavior and to get the current position of each piece before you move it away.

3. Use Modify>Page Properties to turn the background of the parent page to black.

Popup Messages

1. Click the Plus (+) button in the Behaviors inspector.

2. Choose Popup Message from the drop-down list of Actions.

3. Enter any introductory text that comes to mind, perhaps a challenge to your guests to solve the puzzle.

4. Save your work.

Interactivity in the form of entertainment can be a valuable asset to maintain a high site-visitation rate. Keep adding new games and graphics to your site to make sure it never goes stale. Hopefully, with a little word of mouth, your site will become one that is recommended as a great place to visit online.

Macintosh machines prefer the .aiff sound format, while Windows machines prefer the .wav format. Both should work equally well on any browser, provided the browser has an audio plugin to play sounds.

Choose your sounds carefully: music takes up much more space in a computer than most images. For best results, compress the music in a compression program such as SoundForge or SoundEdit 16. A large sound can definitely bring your pages to a standstill.

Action

An action is one of the two components of a behavior; it is what occurs when an event is triggered.

Anchor

A specified point on a page to which you can link so that the pages open to a particular view.

ADN (Advanced Digital Network)

Usually refers to a 56K bps leased-line.

Applet

A Java program embedded in an HTML page. Applets differ from full-fledged Java applications: they are not allowed to access certain resources on the local computer, such as files and serial devices (modems, printers, and so forth), and are prohibited from communicating with most other computers across a network. The current rule is that an applet can only provide a connection to the computer from which the applet was sent.

ASCII (American Standard Code for Information Interchange)

The standard for the code numbers used by computers to represent all the upper and lowercase Latin letters, numbers, punctuation and so forth. There are 128 standard ASCII codes, each of which can be represented by a 7 digit binary number: 0000000 through 1111111.

Asset

An element that is part of a Web site. Dreamweaver displays a categorized list of assets in the Assets panel.

Bandwidth

The amount of data that can be transmitted over specific telecommunication systems. Usually measured in bits-per-second. A full page of English text is about 16,000 bits.

Basefont

The default size of the text you type in a document window.

Baseline

The imaginary line on which the base of letters rest.

BBS (Bulletin Board System)

A computerized meeting and announcement system that allows people to engage in discussions, upload and download files and make announcements without being connected to the computer at the same time. There are thousands (perhaps millions) of BBS's worldwide.

Behavior

A JavaScript that allows you to easily create interactive Web pages in Dreamweaver.

Behaviors Panel

A window that allows you to attach, check and modify any behaviors you have set.

BMP

A Windows bitmap image format that features low-quality and large file sizes.

Browser

A specialized application that interprets HTML code (and other types of media in some cases) and displays it on a monitor.

Cell Padding

In a table, the amount of space between an object contained in a cell and the border of a cell.

Cell Spacing

The amount of space between two cells in a table.

CGI (Common Gateway Interface)

A set of rules that describe how a Web server communicates with another piece of software on the same machine, and how the other piece of software (the CGI program) talks to the Web server. Any piece of software can be a CGI program if it handles input and output according to the CGI standard. CGI is normally written in PERL, C or Java, although there are other languages used as well.

Client

A software program that is used to contact and obtain data from a server-software program on another computer. A Web browser is one type of client; email programs are another.

Color Depth

Maximum number of colors available for an image.

Command

A series of actions saved as a single-named action that you can apply repeatedly.

Cookie

A file sent by a Web server to a Web browser that the browser software is expected to save and to send back to the server whenever the browser makes additional requests from the client.

CSS (Cascading Style Sheets)

CSS styles are custom-created for a site and are used to control the way in which page elements are displayed. These styles should guarantee consistency in a site design.

Cyberspace

Term originated by author William Gibson in his novel, *Neuromancer,* the word "cyberspace" is currently used to describe the entire range of information-resources available through computer networks.

DHML (Dynamic Hypertext Markup Language)

A programming language that provides the flexibility to lay out and create Web pages.

Dither

A process whereby an application attempts to reproduce a color that it cannot otherwise display by using alternating pixels of two other colors.

Docking

The process of combining more than one panel into one floating panel.

Domain Name

The unique name that identifies an Internet site. Domain names always have two or more parts, separated by dots.

DSL (Digital Subscriber Line)

A method for moving data over regular phone lines. A DSL circuit is much faster than a regular phone connection, and the wires coming into the subscribers' premises are the same (copper) wires used for regular phone service. A DSL circuit must be configured to connect two specific locations.

Editable Region

On a template, this is the section designated specifically where changes to be made by the viewer.

Element

In Dreamweaver, any item on a page, such as a graphic or text, is called an element.

Ethernet

A common method of networking computers in a LAN. Ethernet will handle about 10,000,000 bits-per-second and can be used with almost any computer.

Event

An incident that triggers an action.

Exchange

An online site provided by Macromedia to find easy-to-install extensions that will add features and functionality to Dreamweaver.

External Hyperlink

A hyperlink that links to a page within a different site.

FAQ (Frequently Asked Questions)

FAQs are documents that list and answer the most common questions on a particular subject. There are hundreds of FAQs on subjects as diverse as pet grooming and cryptography. FAQs are usually written by people who are tired of repeatedly answering the same question.

Finger

An Internet software tool for locating people on other Internet sites.

Fire Wall

A combination of hardware and software that separates a LAN into two or more parts for security purposes.

Form Field Validation

A behavior that checks whether a visitor to a form has entered the correct information, and ensures that the necessary information has not been omitted.

Frames

Individual Web pages held together in sets.

Frameset

An HTML page that holds all the information that you want to appear together.

FTP (File Transfer Protocol)

A common method of moving files between two Internet sites. When you're working on a remote site, FTP is the most likely way of moving files back and forth.

GIF (Graphic Image Format)

The ideal format for small files that will use minimal colors. GIF files make good buttons, lines and backgrounds.

GIF Animation File

A single GIF file created from multiple frames. GIF animations are good because they remain small in file size.

GIF (Graphic Interchange Format)

A common format for image files; especially suitable for images containing large areas of the same color. GIF format files of simple images are often smaller than the same file would be if stored in JPEG format, but GIF format does not store photographic images as well as JPEG.

Hidden Field

Typically contains information used by the server when it processes a form. Users cannot see or change the information contained in the hidden field.

Home Page

Usually the first page that a visitor sees when they visit your site. In most cases, it's not named "home," however. Most servers require that it be called default.xxx or index.xxx where xxx is .htm, .asp or another extension.

Host

The Internet Service Provider (ISP) that stores your site on a server that can be accessed by the general public; a server at your own location that stores the site.

Hotspot

Defined portions of an image map that are usually linked to another page or site. An image map can contain multiple hotspots.

HTML (HyperText Markup Language)

The coding language used to create Hypertext documents for use on the World Wide Web.

Hypertext

Any text that contains links to other documents; words or phrases in the document that can be chosen by a reader and that can cause another document to be retrieved and displayed.

Image Field

A field on a form that can hold an image or rich media object. Image fields are contained within the <frame>...<frame/> tags.

Instance

Using a library symbol on your page creates an instance of that symbol. Instances can be modified without affecting the stored symbol; changing the original symbol affects all instances of its use.

ISP (Internet Service Provider)

A company that provides access to the Internet.

Java

A network-oriented programming language invented by Sun Microsystems that is specifically designed for writing programs that can be safely downloaded to your computer through the Internet and immediately run without fear of viruses or other harm to your computer or files. Using small Java programs (called applets), Web pages can include functions such as animations, calculators and other functions.

JPEG (Joint Photographic Experts Group)

JPEG is commonly used as a format for image files. The JPEG format is preferred to the GIF format for photographic images as opposed to line art or simple logo art.

Jump Menu

A jump menu is a pop-up list of links; normally used to conserve screen space on complex pages by eliminating the need to show an entire list of links at one time.

Keyframes

Keyframes refers to the frames on a timeline where changes take place. In Dreamweaver, the beginning and end of a sequence of layer movements. Frames between keyframes are called "tween" frames.

Launcher

A panel providing one-click access to any number of Dreamweaver tools or techniques. The panel can be customized from the Preferences dialog box.

Layer

A Dreamweaver object that can be used to quickly lay out page designs. Layers act as containers for images, text or rich media. They are not, however, compatible with all browsers; test your layers-based pages in a variety of popular browser versions.

MIME (Multipurpose Internet Mail Extensions)

The standard for attaching non-text files to standard Internet mail messages. Non-text files include graphics, spreadsheets, formatted word-processor documents, sound files and so forth.

Modem

MOdulator, DEModulator — A device that you connect to your computer and to a phone line that allows the computer to communicate with other computers through the phone system.

Mosaic

The first WWW browser that was available for Macintosh, Windows and UNIX operating systems with the same interface.

Netscape

A WWW browser and the name of a company.

Newsgroup

A discussion group on USENET.

Password

A code used to gain access to a locked system. Good passwords contain letters and non-letters and are not simple combinations such as "my name1". Dreamweaver provides special text-field attributes to simplify the creation of password fields.

Plugin

A piece (usually small) of software that adds features to a larger piece of software. Common examples are plug-ins for browsers and Web servers. Adobe Photoshop also uses plugins.

Server

A computer or software package that provides a specific type of service to client software running on other computers. The term can refer to a particular piece of software, such as a WWW server, or to the machine on which the software is running. A single server machine could have several different server-software packages running on it, thus providing many different servers to clients on the network.

SSL (Secure Sockets Layer)

A protocol designed by Netscape Communications to enable encrypted, authenticated communications across the Internet.

T-1

A form of high-speed connection to the Internet.

TCP/IP

Transmission Control Protocol/Internet Protocol is the suite of protocols that defines the Internet. Originally designed for the UNIX operating system, TCP/IP software is now available for every major kind of computer operating system. To be connected to the Internet, your computer must have TCP/IP software.

WWW

World Wide Web.

Prentice-Hall, Inc.

YOU SHOULD CAREFULLY READ THE TERMS AND CONDITIONS BEFORE USING THE CD-ROM PACKAGE. USING THIS CD-ROM PACKAGE INDICATES YOUR ACCEPTANCE OF THESE TERMS AND CONDITIONS.

Prentice-Hall, Inc. provides this program and licenses its use. You assume responsibility for the selection of the program to achieve your intended results, and for the installation, use, and results obtained from the program. This license extends only to use of the program in the United States or countries in which the program is marketed by authorized distributors.

LICENSE GRANT

You hereby accept a nonexclusive, nontransferable, permanent license to install and use the program ON A SINGLE COMPUTER at any given time. You may copy the program solely for backup or archival purposes in support of your use of the program on the single computer. You may not modify, translate, disassemble, decompile, or reverse engineer the program, in whole or in part.

TERM

The License is effective until terminated. Prentice-Hall, Inc. reserves the right to terminate this License automatically if any provision of the License is violated. You may terminate the License at any time. To terminate this License, you must return the program, including documentation, along with a written warranty stating that all copies in your possession have been returned or destroyed.

LIMITED WARRANTY

THE PROGRAM IS PROVIDED "AS IS" WITHOUT WARRANTY OF ANY KIND, EITHER EXPRESSED OR IMPLIED, INCLUDING, BUT NOT LIMITED TO, THE IMPLIED WARRANTIES OR MERCHANTABILITY AND FITNESS FOR A PARTICULAR PURPOSE. THE ENTIRE RISK AS TO THE QUALITY AND PERFORMANCE OF THE PROGRAM IS WITH YOU. SHOULD THE PROGRAM PROVE DEFECTIVE, YOU (AND NOT PRENTICE-HALL, INC. OR ANY AUTHORIZED DEALER) ASSUME THE ENTIRE COST OF ALL NECESSARY SERVICING, REPAIR, OR CORRECTION. NO ORAL OR WRITTEN INFORMATION OR ADVICE GIVEN BY PRENTICE-HALL, INC., ITS DEALERS, DISTRIBUTORS, OR AGENTS SHALL CREATE A WARRANTY OR INCREASE THE SCOPE OF THIS WARRANTY.

SOME STATES DO NOT ALLOW THE EXCLUSION OF IMPLIED WARRANTIES, SO THE ABOVE EXCLUSION MAY NOT APPLY TO YOU. THIS WARRANTY GIVES YOU SPECIFIC LEGAL RIGHTS AND YOU MAY ALSO HAVE OTHER LEGAL RIGHTS THAT VARY FROM STATE TO STATE.

Prentice-Hall, Inc. does not warrant that the functions contained in the program will meet your requirements or that the operation of the program will be uninterrupted or error-free.

However, Prentice-Hall, Inc. warrants the diskette(s) or CD-ROM(s) on which the program is furnished to be free from defects in material and workmanship under normal use for a period of ninety (90) days from the date of delivery to you as evidenced by a copy of your receipt.

The program should not be relied on as the sole basis to solve a problem whose incorrect solution could result in injury to person or property. If the program is employed in such a manner, it is at the user's own risk and Prentice-Hall, Inc. explicitly disclaims all liability for such misuse.

LIMITATION OF REMEDIES

Prentice-Hall, Inc.'s entire liability and your exclusive remedy shall be:

1. the replacement of any diskette(s) or CD-ROM(s) not meeting Prentice-Hall, Inc.'s "LIMITED WARRANTY" and that is returned to Prentice-Hall, or

2. if Prentice-Hall is unable to deliver a replacement diskette(s) or CD-ROM(s) that is free of defects in materials or workmanship, you may terminate this agreement by returning the program.

IN NO EVENT WILL PRENTICE-HALL, INC. BE LIABLE TO YOU FOR ANY DAMAGES, INCLUDING ANY LOST PROFITS, LOST SAVINGS, OR OTHER INCIDENTAL OR CONSEQUENTIAL DAMAGES ARISING OUT OF THE USE OR INABILITY TO USE SUCH PROGRAM EVEN IF PRENTICE-HALL, INC. OR AN AUTHORIZED DISTRIBUTOR HAS BEEN ADVISED OF THE POSSIBILITY OF SUCH DAMAGES, OR FOR ANY CLAIM BY ANY OTHER PARTY.

SOME STATES DO NOT ALLOW FOR THE LIMITATION OR EXCLUSION OF LIABILITY FOR INCIDENTAL OR CONSEQUENTIAL DAMAGES, SO THE ABOVE LIMITATION OR EXCLUSION MAY NOT APPLY TO YOU.

GENERAL

You may not sublicense, assign, or transfer the license of the program. Any attempt to sublicense, assign or transfer any of the rights, duties, or obligations hereunder is void.

This Agreement will be governed by the laws of the State of New York.

Should you have any questions concerning this Agreement, you may contact Prentice-Hall, Inc. by writing to:
Director of New Media
Higher Education Division
Prentice-Hall, Inc.
One Lake Street
Upper Saddle River, NJ 07458

Should you have any questions concerning technical support, you may write or call:
New Media Production
Higher Education Division
Prentice-Hall, Inc.
One Lake Street
Upper Saddle River, NJ 07458
1-800-677-6337 between 8:00 a.m. and 5:00 p.m. CST, Monday–Friday.

YOU ACKNOWLEDGE THAT YOU HAVE READ THIS AGREEMENT, UNDERSTAND IT, AND AGREE TO BE BOUND BY ITS TERMS AND CONDITIONS. YOU FURTHER AGREE THAT IT IS THE COMPLETE AND EXCLUSIVE STATEMENT OF THE AGREEMENT BETWEEN US THAT SUPERSEDES ANY PROPOSAL OR PRIOR AGREEMENT, ORAL OR WRITTEN, AND ANY OTHER COMMUNICATIONS BETWEEN US RELATING TO THE SUBJECT MATTER OF THIS AGREEMENT.

Resource CD-ROM
MACROMEDIA® DREAMWEAVER® 4
Creating Web Pages
AGAINST THE CLOCK

System Requirements

Windows:

- Intel Pentium class processor
- Microsoft Windows 98, Windows 2000, or Windows NT 4.0†
- 32 MB of RAM
- 135 MB of available hard-disk space (after install)
- Color monitor with 256-color (8-bit) or greater video card
- 800x600 or greater monitor resolution
- CD-ROM drive

Version 4.0 or later of Netscape Navigator or Microsoft Internet Explorer

Macintosh:

- Power PC processor
- Mac OS software version 8.6, or 9.x
- 32 MB of RAM
- 110 MB of available hard-disk space (after install)
- Color monitor with 256-color (8-bit) or greater video card
- 800x600 or greater monitor resolution
- CD-ROM drive

Version 4.0 or later of Netscape Navigator or Microsoft Internet Explorer

To use the additional resources available on this CD-ROM, you will need to have the appropriate applications installed on your system and enough free space available if you copy the files to your hard drive. This product does not come with the application software required to use the data files on this CD-ROM.